It Wasn't Meant to Be Perfect

> These are uncorrected advance proofs bound for your reviewing convenience. Please check with the publisher or refer to the finished book whenever you are excerpting or quoting in a review.

It Wasn't Meant to Be Perfect

A MEMOIR

GAELYNN LEA

ALGONQUIN BOOKS OF CHAPEL HILL
LITTLE, BROWN AND COMPANY

Copyright © 2026 by Gaelynn Lea

Hachette Book Group supports the right to free expression and the value of copyright. The purpose of copyright is to encourage writers and artists to produce the creative works that enrich our culture.

The scanning, uploading, and distribution of this book without permission is a theft of the author's intellectual property. If you would like permission to use material from the book (other than for review purposes), please contact permissions@hbgusa.com. Thank you for your support of the author's rights.

Algonquin Books of Chapel Hill / Little, Brown and Company
Hachette Book Group
1290 Avenue of the Americas, New York, NY 10104
algonquinbooks.com

First Edition: April 2026

Algonquin Books of Chapel Hill is an imprint of Little, Brown and Company, a division of Hachette Book Group, Inc. The Algonquin Books name and logo are trademarks of Hachette Book Group, Inc.

The publisher is not responsible for websites (or their content) that are not owned by the publisher.

The Hachette Speakers Bureau provides a wide range of authors for speaking events. To find out more, go to hachettespeakersbureau.com or email hachettespeakers@hbgusa.com.

Little, Brown and Company books may be purchased in bulk for business, educational, or promotional use. For information, please contact your local bookseller or the Hachette Book Group Special Markets Department at special.markets@hbgusa.

ISBN 978-1-64375-643-1 (hardcover) / ISBN 978-1-64375-645-5 (ebook)

LCCN [TK]

10 9 8 7 6 5 4 3 2 1

LSC-C

Printed in the United States of America

I dedicate this book to everyone who is working to build a more loving, beautiful, creative, just, and welcoming world for all. Never give up hope that a better future is possible.

CONTENTS

Prologue: Musical Alchemy   ooo

1: Major Plot Twist   ooo

2: I Was Born for the Stage   ooo

3: Don't Drop the Baby   ooo

4: Hog Wild   ooo

5: Theater Kid   ooo

6: I Blame *The Baby-Sitters Club*   ooo

7: The World's Tiniest Cello   ooo

8: Fiddle Jam   ooo

9: Leaving the Nest   ooo

10: Medical Mayhem   ooo

11: The Lost Summer   ooo

12: Picking Up the Pieces   ooo

13: Open Mic Night   ooo

14: The Quiet Guy with the Nice Eyes   ooo

15: The Public Forum   ooo

16: Hatching The Murder of Crows   ooo

17: Solo Mission   ooo

18: Safe Harbor   ooo

19: An Unexpected Roadblock   ooo

20: Merry Matrimony   ooo
21: The Infamous Phone Call   ooo
22: Gig Economy   ooo
23: Debut in DC   ooo
24: Tiny Desk, Big World   ooo
25: Hitting the (Bumpy) Road   ooo
26: The Tap Tap   ooo
27: Fiddling in the Isles   ooo
28: The (Nearly) Impossible Staircase   ooo
29: The Legend Herself   ooo
30: Accessibility Is the New Punk Rock   ooo
31: Tabula Musica   ooo
32: Meeting Your Idols   ooo
33: *Sunday Sessions*   ooo
34: Ramping Up RAMPD   ooo
35: The Bard and the Lute Factory   ooo
36: Broadway Baby   ooo
37: Trust in Your Ripple   ooo

Acknowledgments   ooo

It Wasn't Meant to Be Perfect

PROLOGUE

Musical Alchemy

ON TOUR, LIFE speeds up. Moments of brilliance and joy are linked together by the blur of unglamorous monotony.

During a typical afternoon, my husband, Paul, drives while I sit in the back of the van, answering emails and perhaps writing one of my monthly newsletters. The satellite radio serenades us with big band tunes, unbroken by radio static. We stop for gas at another Love's, virtually identical to all the others except that there's a different lady behind the counter. We use the bathroom, and on my way out I buy my guilty pleasure—an overpriced can of Starbucks Doubleshot. We return to the van; only a couple more hours to go. I get back to my newsletter. I must have eaten a granola bar while I was typing because there's a wrapper in my right hand.

At some point Paul says, "Look up!" and I tear my gaze away from the computer. My eyes are met with a gorgeous vista of hills—the autumn-painted leaves are a dazzling patchwork quilt of orange, yellow, green, and brown against a clear blue sky. Or maybe this time it's a winding mountain pass with a crystalline lake below. Or the stark desert sand with saguaro cacti scattered along the horizon like scarecrows standing guard. Whatever the view, we have the same conversation we've had a thousand times: how beautiful it is and how much we love driving through America's varied landscapes.

In no time at all, we're pulling up to the venue. We bicker about parking again, because I can never keep my mouth shut no matter how much I try. As usual, I'm in a hurry to get inside, while Paul is intent on lining up the van perfectly straight in the parking spot. We finally extricate ourselves from the vehicle. Paul unloads my amp, mic stand, looping pedals, and merch. As we approach the door of the venue, my violin case strapped to the side of my electric wheelchair, I feel my energy shift. A little nervous, a little excited. Soon I will get to weave my web of sound. The driving days can feel dull and repetitive, but I don't mind. Because I know what comes next.

When I'm onstage, time stands still—the blur of the day is replaced by an acute sense of clarity.

On one particular evening in January 2020, I'm playing at a funky arts space in New Orleans. I'm on a black wooden stage with a homemade wheelchair ramp that the venue owner built that very afternoon. When we arrived a few hours earlier we made the frustrating discovery that the ramp was only half-completed, but the owner managed to get it done just before the doors opened.

The audience, of course, is none the wiser.

I make my way up the ramp and Paul helps me get situated in front of the microphone. I hold my violin upright in the seat of my wheelchair; it rests comfortably in front of me, like an extension of my body. I smile when I locate a few friends in the crowd. Then the lights are dimmed, just bright enough to make out the audience.

While I sing, I notice every vintage light fixture, every upcycled chair, every tin sign on the walls of this cavernous space. My gaze glides above the faces in the room, not resting long enough to trip myself up, but still, I can see joy in their eyes as they listen attentively.

We rein it in
And there is better understanding
Nobody wins
If there is flight without the landing.

In the middle of the verse about coming out the other side of a conflict with a close friend, I sense a familiar flutter of energy in my belly. The flutters condense and the energy swirls up from my stomach and moves into my rib cage. A warming sensation fills my chest. I focus on the lyrics so that I can really feel their meaning, allowing the song's melancholy to wash over me.

And we learn
To keep our hearts in time.
Try not to burn
The careful ties
That bind us together.

Just then, a second column of energy flows down through the top of my head. Goose bumps form on the base of my neck—it feels almost as if I'd sprouted wings. I push the bittersweet swirl of energy straight out of my chest and into the room, to be absorbed by the audience. If I let myself wallow in these emotions for too long, I might start to cry—but I'm already onto the chorus.

Beauty and sadness blend together when you perform for a live audience. It's such an electric exchange of energy, but you can't force it or hold on to it. These fleeting, alchemical moments are what musicians live for on the road. They make all the unpredictability of pursuing a music career—the twists and turns, the long days, the hope and disappointments—worth it. Of course, you never know when these magical moments will occur—could be any verse, any show.

1
Major Plot Twist

IN 2016, I was earning my living by teaching fiddle lessons and gigging on the weekends at local music venues in Duluth, Minnesota. In the afternoons, I taught Celtic tunes and violin technique to twenty students of varying ages and abilities. I loved it almost as much as I loved performing.

For some reason, Wednesdays were always my busiest lesson day. I had students back-to-back until eight o'clock at night, with barely enough time to snack on bites of my dinner.

One such Wednesday at around 2:30 p.m., I had a little breathing room between students. I was planning to take a bathroom break and maybe eat some of the cheese I'd packed for myself.

Instead, I checked my email.

And there it was, the message I'd never expected to receive:

Good afternoon, Gaelynn! This is Jessica from NPR Music. We want to talk to you about your submission for the Tiny Desk Contest, preferably today. Do you have any time for a call?

A wave of nervous energy made my stomach flip, and I started to shake a little. Could it be? I had daydreamed about getting this email, but I didn't actually think it would happen.

A MONTH EARLIER, two of my fiddle students had separately emailed me about something called the Tiny Desk Contest. I'd never heard of it before, so I did some research. Apparently, it was an annual contest hosted by NPR Music, and to enter, all you had to do was film yourself playing an original song (in front of a desk) and upload it to YouTube. My students urged me to submit a video.

At first, I didn't really feel motivated to do it—I told myself that contests weren't really my thing. But then a couple days later, my best friend, Leah, texted me completely out of the blue: "You should enter this! Who knows?"

Call it superstition, but when the universe sends me a message in threes, it gets my attention.

Now I just had to choose a song. I had narrowed it down to three, but I was having trouble with the final decision. My song "Let It Go" was my initial front-runner, but I wondered if it was too sparse with its simple chord structure and slow tempo. "Watch the World Unfold" was a contender, but it was a happy melody and I wasn't sure it would be taken seriously by the judges. "Someday We'll Linger in the Sun" was my third choice. But it seemed so dark. Or was my hesitation just that I still felt so vulnerable singing it in front of people? It was a very personal song, after all, about my husband, Paul, staying by my side throughout a nightmarish hospital stay a few years back.

So, the next time I was at the pizza shop for my weekly gig, I made the audience decide for me. I told the "crowd" (a group of twenty dine-in listeners) about the impending contest deadline and my song-selection dilemma. I played the three songs in a row and held a vote afterward, by a show of hands. To my utter surprise, "Someday We'll Linger in the Sun" won by a landslide. I doubt I would've chosen it on my own, but democracy ruled the day.

Now that I had my song picked out, I just had to film the video. On the NPR Music website, a lot of the video entries looked like they'd been professionally shot. I asked several music contacts for videographer recommendations, but the contest deadline was fast approaching, and I couldn't find anyone with availability on such short notice.

So instead, I recruited my friend Leah to film my submission video. She met me in my private lesson space, where I already had my violin, looping pedal, and a miniature Orange practice amp set up. All I had for recording gear was an outdated smartphone, and its video quality was lackluster at best.

Despite our limited tech, we tried to be thoughtful about my submission video. We placed everything just so to "frame the shot." I wondered aloud if there was a way to film that didn't immediately reveal my shortened arms and my wheelchair, knowing that the idea of disability comes with baggage for some.

Leah suggested that we begin the video zoomed in on just my hand, as I played my violin. I loved the idea. That would give people a little time to get drawn into the music before forcing them to acknowledge the physical differences of the person making it. It's not that I was ashamed of my disability; it's just that I wanted the judges to consider the music on its own merits rather than having their preconceived notions about my life color their opinions.

We gave it our all. Unfortunately, we had overestimated our cinematography skills. Whenever Leah tried to zoom out from my hand to get the full body shot, my phone's camera got overloaded and the image would jerk. *Glitch, glitch, glitch!* What little artistic vision we'd imagined for the opening moments was rendered almost comical. We laughed hysterically after each take but kept going. We managed to record the full song three times. I let Leah pick which one to submit.

"The second time gave me chills," she said, to my surprise. "Let's go with that one."

We wrapped it up and went to meet our friends for half-price wine night at the bar downstairs.

"If you win this thing," Leah teased, "you'd better remember: You owe it all to me!"

We both laughed. I promised she would be the first person I thanked in my Grammy acceptance speech. "It's just a bummer my phone sucks so much," I lamented. "Oh, well, we'll see what happens!"

And for about a month, nothing much did.

And then, the email. *We want to talk to you about your submission for the Tiny Desk Contest, preferably today.* What could they possibly want? I figured it had to be good news, but *how* good? It was too cryptic for my nerves. Each week the NPR staff highlighted a few fun entries online. Maybe that was it! I'd also read that before choosing a winner, the judges narrowed the list down to fifty finalists. *Don't get too excited,* I scolded myself.

I typed up a quick reply: *I have an opening at 4:00 pm Central Time. Here's my phone number. I am looking forward to talking!* I pressed Send. I sat there frozen as butterflies swarmed my stomach. Just then, one of my adult students walked in for her lesson.

"Gaelynn, you look like you've seen a ghost!" she said, "Are you OK?"

"Remember that contest you told me about? Well, I literally just got an email from them. They want to talk with me!"

Her face lit up. "Are you serious?" she asked breathlessly. "Gaelynn, don't mind me! You should call them right away!" I assured her that we could proceed with the lesson as planned because I had already scheduled a time for them to call me. Nonetheless, we were both so giddy that it was hard to focus on the music during her lesson. We stuck to easy duets while I tried not to explode.

Finally, alone in my office at 4:00 p.m., my phone rang. I answered it, my hand shaking. I had absolutely no idea what to expect.

"Hello, Gaelynn," a deep, vaguely familiar voice said from the other end of the line. "This is Bob Boilen from NPR Music. I've been listening to your album. I just love how you're experimenting on those traditional fiddle tunes. I especially enjoyed 'Swallowtail Jig.'"

I was confused. My entry wasn't from that album. Why did he know about that song?

He didn't leave me wondering long. "The reason I'm calling is because the judges all loved your submission for the Tiny Desk Contest. In fact, it was a unanimous decision. We would like to announce you as this year's winner. How does that sound?"

"What? Seriously?! That sounds amazing!" I heard myself say.

He told me there had been over six thousand submissions. I was stunned.

The entire conversation was surreal, like an out-of-body experience. But at the same time, I felt an inner calm. I took a deep breath, looking around my cheery office. I studied the little white picture frame on my desk. It displayed one of my favorite quotes in bold, colorful font: LIVE ON THE GOOD SIDE, THE BRIGHT SIDE, THE TRUE SIDE OF EVERYTHING!

Remember this moment, I thought to myself. *It's important. Take in every single detail.*

That was the phone call that would change my life. And weirdly, I think I knew it at the time. It was the beginning of a monumental journey—as if a long-hidden path, once shrouded in fog, had magically revealed itself. Now I just had to follow it, wherever it might lead.

2

I Was Born for the Stage

I EXIST BECAUSE of Brigadoon, a magical village in Scotland that rises out of the mist for a single day every one hundred years.

More specifically, I exist because my parents met performing in the musical *Brigadoon*. They were both chorus members in the community theater's 1983 production in Duluth, Minnesota.

At the time, my father, Tim, was twenty-four years old with a quintessential 1980s mustache. He was working as an orderly in a nursing home, where the residents loved his quick banter as he fed them, helped them bathe, and wheeled them around the facility. He was living alone in a tiny rental house and dreamed of going back to school to become a nurse or maybe a teacher.

My mother, Peggy, was thirty-one and working as a secretary. She was just under five feet tall and newly divorced, just scraping by with her two young children, Ben and Corry. They lived together in a little bungalow built in 1912. The back hallway was so slanted that Ben could roll his Matchbox cars from the kitchen to the bathroom. Still, it had the charm of a small cottage, and it's what she could afford.

That fateful (at least for them, and for me) production of *Brigadoon* was quite a spectacle. Much of the music was performed by The Highlanders, a local, kilt-clad drum-and-bagpipe group providing all the Scottish flair you'd expect in *Brigadoon*. My parents and others sang in the chorus on the big musical numbers, but the director brought in Celtic dancers for the extra-fancy footwork. One of the dancers was a sweet girl with curly red hair named Galen, who would later become the inspiration for my name.

My parents' first kiss was on Saint Patrick's Day in 1983 during rehearsal—my mom has often recalled how my dad had worn a KISS ME, I'M IRISH button to the theater that night.

Their relationship was blossoming as magically (and as quickly) as the land of Brigadoon itself.

My mom introduced my dad to her children about a month into the relationship; Ben was five and Corry was two. They responded to him timidly at first, but he won them over with his goofy, childlike jokes and stories. They loved calling his bluff whenever his tales stretched to fantastical proportions.

Just a few months into their relationship, my mother discovered she was pregnant with me. This development certainly wasn't planned, but it wasn't unwelcome, either. My parents knew they would be together forever, and they both wanted to have more kids.

News of my pending arrival, coupled with their fairytale love for each other, prompted my dad to ask my mom if she would marry him. She politely but firmly declined.

"I love you, Tim," my mom assured him, "but I'm just not ready yet." She was still enjoying a blissful oasis after her recent divorce. Besides, they had the rest of their lives to get married.

But a few months later, my mom was ready to take the plunge. The wedding ceremony was a small service, attended by mostly family and close friends. Photos from that autumn afternoon plainly reveal that my mother was six months pregnant at the time. Instead of squishing herself into a wedding gown, she was adorned in a white, flowing maternity top and a pair of white slacks. Her dark brown hair fell around her shoulders, and she held a bouquet of fall-colored silk flowers.

THE EARLY DAYS of my parents' marriage were joyful ones, or so they tell me anyway. And all the while, my mom's due date was fast approaching.

For a few terrifying days in the middle of the pregnancy, my mother experienced some cramping and minor bleeding. My parents visited the doctor, worried that my mom was having a miscarriage. To their immense relief, the ultrasound tech quickly located my heartbeat. Then, just as mysteriously as it had arrived, the pain went away.

No one knew it at the time, but in the womb, I was struggling. My bones were not developing normally. They were fragile—so fragile, in fact, that they were breaking in utero. By today's standards, the ultrasound scans of the early 1980s were fairly grainy. But no matter the year, even a trained eye can occasionally miss a fractured bone (or forty of them, which was closer to the truth in my case). According to their doctor, I was a healthy baby girl with a thick head of hair.

My mother had a C-section scheduled for January 24, 1984. Before Ben was born, her doctor had told her in no uncertain terms that natural childbirth would be impossible for her, owing to her petite frame and narrow pelvis. He scheduled a C-section, and my mother didn't question it.

Looking back, that C-section may well have been a truly lucky break for me, as I doubt my fragile body would have fared well during the physical pressure of labor and a natural delivery.

The Saturday before I was due, my parents planned one last hurrah, a double date at her younger sister and brother-in-law's house. Dinner and card games were the order of the night.

Halfway through a game of hearts, my mom's water broke. My parents quickly gathered their coats, and my dad drove them to the hospital. I was ready to be born, three days early.

This is the only time I've ever been early for anything.

Upon my mom's arrival to the hospital, she was sent in for an emergency C-section. But the delivery did not go as planned.

To their complete surprise, the doctors discovered that all four of my limbs had been broken in utero and healed at unnatural angles. My legs were permanently stuck in the lotus position, my right arm was bent at ninety degrees, and my left arm was twisted around and pinned behind my back. To make matters more stressful, I had inhaled some amniotic fluid, so I was having trouble breathing on my own. I needed to go to the newborn intensive care unit before doctors could even begin to think about a diagnosis.

There was a lot of commotion in the room. My dad sat at the head of the bed, his mind swimming and confused. None of the doctors were addressing my parents, and I hadn't even been introduced to my mother yet. A doctor finally approached my mother, as he administered an unknown liquid through the IV attached to her arm. "What's going on?" she asked frantically.

"There are some abnormalities; we are trying to sort things out," he replied. That was the last thing she heard before the sedative took effect. The doctor turned toward my father.

"Tim? I am going to need you to follow me."

They headed to intensive care.

3

Don't Drop the Baby

FOR THE FIRST day or so, the doctors faced a mystery, and they were eager to solve it. They laid out a bold hypothesis for my parents a few hours after my birth:

We think she has a rare form of dwarfism. She will never walk, her cognitive functioning will be severely delayed, and we doubt she'll live past the age of five.

But the very next day, the doctors returned with a heavily modified diagnosis:

After studying the X-rays more closely, we think your daughter has osteogenesis imperfecta. She will break many bones throughout her life and probably will never walk. But she should be quite bright and very sociable.

How had the doctors come to this new conclusion so quickly? It turns out they'd had a clue in another baby named Julia, who had been born in Duluth the year before.

This baby's limbs had also fractured in utero and healed so that they were permanently bent. Was it possible that two babies, born a year apart in the same city, could share the same rare genetic disorder that affects only one person in every fifty thousand? Apparently, yes.

Osteogenesis imperfecta (OI), also known as brittle bone disease, is a genetic disorder affecting the building-block protein known as collagen, and it causes the bones to be a lot more fragile than usual. Since collagen is present throughout the body, OI can *also* affect one's blood vessels, lungs, teeth, and even hearing.

OI is often traced back through a person's family lineage, but not always. Sometimes it's simply caused by an unexplained, spontaneous genetic mutation, which was the case for me.

There are many variations of OI, ranging widely in severity. Type 1 is the mildest form of OI, and many folks with this type can walk since their bones fracture only occasionally. Type 2 is the most severe; babies with this form of OI frequently die shortly after birth due to trauma in utero. Type 3 is less severe than Type 2, but it often causes fractures before birth, short stature, respiratory issues, and scoliosis. People with Type 3 may experience anywhere from a dozen to several hundred fractures throughout their lifetimes.

Based on my symptoms, doctors have always told me that I have Type 3 OI, though I have never had a genetic test to confirm their diagnosis.

Fortunately, people with Type 3 OI tend to have a relatively normal life expectancy, with two major exceptions. The first cause of premature death is accidents—sometimes a fall that causes a massive number of fractures can be deadly. The second is respiratory failure. People with OI are often smaller in stature and have scoliosis, which means there's little room to spare in the chest cavity for lung capacity. The not-so-secret weapon most people with OI carry is vigilance—against accidents and respiratory illnesses. Our existence is precariously balanced between life and death, beauty and pain, joy and sorrow, audacity and uncertainty. This is, in fact, true for *all* human beings; I only wish society would more readily acknowledge this reality.

I HAVE OFTEN thought about what an emotional roller coaster those first few days must have been for my parents: from the doctor's initial terrifying report that I might die before the age of six, to receiving the diagnosis of OI.

Besides that, I imagine my mother and father must have experienced mixed emotions about the fact that their daughter was born with a disability. Did they cry? Did they pray and ask God why? Did they feel hope, or only fear? How long did it take them to find a sense of peace, even joy, in this unexpected family situation?

In truth, we've never delved too deeply into these questions.

If my surprise disability did initially cause my parents despair, they didn't dwell on it for long. Maybe it was too painful to think about or too awkward to discuss. But most likely, they simply adjusted and moved on; they're a resilient couple. Besides, they weren't alone.

Although there were many grandchildren on my mom's side of the family, the only grandchildren on my dad's side were from former marriages. So for my dad's mom, my Grandma White, I was the first grandchild she could meet right at the start—her own flesh and blood.

And there was no mistaking the family resemblance. I was clearly my father's child from day one. We had the same brown eyes, same rounded nose, same giant forehead, same everything! My parents nervously invited Grandma White to the hospital once I was stabilized. They ushered her up to the medical bassinet, with its tall, clear plastic sides.

There were wires poking out all over my tiny body, monitoring my every vital sign, and I was hooked up to oxygen. My limbs were askew at alarming angles, and my thick, dark hair was sticking up everywhere, its signature cowlicks already defying gravity (thanks, Dad). My mom was exhausted, and nervous about how my grandmother would handle the sight of her new, disabled grandbaby.

Grandma White craned her neck to peer over the edge of the bassinet, staring silently for a few seconds as my mom held her breath.

Then my grandma's whole face broke into a beaming smile. "She's beautiful!" My mom let out a sigh of relief, tears welling in her eyes. "And Peggy," she continued, "I think she has your eyebrows!" My mom knew that was a bald-faced lie, but it was a nice gesture. And she was sure that my grandma would love me exactly the way I was.

BECAUSE THERE WAS no real way to gauge how brittle my bones were in those first weeks, the doctors had to assume I was extremely fragile. It was more or less guaranteed that I would break bones at home, but the goal was to avoid that as much as possible. So doctors showed my parents how to lift me and roll me over. They gave my parents strict instructions to carry me cradled in eggshell foam — akin to a very hot potato, or the Ark of the Covenant. No one else was allowed to hold me or carry me.

I was discharged from the hospital after ten days, and my family started creating their new routine.

My parents say that I was a happy baby in general, curious and alert, but my spine was undergoing compression fractures, the unfortunate effects of gravity on brittle vertebrae. This meant I was often uncomfortable, and I was especially sore by the end of the day. Sleeping soundly was difficult because I couldn't stay in one position too long without growing pained and fussy.

In the mid-1980s, doctors didn't have much advice to offer my parents, except to try and make me as comfortable as possible until my spine settled down. Getting creative, my parents bought a used electric swing that they set up in the kitchen to keep me swaying gently. The back-and-forth movement seemed to distract me from the pain.

As the months went by and my spine gradually healed, it became clear that the rest of me wasn't quite as fragile as the doctors had predicted. My dad eventually ditched the eggshell foam. My parents were still extremely careful with me, but they also wanted me to experience the world around me and to get to know my family. They showed my grandparents and aunts how to hold me safely. And although I couldn't roll over by myself or sit up for over a year, my parents made sure that someone was always there to help me.

My parents adapted to raising a disabled child, often buoyed by the encouragement of others. On one memorable occasion, my mom received a call from a woman she'd never met before. The woman was in her sixties and she also had OI. She had heard about my birth through the medical grapevine, and she reached out to reassure my mom that there was hope for my future.

"Don't worry about her," the woman said in a matter-of-fact tone. "She'll do everything everybody else does—I did too! She'll get a job, fall in love, have kids if she wants to—it'll all happen eventually, just a little later than normal. Be patient, and it'll work out."

My mom says that call stuck with her for years. She told me about it when I was a little older, and the stranger's promise of a fulfilling adult life stuck with me too.

4
Hog Wild

AS A BABY, I couldn't move independently—my left arm was stuck behind my back because of how my fractures had healed in utero. Doctors told my parents that when I was a little older, they could operate on my arm to try to straighten it, but in the meantime, it was impossible for me to crawl, and I didn't have much in the way of muscle tone.

After a few months, my parents noticed that I was starting to permanently lean my head to one side. My neck muscles weren't strong enough to hold up the massive bulb of a head my dad's side of the family had gifted to me. Gravity was winning!

My parents grew concerned that I would have a permanent lean, so they began to encourage me to hold my head up straight, to sit up (with support), and to interact with the world from a more upright position.

Shortly after my first birthday, my doctors decided that it was time to correct the position of my left arm.

The doctor sawed my humerus bone at two different points, one right below my shoulder and one above my elbow. Then they rotated the bone so that instead of pointing backward, my arm was angled forward, no longer pinned behind me. They placed rods in my arm bone and allowed it to heal in this corrected position.

After the surgery, the arm itself was still permanently bent at the elbow, but at least I could use both hands now. Even with my left arm in better working order, though, I still wasn't strong enough to crawl by myself as a toddler, and it was pretty clear that I'd never be able to walk without some fairly drastic surgical interventions.

One day, when I was about eighteen months old, my parents had an appointment with an occupational therapist, who had crafted me a rather ingenious scooter that sat very close to the ground. It looked like a cross between a wheelchair and a skateboard—it had a caster wheel in the front and two larger wheels on either side in the back. My hands could reach the big wheels from my seat, and the scooter was light enough for me to push by myself.

The afternoon I was fitted for my new mobility device, the therapist put me into the seat and buckled me up so I could test it out, then she and my mom started chatting as I sat there. They got lost in conversation, and I wheeled away to explore the clinic. The next thing they knew, I was nowhere to be seen.

"Gaelynn, come back here!" my mom called to me in a singsong voice when she spotted me from the doorway. With a gleam in my eye, I took a hard right down the nearest corridor. *If they wanted me so bad, they'd have to come get me!*

When my mom realized I had just shown my first outright display of disobedience, she was ecstatic—I had never been able to move on my own, let alone ignore her commands like other children my age. I got my inaugural taste of freedom that day, and I have never stopped moving since.

IF THAT THREE-WHEELED scooter was a ticket to freedom in our house, then my electric wheelchair was a passport to the rest of the world. I was a mere two and a half years old when I was fitted for my first chair, which seems a bit preposterous in retrospect. I have since watched all my siblings raise kids, and toddlers seem hell-bent on destroying themselves if you so much as turn your back for a second. I can't imagine handing any of them a bona fide motor vehicle at that age! But with great mobility comes great responsibility. I cherished that chair; it was like an extension of my own body.

Back in the late eighties, electric wheelchairs were pretty low tech. Mine was built with a metal frame and adorned with blue faux leather on the slingback, seat, and armrests. The joystick that steered the chair looked like a video game controller mounted to a large rectangular silver box, approximately the size of a pencil case. I was so tiny at the time that the joystick box had to be mounted *inside* the right armrest, because otherwise I couldn't reach it.

But who knew a clunky, battery-powered machine could lend such a sense of normalcy to my life?

My independence grew tremendously with my first wheelchair. I could drive it on the sidewalk and the grass, so I could go pretty much anywhere I wanted with my siblings, cousins, and friends.

One of my first memories in my new electric wheelchair was skunk hunting with my little brother, Greg. The two of us would don the appropriate accoutrements from my mother's costume bin in the attic: a pair of Styrofoam safari hats, matching khaki multipocketed vests, two sets of binoculars, and a big green butterfly net. Once outfitted, we bade our parents farewell, setting out on our expedition to catch a skunk.

Why did we want to catch a skunk, you ask? I honestly do not know. How do you actually catch a skunk? I still have no idea. But at the ages of six and four, we believed that if you poked a stick down a hole in the yard—or even a slight divot—a skunk might come charging out. Greg would hold the net while I'd lean over the edge of my chair with the longest stick we could find. Feeling both nervous and expectant, we'd count in unison: "One, two, three!" In that stick would go... but no skunk would appear. Slightly deflated, but not defeated, we would search for a more promising hole in an even more distant land (our neighbor's yard).

My wheelchair quickly became part of my identity. One morning, my siblings and I found a prize in a cereal box—a mini license plate that read HOG WILD. Since I was the only one with a motorized vehicle, we all agreed that I needed to have it. I proudly hung the license plate on the back of my wheelchair so that it would be the last thing you saw as I drove away from you (that, and a cloud of dust). I felt truly unstoppable in that thing.

But just because I loved my new electric wheelchair didn't mean I was good at operating it. During those first few years of learning how to drive, I destroyed all the door frames in our house (my mother discretely replaced them after I left for college). My back wheel would catch on the corner of the doorway as I was zooming into the kitchen, and—*crack!*—you'd hear the sound of wood being pried off the wall. What's more, countless toenails were collateral damage to my ruthless back tires and young driving age. My family and friends got used to keeping my wheels in their sights, and they would deploy some fancy footwork when necessary.

THE FREEDOM OF mobility quickly became my new normal. For the most part, I simply stopped being aware of it and carried on with the exciting business of living. But annoyingly, other people couldn't seem to contain their discomfort and curiosity about my new wheelchair. Strangers of all ages would stare or make silly jokes about it or sometimes ask rude questions. I sensed a disconnect between how *I* viewed my wheelchair and how others did.

Deep down I knew that the disproportionate focus on my wheelchair was often an awkward or misguided attempt to make small talk and connect. But still: *Slow down or I'll give you a speeding ticket, You need to get chains on those tires!* and *Do you have a license to drive that thing?* soon became three of my least favorite sentences in the English language.

Sometimes I would engage with folks fully when they asked invasive questions or made what they considered to be witty comments about my wheelchair. Other times, I would give one-word answers or smile. On the really bad days—when I just didn't have the energy—I simply pretended not to hear them.

From an early age, I wished that I could wave a magic wand to help people see my wheelchair through *my* eyes instead of theirs. Far from confining me, my wheelchair was my trusty companion. Not only did it give me much-cherished mobility, but it provided a place to hang my purses and to sit comfortably in a chairless room—plus it was great at splashing through puddles.

REGARDLESS OF HOW others responded to my wheelchair, it did not dominate my consciousness growing up. Occasionally I even experienced wonderful adventures *without my chair!*

One afternoon, when I was about nine years old, my mom needed to attend a meeting a few blocks away, and she left my older sister, Corry, to babysit Greg and me. Corry wasn't often put in the command zone, let alone for two whole unsupervised hours. It felt electric, almost dangerous, as we watched my mom drive away from the house.

My wheelchair happened to have no battery power that day, and it was plugged into its bulky wall charger. But the exact minute my mom left, we three kids began discussing how it was absolutely necessary that we buy candy at the neighborhood gas station.

Saddled with Greg and me, Corry knew she couldn't be so irresponsible as to leave us behind to load up on sweets. But how could we make the three-block journey together without my wheelchair? The perfect plan began to crystallize.

We dug out an oversized, hand-me-down camping backpack—it was one of those M*A*S*H-like military-issue bags made of thick olive-green canvas and supported by an external frame of metal bars.

"Gaelynn, do you think you can fit inside?" my sister asked, setting the backpack next to me so that we could gauge its height and width. I eyed it hopefully.

"I think so! But are you strong enough to carry me that far?"

"Don't worry. I'll make sure we do this safely!" Corry replied confidently. "We can try it out first; I'll carry you around the house."

Corry was smart, responsible, and true to her word, so I trusted her.

"Let's try it!" I urged. "Hurry, before Mom gets back!"

Corry carried me over to the couch and laid the backpack on its side, the mouth of the bag facing me. We put a few towels at the bottom of the bag to cushion me from the metal bars. I flattened down and shimmied myself inside, butt first, until my legs touched bottom.

"OK, you can lift up the bag now!" I called from within my canvas cocoon.

Ever so carefully, Greg and Corry rotated the bag upright. I slid down the last few inches until I was resting on the towels. To my surprise, I couldn't see anything, as the upper rim of the bag was virtually level with the top of my head. We all started to giggle. I could hear them (and breathe) just fine so long as we didn't close the bag.

So we forged ahead. Corry knelt down in front of the couch and slipped the two thick straps over her shoulders.

"Greg, help me up!" she directed.

I felt my body stiffen and rise as the bag seemingly levitated from the couch.

We had liftoff! Although I only weighed about forty pounds, Corry was a veritable twig of a girl, so none of us were really sure if she could lug me all the way to the gas station.

"Do you feel steady on your feet?" I asked nervously from within my sack.

"Yes!" Corry said, demonstrating the command of her muscles by flexing and straightening her knees in a quick dip.

"But let's do a test run," she said. "Greg, spot me, OK?"

Arms outstretched under the bag, Greg followed Corry from room to room, akin to prepping for a NASA launch.

"Are you tired?" I asked.

"No, but if I get tired, I'll sit down to rest on a curb."

That satisfied me. We were good to go!

We bravely made our way to the front door, feeling gleeful that our ingenious idea was actually working. We then made our way outside. I couldn't see anything.

"Where are we?" I asked.

"We're walking down the ramp now," Corry said.

"Now we're turning right on the sidewalk."

We started talking about what candy we were going to get. Airheads for Greg, Three Musketeers for me, Rolos for Corry.

"We're approaching the end of the block," Corry told me. "Then we'll cross 46th Avenue."

I was feeling quite content in my canvas cocoon as we plodded along. Everything was going swimmingly. Suddenly Corry exclaimed, "Oh, no!" and stopped dead in her tracks.

"What is it?!" I called out frantically.

"It's Mom," Corry said. "She's back early for some reason!"

My stomach dropped.

"OK, guys, just don't say anything," Corry told us. "Let me handle this."

I strained to listen, and sure enough, there were tires rolling on the pavement. They stopped. A car door opened, a familiar dinging. A seat belt unclicked.

Then, just as I'd feared, the loud, piercing words of my flustered mother:

"What are you two doing?!"

Corry tried her best to play it cool. "We're just walking to the gas station. Why are you back so early?" she asked in her most innocent-sounding voice.

"I ran back to grab something I forgot at the house," Mom snapped. She was not having any of it. "Never mind that! You two left Gaelynn at home, all by herself?"

"No!" Corry shot back desperately. "She's with us!"

There was an unbearably long pause. The absurdity of the situation began to dawn on me, and a round of giggles began building inside.

"What do you mean?" Mom asked, completely baffled now.

An even longer pause followed.

Corry realized the game was up and blurted out her confession. "She's in my backpack!"

The three of us kids quickly unraveled, laughing uncontrollably. Mom squinted at Corry's back, and sure enough, she could just make out the top of my head, bobbing up and down while I belly-laughed from deep within the canvas hiking bag.

"Well, get inside the house!" she sputtered incredulously, trying to hide her own amusement.

We turned to head back home. Our plans were foiled, but our spirits remained high. My mom didn't have the heart to punish us. Maybe she knew then what seems so clear to me now: that a deep sense of well-being can spring from even the tiniest act of inclusion. Even if that looks like stuffing your sibling into a backpack.

5

Theater Kid

MY PARENTS' LOVE of theater extended well beyond their initial meeting in *Brigadoon*. One or both were always performing in a show, mostly musicals, for as far back as I can remember. More than soccer leagues or PTA meetings or the pressure to get good grades, musical performance was a staple in our household. One of my earliest memories was my dad playing musical games with me in the car.

"Hey, Gaelynn," Dad would say as he glanced up at four-year-old me from the rearview mirror. "Sing this back to me."

Then he'd belt out, in an ascending arpeggio, "La-la-la-laaaaaaa!"

Perched atop the booster seat in the back of our old Crown Victoria, I'd listen carefully to the notes he sang so that I was sure I'd remember. Then I'd blast them to the front of the car with a volume that quite exceeded my tiny frame: "La-la-la-laaaaaaa!!!"

"Correct!" Dad would answer enthusiastically, and then I'd sing him a phrase to parrot back to me. We would trade off roles in this call-and-response, each trying to stump the other. The string of notes would get progressively more complex, and sometimes I'd have to ask him to repeat the phrase or break it into parts before I could accurately sing it back to him. But I couldn't get enough of it.

Little did I know, this was just ear training disguised as a game.

There was no escaping music in my family. During the early 1990s, parents and children alike participated in our church's cantata—a musical theater–style retelling of the Christmas story. It was not uncommon for spontaneous sing-alongs to erupt at the kitchen table in the weeks leading up to the "big show."

One year, when my dad was playing King Herod, my seven-year-old brother, Greg, belted out King Herod's solo over dinner, and the rest of us joined in on the refrains. Greg had the whole thing memorized, down to its ominous last line: "I won't stop till I know he's dead." (He slowly clenched his fist for added dramatic flair.) We all clapped over our plates as Greg grinned at us.

Then Corry and I took the stage, trading off verses of "Mary, Did You Know?"—occasionally bickering over the correct lyrics—until Greg joined in with the harmony on the last refrain. (Yes, harmonizing at the dinner table is a little over-the-top *Brady Bunch*, and there is unfortunately film evidence for many of these evenings.)

Making music wasn't just reserved for holidays. Greg and I absolutely loved to record ourselves singing together on cassette tape (always with harmonies, of course). On rainy afternoons we'd spend hours huddled next to the cassette recorder, doing take after take until we had finally locked in a masterpiece. One of our favorites was the brother-sister duet "Somewhere Out There" from the mouse-themed cartoon movie *An American Tail*. If you know, you know...

SINCE I WAS raised by thespian parents, it's no surprise that I was also interested in theater at an early age. And as a benevolent gift from the universe, there happened to be an inclusive, all-ages theater company already up and running in Duluth called Access Theater, which cast both disabled and nondisabled actors side by side. American Sign Language interpretation was included at *every* Access Theater performance—this meant deaf people could attend the shows whenever they wanted, not just on a few, select evenings.

It wasn't until adulthood that I realized how rare this kind of theater production company was back in 1989. After all, this was a full year before the Americans with Disabilities Act—the law requiring that public spaces become accessible to people with disabilities—was even passed. Duluth was some kind of disability haven; at least, that's how it felt growing up.

Duluth is a city of ninety thousand in northern Minnesota, situated on the rocky shores of Lake Superior. If you were to study a map, imagining the lake as a wolf head, we'd be right on the tip of the wolf's nose. But the word *lake* hardly does it justice—Unsalted Sea, as it has lovingly been referred to in the past, comes closer. Lake Superior alone holds 10 percent of all the earth's fresh water. Views from the glistening shore are vast and majestic, and there are many places where you can't see land across the water.

Duluth also hosts thriving art, music, and theater communities. And Duluthians are *very* proud of the fact that Bob Dylan was born there, as evidenced by the annual Bob Dylan Days (Bob himself seems markedly less enthusiastic about this fact).

But Duluth is far from perfect. Around the time I was born, there was a mass exodus of young people, thanks to a crushing recession. On the bridge to our neighboring state of Wisconsin, travelers passed a billboard with a chilling message: WILL THE LAST ONE LEAVING DULUTH PLEASE TURN OUT THE LIGHT?

Even in 2025, Duluth has a poverty rate of over 17 percent, and its racial and economic disparities are significant. There are several areas of town with empty shop windows and dilapidated houses. A reporter from *Rolling Stone* once went so far as to write that "a thin layer of grime covered the downtown." And while this may be a little true, it's not a very nice thing to say as a visitor. But the sight of cargo ships, iron ore docks, railroad cars, and manufacturing plants *does* give Duluth a distinctly industrial feel against its backdrop of rustic, natural beauty.

Most notably, the winters are severe enough to make grown adults cry. Duluth is one of the snowiest cities in the United States, receiving close to ninety inches of snow in the average winter. The snow starts in October, sticks by November, and won't completely melt until mid-May. During the winter, temperatures drop to minus twenty degrees Fahrenheit (minus forty with the wind chill). These extreme temperatures can last for weeks, wreaking havoc on the roads—and souls—of Duluth. Though it is a lovely place in the summer, living there year-round is not for the faint of heart.

But the Duluthians surrounding me as a kid—especially the artists and musicians—were kind, quirky, and creative. I know that many disabled people grow up feeling unsupported by their communities, but this wasn't my childhood experience. I'm still not sure why, but the small Midwestern city of Duluth was ahead of its time in a number of ways, including Access Theater.

I was elated when my dad told me I'd been asked to perform in my first-ever play with the theater troupe. I was only six years old (apparently I'd been fast-tracked past the auditions). My first role was reciting a short, satirical Mark Twain monologue called "Advice to Little Girls." The problem was, I couldn't read very well yet! But my dad was a resourceful guy. He recorded himself reading the monologue, and I memorized the lines by listening to them on repeat.

Twain's tongue-in-cheek missive on good behavior contained gems such as this one:

If at any time you find it necessary to correct your brother, do not correct him with mud—never, on any account, throw mud at him, because it will spoil his clothes. It is better to scald him a little, for then you obtain desirable results.

I was portraying an unusually sadistic child!

Anyway, I must have been quite the sight up there, a tiny wisp of a thing seated in an electric wheelchair, all alone onstage. But I was no wallflower: I'd belt out my lines into the darkness, projecting louder than many full-grown adults. My costume was a frilly gown, as if I'd been playing dress-up and stopped to tell the audience my take on female etiquette.

To that end, I was allowed to do my own makeup each night, my messy lipstick visible from the back row. The monologue's old-fashioned language and subtle humor were both beyond my childhood comprehension, but I easily connected with the joy in the room as the audience roared with laughter every time I delivered my lines. The reviews—from my parents—were glowing. I was forever hooked on performing after this first theater experience.

Over the next dozen years I was in about as many plays, sometimes at school and sometimes at our local children's theater.

My favorite plays were always at Access Theater. This forward-thinking theater troupe not only introduced me to the thrill of performing onstage—a delight that would someday cross over to my concerts—but also introduced me to a true disability community. I got to know some really cool disabled adults, which basically never happened otherwise. One such individual was Russ, who also had OI. Even though we had the same disability, our physical situations were far from identical. His arms were much longer than mine, so he could push a manual wheelchair and take care of his daily needs without assistance. He was about forty years old at the time and lived a very independent life: He drove a car, owned a home, and was even elected to our city council. Russ was a good OI role model for me during my formative years (he also happened to be the only one).

And then there was Jeff, who made a huge impact on me as a kid. Jeff was a tall, quiet man in his mid-forties. He had kind eyes, a friendly smile, and a deep laugh. A surgery to remove a benign brain tumor in his twenties had left him completely, unexpectedly deaf. He could still speak, of course, so for two decades he navigated the world through lipreading. By the time we met, he was starting to learn American Sign Language (ASL), and seeing ASL used in conversation blew my ten-year-old mind.

I know now that it can be annoying for deaf people when hearing folks treat ASL as though it's a visual novelty rather than a true language, a method of daily communication. I imagine it's similar to the way I feel when people make unnecessary comments about my wheelchair in the grocery store. Responses to signifiers of one's disability can make people feel on display.

Hindsight, however, is 20/20. The moment I met Jeff at our first rehearsal, I was drawn to ASL like a moth to flame, and I became determined to use it to communicate with Jeff.

My favorite ASL interpreter at Access Theater, Nancy, was a kind woman in her forties with a dark-brown bob and thick glasses. By day she worked at the local university in the Disability Services department. She was always keen to indulge my interest in the beautiful, mysterious, enthralling gestures of ASL, so she lent me one of her ASL dictionaries.

First, I memorized the alphabet for finger signing, and then I moved on to basic phrases. But there were so many words I didn't know! I had to stop and spell out a word every few minutes, which was a painstakingly slow way to communicate.

I'm lucky that Jeff had the patience of a saint and a very kind heart. Perhaps he understood that people can be both foolish and loving at the same time, or maybe because he was a student of ASL himself he was willing to cut me a little more slack.

Either way, even if the initial draw to Jeff was ASL, we soon developed a genuine friendship. I found him hilarious, and we really enjoyed each other's company. As the weeks passed, ASL became less of a hobby and more a useful tool to communicate with Jeff backstage, where it really was too dark to lip-read. I have many fond memories of laughing with Jeff at rehearsals, after he would deliver a perfectly timed punch line.

Jeff and I have kept in touch over the years. Even though we only see each other occasionally, he is like an uncle to me. I think some people have an outsized impact on your life, because they introduce you to a new perspective or an interest that fundamentally alters your life's course. Jeff opened my eyes to the world of Deaf Culture. And *that* was my first taste of Disability Culture, a concept that has been weaving itself into the fabric of my life ever since.

WHEN MY MOM turned forty, she had a bit of a midlife crisis. She wanted to do theater professionally, but she wasn't sure how to make her dream a reality. She had many years of experience onstage and behind the scenes, and one of her part-time jobs was selling print advertising for the playbills at the Duluth Playhouse.

One afternoon, she was making calls to businesses in the area to sponsor the next big play. She called the owner of an old brewery building downtown that had been repurposed to house a shopping complex, several restaurants, and a hotel. When asked if he'd be willing to take out an ad, the owner sighed.

"What I really want is to have my own theater *here,* not advertise in a theater across town."

He had piqued my mom's curiosity.

"But where would you do the plays?" she asked.

"There's an eighty-seat theater up on the third floor, and it's hardly ever used. And I'd want to make it a dinner theater too. We'd serve a meal in the banquet room ahead of time, from the restaurant downstairs. I think it could bring new people in, but I don't know the first thing about theater. You don't know anyone who could open a theater here, do you?" he said, laughing wistfully.

My mom didn't know what came over her, but she heard herself saying, "I could do that!"

"Really?" he asked.

"Yes, I could definitely do that," she said, reassuring him and herself simultaneously. "How hard could it be? Just give me a little time to draw up some plans."

The call ended without a sale that day, but my mom had definitely made some moves.

That night, after my dad got home from work, Mom announced, "Tim, I'm opening a dinner theater!"

He shot her a quizzical glance. "You mean *we're* opening a dinner theater?" My dad was teaching high school math full-time, so it's not like he had a lot of free time for a side hustle.

"You can help if you want to, but I'm doing it either way," my mom replied with stubborn confidence. A few months later, my parents launched Change of Pace Productions.

Their first play was *I Do, I Do,* a musical chronicling the life of a married couple from newlyweds to old age. It starred both of my parents, of course.

It turned out that my mom and dad made a good team in business as well as in marriage. They each had their roles: Mom advertised and costumed all the shows, and Dad directed and built all the sets. One or both of them acted in almost every show, and together they produced three plays a season for the next two decades.

Since they couldn't afford babysitters, my parents brought me and my little brother, Greg, with them to every rehearsal. Up way past our bedtime, we'd run feral all over the shopping complex where play practices were held. Mom brought mats so that we could nap on the floor by the stage when we got too tired.

Greg and I always ushered at the shows. My parents would pay us each five dollars a night, which was a lot of money back then! By the end of the run of a musical we'd have every song memorized. The whole family folded playbills and stamped the thousands of postcards that were mailed out to advertise, before the rise of social media. It was more than a family business: Theater was a family identity.

In junior high, I started bringing my friends with me to rehearsals. Each night, we'd watch the first half, then go downstairs to get a "coffee" (mocha with extra chocolate and whipped cream) and talk for hours. When the show finally opened, my friends and I would watch every performance, more often than not swooning over whatever young male actor my parents had hired to sing the tenor parts. The theater was pretty tiny, so my parents stuck to small-scale musicals like *Forever Plaid, Beehive,* and *The Fantasticks.*

As I grew up, I became involved in the theater in other ways. My friends and I operated the light booth in high school, and once or twice I played violin in the band. When I was in college, my parents started staging audience-participation murder mysteries. They even hired me to write one for them. The resulting script, *Murder at Casino Royale,* involved a Mafia family with twin brothers, a couple of feuding showgirls, and a poisoned drink. While my original script certainly didn't win any awards, writing a murder mystery was a good creative challenge.

My parents' last production was a reprise of *I Do, I Do,* twenty years later. As a kid, I had always grumbled about how we were stuck at the theater and how the rehearsals would never end. But as my parents sang their closing number—a poignant duet called *Our House*—I was man-sobbing next to my siblings in the front row. Theater had become part of our family's fabric, and now I wouldn't trade those memories for anything.

6

I Blame *The Baby-Sitters Club*

I'M PART OF what's referred to as the ADA generation.

As I mentioned earlier, the Americans with Disabilities Act (ADA) is a civil rights law that prohibits discrimination on the basis of disability and ensures access for disabled people in all areas of public life.

This important bill was signed into law on July 26, 1990, when I was six years old.

Because of the ADA, I grew up in a world full of accessible buses and curb cuts and ramps and elevators. That's not to say everywhere I went was wheelchair accessible—far from it—but if I'd been born just one generation earlier, virtually none of those accommodations would have existed.

Even though it hasn't always been adequately enforced, the ADA's existence meant that I grew up knowing that I was entitled to equal rights as a disabled person. This seems like a small matter, but it really isn't. I've often wondered what it would have been like to grow up without those rights, or without a means of legal recourse if they are violated.

For example, Russ—the man with OI whom I had gotten to know through Access Theater—grew up in Duluth in the mid-1960s.

"*Nothing* was accessible back then," he told me during one of our play rehearsals. "It's a good thing I only had a manual chair instead of a big electric chair like yours. I wouldn't have been able to go anywhere. People were always carrying me and my wheelchair up flights of stairs."

"What about school?" I asked.

"Same thing," he replied. "A couple of my buddies would carry me up those steps too. The old high school was *big*—with a huge stone staircase at the front door. They'd bring me and my wheelchair inside and then I'd wheel off to the classroom for kids with disabilities—they lumped us all together in those days, even if you didn't need help with your homework or anything. Then my friends would pick me and my chair up at the end of the day and carry me to the sidewalk."

I couldn't believe my ears. Having to be carried up the stairs at school (and be separated from your friends!) sounded more like the 1800s than the middle of the twentieth century. That conversation with Russ awakened a keen sense of gratitude that I was born in 1980s America, just as the fight for disability rights was starting to come to fruition. What a difference a generation makes!

Thanks to the ADA, elevators were being installed in the local public schools while I was growing up. When I was old enough to enter kindergarten, only two elementary schools in Duluth had elevators. I went to the closest one, about a mile away, even though our neighborhood elementary school was a mere block from my house.

At school I was entitled to an aide who could assist me in the bathroom, lift me in and out of my wheelchair, reach my books, and carry my lunch tray.

Having an aide meant that my mom didn't have to attend school with me or worry about my safety while I was there. My aide would, of course, be trained on how to properly lift me so as not to fracture my brittle bones. With this extra support, my mom could work part-time once I started school.

Ultimately, having an aide meant I could be in the same classroom as my peers, learning alongside them rather than being hidden away in a "special" room for disabled students, like my friend Russ had experienced when he was in school four decades earlier.

My first aide had a distinct grandmotherly air about her. Her appearance was not unlike my own grandma, although she smiled less and didn't offer me Werther's Originals from her purse. She was stuffy, prim, and proper; never mean, but always formal. Although I'm sure she was doing the best she could, this first aide severely hampered my style. This was most evident at lunch.

The lunchroom is where social learning happens. You swap desserts and gossip like currency. You reveal crushes to your girlfriends, who immediately pass them on to the poor boys' lunch table.

My first aide, however, insisted on joining me for lunch every afternoon. She sat at the end of the table with me and my friends, presumably so that she could be nearby if I needed something. It was embarrassing to have her at the table, especially when she would interrupt our fun.

"Gaelynn, don't talk with your mouth full."

"Gaelynn, use your inside voice, please."

"Gaelynn, please compose yourself. We must behave like ladies."

The absolute worst was when she'd ask, right in front of my friends, "Gaelynn, do you have to go to the bathroom?"

Nothing can make a kid feel more mortified than publicly advertising that they need help to use the bathroom. One minute I'd be hamming it up for my friends, telling some goofy tale from the weekend, and the next I'd be bright red, wanting to melt into the floor.

I complained to my mom, but since unintentional embarrassment isn't the same thing as abuse, there wasn't much she could do. My mom didn't pick the aides; the school assigned them.

In third grade, however, my luck changed. I was paired with a new aide named Mary Stromdahl, who felt like a breath of fresh air. She'd been a surgical nurse before working in the schools and was around fifty when I met her. One of the first things I learned about Mary was her love of animals. She fostered kittens for the humane society, and she also had a dog and *nine cats* of her own.

Mary was a short, sturdy woman with close-cut curly hair that was still black in the back but going gray in the front. She wore sweatshirts (often adorned with portraits of cats), jeans, and tennis shoes. But her most memorable feature was her infectious smile. Mary had one of the goofiest senses of humor I had ever encountered. Around adults she could appear serious, but the second we were alone together, Mary was just as playful as any kid.

Because I didn't need help with homework, Mary and I mostly interacted between classes, and almost all of our deep conversations happened in bathroom stalls.

Having to get help in the bathroom might seem incredibly awkward (and it is always a little weird for the first week or so). But if the person helping you is someone you like and trust, eventually the oddness of the situation fades away and you hardly even notice the assistance.

As we grew closer, those short bathroom breaks became a highlight of my days in many ways.

Mary was always on a mission to make me laugh. One of my quirks was that I would gag loudly at the thought of pretty much anything that made me squeamish. Mary delighted in exploiting this weakness by grossing me out with "war stories" from her days as a nurse in the operating room.

"Did I ever tell you about the one time we were doing an abdominal operation on a guy who got the hiccups in the middle of surgery?" Mary asked, as she was helping me. "Every time he'd hiccup, his small intestines would fly out everywhere and we'd have to cram them back inside!"

I gagged, as expected, and Mary let out her signature cackle.

At one point, Mary bought me the children's book *Grossology* with the express purpose of torturing me with disgusting facts involving mucus and farting. Of course, I feigned protestations when she read it aloud, but my resulting gags always left us both in fits of hysterical laughter.

When I would occasionally break my bones, Mary was always there to help get me through it. Once I took a particularly bad fall—my dad was carrying me down a flight of stairs and slipped on a pair of snow pants—and both of my arms and a leg were fractured. I returned to school after a few weeks of at-home recovery, but for several additional weeks I would still get too sore to stay upright in the classroom all day long. For weeks, Mary read me books in the nurse's office in the late afternoons. Another time in junior high, I broke my writing arm after falling out of my wheelchair at Sam's Club, so Mary had to write for me as I dictated my French homework.

"Which accent goes above the letter *e* again?" she asked.

"The one pointing up, the accent *ah-goo*," I said, overpronouncing the accent *aigu*. "The other one is pointing down. That's an accent *grave*." She insisted on calling them *Ragu* and *gravy*.

Aides are typically assigned to students at random, and rarely do they travel from elementary to middle to high school with the same student. But by the time I was getting ready for middle school, it was clear that Mary played a hugely important role in my life—she was somewhere between a best friend, an accomplice, a mentor, and a second mom. It would have been stressful to start over with a new aide every time I changed schools (even though that is—unfortunately—often the case for students with disabilities). Thankfully, my mom managed to convince our school district to let Mary follow me all the way through high school. Once I got to high school, Mary had to juggle several students throughout the day, but she always made enough time for me, and our friendship only deepened as the years progressed. I look back on the years I spent with Mary as being a uniquely positive part of growing up with a disability.

DESPITE HAVING SUCH a supportive environment, there was a dark spot in my childhood:

Hypochondria.

Does every kid worry about getting a deadly disease, or was that just me? Either way, I took it to another level. Long before WebMD existed, I scared myself with symptom lists.

After everyone was asleep, I'd climb out of bed and quietly scoot myself across the floor, sneaking into the living room. I'd pull my family's massive hardcover copies of *Encyclopedia Britannica* off the lowest bookshelf so that I could look up things like brain tumors and diabetes.

Back in those days, I didn't use my electric wheelchair in the house very often. I had long since graduated from my three-wheeled scooter, and by then I'd grown a lot stronger, so I could propel myself across the floor with my legs from a seated position, a method we dubbed "scooting."

It wasn't that my parents didn't allow my wheelchair in the house—they simply wanted me to move around on my own to gain and maintain physical strength. To that end, we had arranged my bedroom to accommodate me on the floor. My clothes, toys, and books were all on low shelves just off the ground. I did my homework and read for hours sitting on a cushion alongside a folding lap desk. It was the perfect height for me, tucked neatly by my favorite bookshelf, with a small lamp on the desk and a homemade privacy curtain.

From the age of four until about eleven, I could scoot on the floor almost as fast as someone could walk. I still used my wheelchair outside, of course, but I prided myself on my speed and strength indoors. I loved dancing and doing gymnastics routines with Greg in our living room; I could even do a modified handstand!

It seemed my parents' hunch had been correct—putting weight on my bones through exercise appears to have helped them develop as solidly as possible, despite their genetic makeup.

Still, I was always concerned about my health. Even though I was remarkably robust for a kid with my disability, if I had even the slightest headache, I'd become convinced it was a brain tumor. Thirsty? I'd immediately think: diabetes.

In part, I blame my health anxiety on *The Baby-Sitters Club* series and Lurlene McDaniel's books. Although I absolutely adored reading, I just wasn't cut out to handle the medical details of Stacey McGill's diabetes diagnosis, and no prudent school librarian should have let a kid as obviously anxious as me check out books with titles like *Six Months to Live* and *A Time to Die*.

With every "symptom," I felt compelled to check in with my mom, to make sure I was OK.

"Mom, I'm feeling kind of nauseous. Do you think that means I have a brain tumor?"

"No, Gaelynn, you have a sinus infection. That's why you're dizzy." Temporarily reassured but never fully convinced, I subjected my mom to these disease screenings on a weekly basis.

Things got even worse after my aunt was diagnosed with breast cancer when I was ten years old. She was a beautiful, adventurous, vibrant woman in her forties, and all of us kids adored her. It was extremely jarring to watch her lose all her hair and be so worn out as she battled through chemo. The cancer went into remission for a while after that, and she was back to her spunky self. But the respite wouldn't last.

Six months later she was diagnosed with an extremely aggressive brain tumor, and she died within the year. My siblings and I visited her in the hospital during the last week of her life; her face was all puffy, her skin was ashen, and she could barely talk. She still had that tenderness and sense of humor we recognized, but the cancer had taken almost everything else.

I was terrified of cancer after that. I badgered my mom nonstop about what I believed to be a tumor in my breast. I can still hear her exasperated reply, "Gaelynn, eleven-year-olds just don't get breast cancer!" But I finally wore her down, and she took me to see my pediatric doctor.

I showed him what I was convinced was the tumor. Somehow, with a straight face, he managed to say, "Gaelynn, these are called breast buds. You are developing breasts. Don't worry, there's nothing wrong with you!"

My hypochondria was, no doubt, subconsciously exacerbated by my disability. Even though life expectancy for people with OI is relatively normal, breaking bones in a fall that would typically cause only minor injuries is a pretty stark reminder of one's mortality. There was always a fear simmering slightly below the surface that the next terrible accident was right around the corner.

7

The World's Tiniest Cello

WHEN I WAS in fourth grade, a middle school orchestra visited our elementary school. I had never given the idea of playing a musical instrument much thought, even though I loved to sing. But that afternoon's concert had an immediate effect on me.

I sat in my wheelchair in the back of the school's "gymnatorium," parked beside my classmates as a sea of noisy students crammed themselves into untidy rows on the floor ahead of us. At the far side of the gym, approximately eighty students were onstage, holding wooden stringed instruments of varying sizes. I had never seen anything like it.

"We're here to introduce you to the instruments of an orchestra," the redheaded orchestra teacher announced, from the edge of the stage.

A few of the students gave demonstrations on their instruments. I knew right away from the deep, rich tones and the graceful, sweeping movements of the bow that, were I to ever join an orchestra, I'd play the cello. What a gorgeous, mellow sound it made!

The teacher took her place at the front of the ensemble, white baton in hand. She tapped it against her metal music stand, and eighty young musicians positioned their instruments. Then, on a magical cue that was little more than a collective in-breath, the music erupted. Their joyful cacophony was unlike any other ensemble I'd ever heard.

It was elegant and lively, and the harmonies swirled around the cavernous room. What's more, it was mesmerizing to watch. The rich, brown wood gleamed in the gym lights, and even better, the eighty delicate bows moved back and forth in what appeared to be unison. Upon closer inspection, it was really a rhythmic dance, with each group carrying out their own choreography with their bows, swaying along with the other players in their section. I found myself air-conducting from my wheelchair—I couldn't help it! I was caught up in the spectacle before me, and I desperately wanted to participate.

Never mind that these were eighth graders, most of whom had only been playing for four years themselves, and that the only song I'm certain I remember from that afternoon is a fancy version of "Old McDonald Had a Farm." To me, their performance was a revelation.

That night when I got home, I couldn't wait to tell my mom about the beautiful concert I'd just witnessed.

"I want to join the orchestra next year, Mom!" I exclaimed. "I really liked the cello, and I think I could play it from my wheelchair!"

I mimicked pulling the bow in long strokes in front of me with my right hand as my other hand played the imaginary fingerboard up by my left shoulder.

She gave me an encouraging smile as she said, "If you really want to do it, I'm sure you'll figure out a way."

Many years later, my mom told me that my jubilant announcement about wanting to play the cello had actually filled her with a sense of dread. Not only did she know nothing about string music, but she simply couldn't envision someone my size handling such a large, unwieldy instrument. But she kept her reservations to herself that day, allowing visions of symphonies to dance in my head.

ONE AFTERNOON, AT the beginning of the following school year, the intercom squawked out an important announcement to the new fifth graders: *If you want to be considered for strings, sign up for a music listening test with Mrs. Sommerfeld.*

I eagerly added my name to the list of orchestra hopefuls.

A few days later my teacher quietly dismissed me from class so that I could go to the orchestra room for my test. I felt a sense of awe and excitement when I passed through the imposing double doors and saw the gleaming stringed instruments standing in racks along the walls.

Mrs. Sommerfeld—the orchestra conductor I'd seen that previous year—was seated on a bench next to a baby grand piano. She was wearing a blazer and a pencil skirt. An air of formality surrounded her.

"Come in, children," she said. There were five or six other kids up there with me. I didn't recognize any of them.

"Today we are going to do a music listening test," she began. "Playing a stringed instrument requires that we really hear the notes we are trying to play."

We timidly approached the piano in a cluster, like a nervous school of minnows. She handed us each a half sheet of paper and a pencil and asked us to number it from one through ten down the side.

"So today I'm going to play you different pairs of notes, and you're going to tell me if they are the same or different. Like this," she said. She proceeded to play two notes on the piano in turn, the second being noticeably lower in pitch than the other. "Which one is higher?"

I raised my hand eagerly, and she nodded at me to proceed. "The first one!"

"Very good!" she replied. "But obviously you could have just looked at the keyboard while I was playing. So before we begin, I am going to ask you to spread around the room with your backs to the piano, so there's no chance of cheating."

We did as we were told. My mind was spinning. Clearly there had to be more to it than this. What an easy test!

Thanks to my dad's ear-training game, I had unwittingly been practicing for this moment for years. By now the task of differentiating between two notes was quite literally child's play. Mrs. Sommerfeld went through the ten pairs of notes, clearly trying to trip us up with close intervals and even octaves, but I felt confident in my choices as I wrote my name on the top of the paper, handed it to her, and returned to class.

A couple of days later, my fifth-grade teacher told me that Mrs. Sommerfeld wanted to see me. I nervously made my way back over to the orchestra room, but to my surprise, I was the only one there.

"Hello, Gaelynn. I wanted to talk to you about orchestra. You did a really good job on the music listening test, and I'd like to find a way for you to play an instrument."

As I would learn later, Mrs. Sommerfeld confided to my mother that I had been the only student to get a perfect score on the music listening test that year. My natural inclination for music had gotten her attention. Of course, she didn't want that to go to my head. Instead, she focused on the practical challenges ahead of us.

"I want to be up-front with you, Gaelynn. I'm not sure if this is going to work. I've never taught a student with a disability before. But I'd like us to experiment together. Is that OK with you?"

I was surprised and just a bit perturbed that she seemed so hesitant, but I brushed it off. What was the big deal? Of course I was game! She asked me which instrument I was most interested in, and I confidently answered "cello." So she took one off the rack, brought it over, and held it against my wheelchair. It was clearly too close to the ground, so she extended the endpin, a kind of retractable appendage that allows you to adjust the height of the instrument.

Now it was high enough for me to grasp the long, slender neck of the instrument. "Try placing your hand on the fingerboard, like this." She demonstrated on another cello she took from the wall, spreading her four fingers each at least an inch apart, pushing down firmly on the taut strings so that they touched the strip of black-hued wood below. I tried my best to mimic her, but my fingers couldn't spread that far apart, let alone push down hard enough to depress the string completely.

Nonetheless, I wasn't discouraged. Surely with enough practice, I could gain the dexterity and strength I'd need. A new difficulty arose, however, when she introduced the cello bow. She held her bow gracefully from above, with her four fingers stretched impossibly far across the top of the wooden stick. I was able to achieve a loose approximation with my own bow. But the impasse came when she demonstrated how to set the hair of the bow on the strings and pull it across.

My arm was way too short to reach the area below the fingerboard, where you pull the bow across the strings. After several minutes of unsuccessfully trying to extend my arm far enough, Mrs. Sommerfeld switched tactics.

She took a violin down from the rack on the wall.

"Here. This is a half-size violin. See if you can fit it on your shoulder, tucked under your chin." I lifted the instrument up awkwardly, but it was pretty heavy. When she asked how far I could stretch out my arm, the tips of my fingers barely cleared the body of the instrument. There was no way my hand would reach all the way to the fingerboard.

"OK, so that one is too big. Let's try a smaller size. This is the smallest one I have here—it's a one-eighth-size violin." She reached over for a miniaturized version of the instrument I was holding and traded with me.

This one was significantly lighter and fit under my neck better, but again, the angle of my hands became an issue. I couldn't turn my wrist sufficiently so that my fingers could make contact with the strings.

Stumped and slightly dejected, we sat quietly for a few moments, both of our wheels furiously turning as we tried to come up with a solution. I'm honestly not sure who had the idea first, but one of us eventually broke the silence: *Maybe I could hold the violin upright in my wheelchair, like the world's tiniest cello?*

"Why not try it?" Mrs. Sommerfeld said encouragingly. She took the half-size violin back down off the wall and handed it to me. It was large against my small frame, but proportionally it was strikingly similar to the size of a cello compared to a typical person. And what was even more exciting was that I could easily press three of my fingers down on the strings with my left hand!

I couldn't quite stretch my pinky far enough to make contact due to the angle of my wrist, but that didn't seem to faze Mrs. Sommerfeld.

"Three fingers is plenty! We can work around your fourth finger."

I was elated. We seemed to be making progress—until she handed me a bow.

Once again, I ran into problems. My bendy arm just couldn't rotate enough to grip the bow from above. It was frustrating being so close to a solution, but the bow hold was proving to be quite the barrier. Discouragement washed over me.

Mrs. Sommerfeld stepped back to watch me struggle with my bow hold, clearly deep in thought. All of a sudden, a huge smile broke across her face.

"I have an idea! Usually I teach both cello and bass players to hold their bow the same way, from above. But there is another way some bass players hold their bow. It's called a German bow hold instead of a French bow hold, and in the German bow hold you hold the bow underhanded, like this."

She took the violin bow from me to demonstrate. Instead of

clutching the stick from the top, she cradled the end of the bow from underneath, so it rested between her thumb and index finger, almost like holding an oversized pencil. She handed the bow back to me so that I could try it out for myself. To my utter delight, this new bow hold worked with my anatomy a hundred times better. Finally, the angles aligned!

I often get asked about whether I doubted my ability to adapt to my instrument when I was first working with Mrs. Sommerfeld. And while I can understand why reinventing the violin may sound daunting, I believe this is mostly based on the adult perspective of learning new things. If a child grows up in a supportive and enriching household—which mine certainly was—then learning new things is just par for the course.

We've all seen how quickly children take to new activities or how they can, with seeming effortlessness, create whole new galaxies with a cardboard box and some Crayola markers. Being afraid to explore new things is an adult problem foisted upon unsuspecting young minds.

Ultimately, it wasn't a matter of *if* I could play the violin, but of *how*.

Playing the violin upright like a tiny cello was clearly going to work, but over the weeks, months, and years to come, we'd make numerous tweaks to our newfound method.

For one thing, the violin didn't stay in my wheelchair very well at first. I'd be happily bowing alongside my peers, my violin resting upright on the seat of my wheelchair in front of my legs. The next thing I knew, my violin would start sliding on the smooth fabric of my wheelchair seat, threatening to escape my grasp. A few times my reaction wasn't fast enough, and the violin would slip out of my wheelchair, landing with a loud clatter on the orchestra floor.

Eventually we solved this problem by mimicking the cello itself.

We re-created the endpin by drilling a small hole into the wooden button on the bottom of the violin and inserting, of all things, the pointy part of a Bic pen cap. We also installed a metal grommet into my wheelchair's canvas seat. This provided a round divot into which the pen cap could rest, imitating a traditional endpin stop.

Something else my teacher and I discovered was that the half-size violin bow wasn't the same shape as the German bass bow, whose hold I was using. A full-sized German bow had a curved piece of wood that you cradled between your thumb and your index finger. My violin bow, however, had a pointy corner that was forever jamming itself into the soft tissue of the palm of my hand.

One day, Mrs. Sommerfeld pulled me aside after class. "With your permission, I'd like to introduce you to a local violin-maker," she said, smiling. "I told her about the problems you've been having with your bow, and she wants to design one for you that's shaped like a mini German bass bow!"

This was amazing news, but I certainly didn't have any savings on hand. "I'm not sure if my family can afford that," I said, hesitantly.

"She wants you to have it as a gift," Mrs. Sommerfeld replied. "It's something you should be able to own for many years, maybe even forever, and she wants to do this for you."

I didn't know what to say other than yes and thank you. A week or two later the luthier met me after school to design my new bow. She measured my arms, watched intently as I played, and asked what color wood I preferred. About a month later, she returned with the most beautiful bow I'd ever seen. It fit my hand precisely, with no pointy edges. It made playing so much easier now that the poking sensation was gone. I loved that custom bow instantly—and I still use it to this day.

Other adjustments to my playing were more subtle. For example, when Mrs. Sommerfeld was teaching us vibrato, that lovely way of bending notes to make them sound gentler, it became clear that the cello technique was going to work a lot more naturally than a violin vibrato. Because of this slight modification, my whole sound has a different, more relaxed tone. It is uniquely my voice—not despite my adaptation or my disability, but because of it.

I also had to vary my bowing patterns. Since my half-size bow is much shorter than a regular violin bow, it often takes me two or even three smaller strokes to complete what most violinists can do in one long bow stroke. This might not seem like a big deal at first, but in an orchestra, all the players are supposed to be pulling their bows up and down at the same exact time. This creates a sort of dance onstage, everyone moving in unison. It's one of the things I'd loved when I first saw the orchestra play at my school.

This clearly was not possible for me, but Mrs. Sommerfeld still emphasized the importance of starting and ending each phrase by steering my bow in the same direction as the players around me. She said people in the audience likely wouldn't notice the extra bows in the middle of the passage, but if I ended the last note pushing my bow up while everyone else was pulling downwards, it would feel jarring to the audience. So she'd help me create my own set of bowings that loosely aligned with the rest of the class but allowed me to play my own instrument in a way that worked.

I also had to adjust my fingerings to keep up with the orchestra. I used only three fingers instead of four, so I became adept at crawling up and down the fingerboard to hit all the notes. Just like with bowing, my fingers weren't always in sync with my fellow players in the orchestra. A certain passage might be relatively stationary for a four-fingered player, but I might have to slide my hand to three different places on the fingerboard to reach the same notes.

This additional movement required extra practice on my part, especially on the faster songs, when our fingers were really flying. I even had my own set of sheet music instead of sharing with a partner, as was customary, because my notations were different from those of my classmates.

Mrs. Sommerfeld marked down my unique fingerings and bowings on my sheet music after class. The music was pretty simple during those beginner years, and we all sounded terrible anyway. I squeaked and squawked happily alongside my peers twice a week during orchestra class.

For the first couple of years, I didn't touch my violin outside of school, and my parents didn't force me to practice. Sometimes I regret not practicing more at first, but I have come to believe that it's more important that I never fought with them about it. Music was just a fun thing that I did with my friends, and it was never tainted by parental strife.

By the end of eighth grade, I was completely enamored with the violin. I had just mastered vibrato and was finally really liking the way my violin sounded. Orchestra was my favorite class by a long shot, in part because making music in an ensemble felt thrilling, and also because all of my friends were in class with me.

It was then that I really started practicing at home. After dinner I'd go into my bedroom, close the door, and lovingly place my sheet music on the stand. I'd unpack my violin and practice for about an hour every night. Sometimes I'd run through whole pieces, and occasionally I'd just repeat the same few measures dozens of times until my fingers knew what to do. This muscle memory was crucial, especially on the faster pieces.

It was on one such evening, upon exiting my bedroom, that I saw my mom grinning at me.

"What is it?" I asked, as she was clearly very excited to tell me something.

"You're just sounding so good, sweetie," she said with a gleam in her eye. "It doesn't hurt to hear you play anymore!"

WHEN I ENTERED high school, our orchestra music got significantly harder. This meant that I had to practice even longer if I wanted to keep up with my peers. The bigger ensemble meant there was less one-on-one time with my orchestra conductor, yet I still needed guidance making adjustments to my fingering and bowing.

Luckily, I didn't have to figure this out on my own.

At the beginning of ninth grade, I started taking private lessons every week.

Technically, lessons were way outside my family's budget, but my parents had a secret weapon: dinner theater! Since they owned and operated Change of Pace Productions, they could easily gift my private teachers four tickets to each of their shows, with meals included, several times a year. Fortunately for me, this barter was accepted.

For the next four years, I had one-on-one lessons every week for an hour. I switched teachers a few times, but no matter who it was, the general process was the same. We focused on basic technique, music the orchestra was playing, and at least one solo piece chosen by the teacher specifically to stretch my limits.

A large percentage of our lesson time was spent reworking bowings and fingerings so that I could play the orchestra music alongside my peers. There's no way I would have been able to modify the sheet music successfully on my own—I just didn't have the experience or expertise.

Each of my private teachers did a great job of pushing me to continually improve. None of them ever made me feel inadequate if there was a skill I was struggling with, but once an adaptation had been made, they expected me to try my hardest, no excuses.

For example, when I was practicing my solo piece for the final orchestra concert of my senior year, my private teacher at the time would videotape me performing the piece in his office. If I winced when I made a mistake, he would stop the recording and make me start the whole piece over again. Although that may seem like a lot of pressure to put on a high schooler, learning to maintain my poise and perseverance while performing later became one of the greatest gifts my private teachers ever gave me.

This support is something I wish more teachers and parents understood about disability. For every "success" story of a disabled person breaking barriers, there is at least one person—most likely, many—helping them to navigate, adapt, and stay motivated in real time behind the scenes. In no way does it diminish the disabled person's often tremendous efforts, but it does mean that proper support is crucial to success.

Unfortunately, the reverse is also true. One summer, I practiced nonstop for an audition to join an elite youth string ensemble. Finally, the day of tryouts came.

My audition went as well as I could have hoped for, although playing for the director in such a scrutinizing context was very unnerving. After a few agonizing days of limbo, I got the news, delivered by the director on a phone call.

I didn't make the cut.

I was heartbroken, though I tried to be stoic. I asked him what factors had gone into the decision, in part to find out where I needed to improve in the future.

There was a thoughtful pause, and then he began. "It was a really hard decision," he said. "I knew that if I let you in, people would assume it was because of your disability. But if I didn't let you in, they'd also think it was because of your disability. So I was stuck between a rock and a hard place."

I was stunned by his response. How had he envisioned this explanation coming off as anything other than callous and prejudiced? Tears began to well in my eyes as I grappled with a mix of sadness, rage, and confusion.

"Thanks for the explanation," I mumbled.

Now I just wanted to escape, to get off the phone as soon as possible.

"Hey, it's OK," the director said, undoubtedly hearing my sniffles. "You're a talented player. I'm sure that if you audition again next year you'd have a good shot at getting in."

Despite my anger, I did decide to audition again the next summer, and I did get in that time around. But internally, something had snapped. My admittance into this so-called elite ensemble didn't feel like the joyful affair it should have been—my victory had been cheapened by the director's comments from the previous summer. I knew he didn't look at me the way he did the other musicians, all because of a part of my identity I could never change.

Up until that point, I'd believed that if I just put in enough hard work and had enough enthusiasm, I would be able to soar, disability or not. But that director had plucked me out of the sky, pressing and smudging my wings between his fingers.

I WISH I could say that this kind of response from educators is a rare occurrence. But in adulthood I have since met so many other disabled people—artists and those who *could have been* artists, with the right mentors—who have expressed pain and regret over what felt like dismissal from a teacher or program director in the creative arts.

How do we prepare educators to think outside the box in creative disciplines? To examine and then challenge their own, possibly prejudiced thinking about disability—especially when a student has to do things differently?

To start, it's important for all educators to remember that different is not always bad; rather, different can be a vehicle for innovation.

Technique and traditional methods are only part of the creative story. Art is also meant to be subversive, to surprise and move you and make you think. Disabled people are just as capable at tapping into creative impulses and of making art that speaks to people, but apathy or disdain or a rigid adherence to technique or "normal" ways of doing things can easily squash their desire to create or express themselves.

These types of fleeting, unfortunate interactions with teachers can create baggage that lingers for years, even a lifetime. I would urge any educator to examine their own behavior and rigid thinking when they are faced with a disabled student. No one involved in music education truly believes that every student they teach will go on to become a professional musician, let alone even continue their artistic endeavors after high school.

Instead, educators are there to impart knowledge, skills, and passion to those who wish to learn. Disabled students are no different: They don't need limiting beliefs that chain them down or a "dose of reality" from teachers unable to visualize what is possible. They simply need to be taught, believed in, and encouraged to create, as much as every other student in the room.

8
Fiddle Jam

WHEN I WAS seventeen, I met my first true love.

Elliot was an incredibly skinny boy with shaggy brown hair, glasses, ratty flannel shirts, and the distinct smell of patchouli. He played violin in the orchestra that met during the hour right after mine. Our friendship started with brief conversations between music classes, and soon it blossomed into what would become a revolutionary relationship, for me at least.

Elliot was a little younger than I was, but he possessed wisdom and wit far beyond his years. Our conversations expanded my mind and showed me new ways of looking at the world. I loved it. Plus, he was quirky, funny, and accepting—quite unlike the other boys I knew.

His parents were true hippies—they'd given birth to Elliot and his siblings in their living room, never ate fast food, and gardened and composted. My family did none of these things. During the summer, Elliot and his family visited a cooperative campground north of Duluth called Mesaba Co-op Park.

The first summer after we met (and many summers after that), Elliot brought me to his fabled Mesaba Co-op Park for its annual solstice festival, Midsummer. I was hooked instantly. I had found a homeland I'd never realized I was missing—like the Shire in *Lord of the Rings* or Sherwood Forest in *Robin Hood*.

The park was located at the end of a long dirt road that was surrounded by piney woods, the forest floor covered with trilliums, ferns, and blackberry bushes. We came to an old metal gate, where two middle-aged ladies in charge of reservations sat behind a white folding table.

"Set up your tent in any open patch you can find," they said cheerfully as we paid the thirty-five-dollar annual membership fee. We didn't need meal tickets so long as we did our share of kitchen duty.

Near the registration table was a large wooden mural with WELCOME TO MIDSUMMER written in colorful, sloppy letters. It was decorated with stick figures and the yellow circle of a sun hovering above. Elliot showed me his childhood scrawl among the mural's signatures.

We parked the wheelchair-accessible van that my parents let my friends drive and got out to explore. A number of tents, a few small to midsize RVs, and the quintessential Volkswagen bus were all spread out on either side of the gravel road. We followed the road down a steep hill until it ended in front of an imposing wooden building. A pristine lake glistened behind it.

"That's the pavilion," Elliot said as we gazed at the massive two-story structure. "We'll eat downstairs, and the contra dance will be upstairs in the dance hall—there's a door to that floor that's level with the hill on the right side of the building. After the dance we'll have a midnight bonfire, away from all the buildings." He motioned to a giant pile of brush that I hadn't yet noticed in the grass.

Elliot then led me down a narrow dirt path to show me the cabins, as well as a large sauna with its wood stove. The sauna's walls were lined with benches made of aromatic cedar planks.

"We'll try it out later tonight," Elliot said. "There's a path down to the lake over here and we can carry you down to cool off when you get too hot."

Last, but not least, Elliot gave me a tour of the bathroom facility, which was not much more than a rundown shack with two doors side-by-side—one for men and one for women.

There were stairs leading up to both entrances.

During our first day at the park, Elliot carried me up the bathroom stairs whenever I needed to use the facilities. Then he'd set me on a wooden chair by the toilet so that I could climb over safely.

But that was just the first day. One of the things that endeared me to the park was the members' creativity and willingness to fix things. On my second morning there, I woke up to my own personal facilities. A boisterous man with smiling eyes—who introduced himself as an elder of the park—had constructed a makeshift outhouse for me in the early hours of the morning.

He started with a commode (I'm not sure why the park had one of these lying around) and sat a five-gallon bucket underneath, which he'd lined with a large trash bag. For privacy, he'd strung up thick brown tarps between three trees so that they formed a triangular bathroom stall. Two of the tarps were staked down with tent poles and the third was left to flap open and shut as the door. He'd outfitted the bathroom with toilet paper and sawdust to cover up the evidence.

This was certainly an unconventional bathroom setup, and I wasn't sure if I should be delighted or horrified. I was certainly touched that he'd wanted to give me more independence at the park, but I couldn't help but laugh out loud the first time I used this handmade outhouse—I was ridiculously exposed to the elements. Apparently being disabled is not for the faint of heart!

That solution, however, was only temporary. Before we left that weekend, the elders were already making plans to add a ramp to the front of the bathroom and to widen the doorway so that I could get in. The next summer I arrived just as said ramp was being completed. The elders were excited for me to try it. For years it was called The Gaelynn Ramp.

Every year after that—subtly and without fanfare—more ramps began to appear around the park. A plywood ramp to the dance hall, small boards angled up to bridge the single steps into the dining hall and the sauna, and little ramps to a couple of the cabins.

Certainly none of these constructions were fancy. But to an eighteen-year-old kid, seeing people take the extra steps necessary to make sure I could enjoy Midsummer alongside my friends meant the world to me.

ASIDE FROM INTRODUCING me to Mesaba Co-op Park, Elliot also showed me the joy of fiddling.

Unbeknownst to me, Duluth was home to a weekly Old Time Jam at a cozy English pub downtown. This long-standing gathering was the preferred meeting place for hippie fiddlers in various stages of the aging process—including many of the same folks who attended Midsummer.

One Thursday evening, Elliot invited me to meet him there. My parents dropped me off, violin in tow. I soon found myself surrounded by a rowdy, somewhat unkempt circle of musicians. Everyone in the circle was playing the melody in unison as though on some secret wavelength. They shared several pitchers of beer in between tunes that they all seemed to know by heart.

I felt instantly lost.

By this point in my musical journey, I had become fully dependent on reading sheet music to learn new songs. Even though I had delighted in my dad's call-and-response ear training as a kid, my subsequent years of classical conditioning made the idea of improvising on my violin feel completely foreign to me now.

"What do I do? I don't know any of this music!" I asked Elliot, rising panic evident in my voice.

"Don't worry," he replied in a relaxed manner, having grown up around this strange culture of playing by ear. "Just listen to it a few times and you'll pick it up." He might as well have said, "Just hold this physics book for a few minutes and you'll be able to solve the equations inside."

However, because I quite fancied Elliot, I didn't want to seem like a stick in the mud.

So I did what he suggested. I listened carefully as the group played an upbeat tune several times in a row. Sure enough, as they were approaching the third repetition, I thought, *I actually remember how this song goes!* I boldly attempted to play when the beginning came around.

But even if my *brain* knew the tune, my fingers were embarrassingly tongue-tied. What came out was a jumbled mess of notes not even resembling the melody a little bit.

I stopped playing and leaned toward Elliot to whisper-shout, "I'm terrible at this!"

"No, you're doing great!" Elliot shouted back over the din. "But if it's too hard to play the whole melody right now, just try to hit a couple of notes of the first phrase whenever it comes around. You'll eventually learn the whole tune. Besides, no one's listening! There's too many of us."

And with that, he turned back to the group and resumed playing. As much as I wanted to match his laid-back energy, I found it too hard to believe that no one was listening. All I could hear were my horrendous attempts at keeping up with their flying fingers, even for just a few measures. I was sure they could hear that I was ruining the whole thing. I wanted very badly to escape.

Elliot must have sensed my discomfort, because he helpfully suggested a new tactic. "Instead of trying to play the melody, don't worry about your fingers. Try bowing on the open strings whenever you think they sound good. Just make up your own harmonies!" Now this did seem more manageable. It was easier to keep track of four notes, one for each string.

So rather than focus on keeping up, I switched my attention to playing long, slow, complementary notes. If the particular string I'd chosen sounded bad, I'd simply try another one. With only four notes to choose from, this was pretty easy; I could find a note to fit almost every melody. I grew more comfortable with this extremely simplified form of improvisation. I eventually got brave enough to try playing the melody again and gradually picked it up, bit by bit.

As I relaxed, I studied this ragtag team of musicians a little more closely. It was clear all of them knew the songs, but no one seemed too uptight about playing them perfectly. Sometimes folks missed notes, bowed sloppily, or even dropped out entirely. They seemed to understand that the focus was not on them as individuals—instead, they were creating ambience for the pubgoers to enjoy with their beers. Folks enjoyed playing as part of a collective rather than standing out as individual players. This had always been a theoretical concept in orchestra, but the air of competition was too thick.

My high school orchestra conductor, in particular, was extremely focused on precision, technique, and a progressive mastery of the instrument. These exacting standards admittedly resulted in many of his students becoming technically proficient musicians. But at what cost?

Like many orchestras, ours had an assigned-seating arrangement in each section based on merit. At the start of the school year, every student took a playing test. The best-performing player of each instrument was given the coveted title of "first chair," while the rest of us were ranked from best to worst.

There was simply no escaping the reality of your worth in the orchestra. The most ambitious musicians were even encouraged to challenge the people seated just ahead of them. If you won your challenge, you moved up the ranks. This somewhat ruthless progression motivated some folks—like me—to practice, but for many other students, it was immensely damaging to their self-esteem and created a lot of unnecessary baggage. Either way, your place was never really secure.

More than anything, the concept of chairs created a competitive and individualistic approach to music that gradually squashed some of the unbridled joy I'd felt when I was first learning the instrument.

But during the Old Time Jam, I didn't sense any of that competitive edge that had become so familiar to me. On the contrary, these weekly gatherings were *communal* musical experiences. They reminded me of a very important truth that had faded from view — you can make music solely for the joy of playing, not just to be recognized as exceptional or to be hailed as a virtuoso.

As the weeks went on, the pressure for perfection I had unknowingly internalized began to dissipate. My previous veneration for classical music was gradually replaced by a deep appreciation for traditional fiddle tunes. Not only were the melodies catchy and fun to play, but I had finally learned to *enjoy* improvising instead of fearing it — now I absolutely loved creating interesting harmonies by ear.

Occasionally (and quite blissfully) I'd find myself "in the zone." My fingers would fly confidently from one note to the other, and my bow would sail effortlessly across the strings in straight, long strokes. Each movement connected smoothly to the next, as if my body played on autopilot.

I could only witness these ephemeral moments of musical Zen with a light sense of awareness, or else they crumpled like the delicate petals of a wildflower. If I focused too much on what I was playing — or if I let my mind wander too far from the music — my fingers would inevitably stumble, and my bow would grind unpleasantly against the strings.

What I loved most about the fiddle jams was how every tune we played was a relic from a bygone age. Many of the classic Irish fiddle tunes we learned at the fiddle jam had been passed down—largely by ear—since the 1800s.

One night, we were playing a favorite of mine, "Swallowtail Jig." I liked the tune's quick-flowing tempo and how its minor key gave it a haunting feel. As I wove my harmonies around the melody, I wondered about all the people who had loved it before me. How many generations of soldiers, travelers, grandparents, children, and musicians all over the world had played the same notes we were playing now? How many parties, dances, campfires, or solitary moments had this melody graced? I'd never felt the power of music to connect people through time and space so keenly until that moment—the tune was a musical portal to the past. I soon brought myself back to the present and smiled over at Elliot, the singular human bowing alongside me.

9
Leaving the Nest

MY PARENTS AND I had long known I had scoliosis, which is a pretty common feature of OI. During every annual physical I had growing up in Duluth, the doctor would X-ray my spine and we'd discuss my prognosis. The orthopedic surgeon would invariably tell me that I would need a spinal fusion someday, but that it didn't really matter when I did it; they could correct it whenever I wanted.

"Just let us know when your spine starts bothering you, and then we'll address it," he'd told me.

Well, during my junior year, I started to notice difficulty in sitting up straight—I always had to lean my right arm against something for support. Resigned, I figured the time had finally come to face the music and look at getting back surgery.

We had a new set of X-rays taken, but instead of meeting with my doctor in Duluth, we consulted a surgeon in Saint Paul named Dr. John Lonstein, a middle-aged man with graying hair and a South African accent. He was serious and even stern upon first meeting, but over time the gleam in his eye and clear dedication to his patients revealed a soft, squishy center. That first meeting, however, he was all business. He immediately placed my X-ray films up against the light box on the wall.

"Now, Gaelynn," he began, after brief introductions. "I am very concerned about your spine. Do you see this bend here?" He pointed with a pencil to the curviest part of the S shape, which was my spine.

I nodded.

"Well, right here the curve of your scoliosis exceeds 90 degrees." And then he looked me squarely in the eyes. "Why did you wait so long to come see me?"

"My doctor said it was up to me," I said. "That whenever I was ready, you could straighten it."

He let out a deep sigh. "Unfortunately, that's not true. You probably should have had this operation around eight years ago. I won't be able to correct your spine."

Terror flashed across my eyes, and he quickly continued.

"What I mean is, I won't be able to *fully* correct it," he said, in a slightly more reassuring tone. "The best we can hope for is about a 30-degree improvement. But I should be able to keep your spine from getting worse."

This certainly wasn't the conversation I'd been expecting to have. "Will I be OK if you stabilize it? Am I in danger?"

He lifted his pencil to the X-ray again as he talked: "See this gray area at the bottom of your rib cage?" he asked. Again, I nodded. "That's lung tissue that has nowhere to expand, because your spine is taking up space where your lungs should be. Your spine is cutting into your lung capacity, but it seems your body's able to handle it. If I can stop the scoliosis from getting worse, yes, you should be able to function normally. But if you wait any longer for this operation, your lung capacity will become even more compromised, which will eventually impair your ability to get enough oxygen. *That* is life threatening. You need this operation as soon as possible."

I felt strangely betrayed by my doctor in Duluth. Why did he leave it up to me? Of course I didn't want to have surgery, but if I'd known my scoliosis would eventually be life threatening, I would have done it sooner.

As is always the case with poor medical advice, there was nothing I could do about it now. Surgery, it was. And it was going to be a big one. To make sure my spine was totally immobilized, Doctor

Lonstein would fuse all the vertebrae from just above my hips all the way up to the base of my neck. That way I could still turn my head and swivel my hips, but the rest of my spine would be transformed into a solid, albeit bendy, pillar.

My vertebrae would be held up on either side with metal rods, and the cracks would be filled in with donor bone.

The earliest they could schedule the operation was eight weeks later, during the second week of August. I'd be in the hospital for a few days after surgery, followed by an intense two-week recovery. I was told that as long as things went according to plan, I should feel good enough to start my senior year of high school on time, in early September.

MY SURGERY TURNED out to be a lot trickier than expected.

When he opened up my back, Doctor Lonstein had been prepared to deal with the extreme curvature of my spine, but he hadn't expected the *texture*: My spine was the consistency of Jell-O. Placing rods alongside it simply wasn't going to work—the vertebrae would have slipped out of place almost immediately.

Doctor Lonstein had to think fast. He decided to connect every single vertebra to the two rods using thin metal wires, not unlike twisty ties. This way my vertebrae would hold firm—snugly attached from both sides—to the rods. Donor bone, inserted between the vertebrae, added more support. By the end of this much longer surgery, my spine was finally secure.

I was relieved to hear my surgery was a success, but there was still a nasty surprise in store for me.

Because the surgery had been so much more involved than planned, Doctor Lonstein informed me, as gently as possible, that I'd have to be on strict bed rest for the next six weeks. No sitting up whatsoever. I was going to miss the first month of my senior year.

I was crestfallen, but there was no other option. I had to give the donor bone time to fuse to my vertebrae. If it didn't calcify properly, the whole house of cards would collapse and we'd be right back where we started. So instead of shopping for school supplies that August, I braced myself for a long, slow recovery.

THERE IS SOMETHING magical about close girlfriends in adolescence.

In high school, I had a small group of friends who shared the same nerdy sense of humor as me. We all played in orchestra, of course, and most of us partook in other uncool hobbies like debate club and math league. Perhaps unsurprisingly, none of us dated in high school. It didn't matter much to us, because we quickly became each other's solar system.

My friends and I were all good students. But by our late teens, we were decidedly less focused on our classes than on our own immature antics. We enjoyed our fair share of (mostly) innocent mischief. For example, one night we drove my parents' red wheelchair-accessible van three hours north, all the way to Canada. We did it secretly, and on an absolute whim, while my parents were busy at a play practice. We headed back to the United States just as soon as we'd crossed the border—it was mere foolishness, not the lower drinking age, that had called us there. I still remember the giddy exhilaration we felt as we cruised through the pines lining the shore of Lake Superior, heading back home. That night, we proudly dubbed ourselves The Van Girls.

This same tight-knit group of teenage girls took it upon themselves to make sure that I was as entertained as possible while I was on bed rest. My parents had rented a hospital bed for me to use after surgery, and the school days in bed passed incredibly slowly. But as soon as class was out for the day, anywhere from one to six of my friends would come over. They'd grab snacks from our fridge, then bring them into my room and immediately crawl into bed with me.

The gossip of the day was dished, with as much dramatic flair as possible (usually about how a teacher was being unfair or which celebrity was the hottest). Then we'd spend the next hour making inane jokes and cracking ourselves up. We'd listen to music too, often playing the same familiar songs on repeat—this was my preferred method of music consumption.

Although I have always loved music, I'm not a true audiophile. Some people, for example, are musical encyclopedias. They can identify pretty much any hit ever made by listening to the first three chords. Others are seekers, always devouring new albums in search of the next gem. Both types of aficionados have an innate sense of musical curiosity, an adventurousness of taste, and an insatiable hunger for songs.

That is decidedly *not* me.

I have never been on a quest to consume large quantities of music, and I come across my favorite music haphazardly. But whenever I do find a song or a band that resonates with me, I thoroughly digest the music until it becomes part of my DNA. I listen to it on repeat for weeks; it tumbles around inside my head until it's well-worn and familiar. Then I tenderly place it in my collection of favorite songs, from which it shall never be removed. This collection grows just a little bit larger with each passing year, but I am in no hurry to fill it. The right songs will find me when I am ready to hear them.

My peculiar listening habits had started back in junior high school. I heard Simon and Garfunkel's gorgeous harmonies and captivating lyrics, and I was instantly hooked. Thirteen-year-old me saved up and ordered their *Complete Works,* a box set of three CDs, from a catalog. I listened to those CDs until they were scratched up. But I'd found two songs that would stay with me forever—"Bookends" and "Old Friends"—and a host of other poetic folk songs that I adored.

Around this time—during the early aughts—I was obsessed with The Decemberists. Their music, too, had been love at first listen. Some of my favorite lyrics are on their first EP, in the song "Red Right Ankle." Over the next few years I devoured their albums. Their melancholy ballads often brought me to tears—the good kind of tears!—especially at that age.

Wilco was next in my succession of musical fixations. I loved many of their songs, but for some unknown reason it was "I Am Trying to Break Your Heart"—with its hint of nihilism and deliberately sloppy arrangement—that got permanent residence in my mental catalog.

My love language in those days was making mixtapes for friends and family. I tried to make each compilation feel personalized for the occasion, but I could never resist populating at least half of it with songs by those three bands. It became a running joke among the hapless recipients of these musical artifacts: "O-o-h, I think the track order is a little bit different this time!"

Usually, during our afternoon hangout sessions, there'd be two girls lying at odd angles in the hospital bed with me and another two sitting in chairs pulled up to the railing. We would talk for hours on end. When dinnertime arrived, there was never a question if they could eat with the family—we *always* had extra people crammed together for meals while I was recovering. If needed, we set up card tables and folding chairs for extra seating. It felt like one big holiday.

To accommodate the crowd, my mom made enormous hotdishes. Tuna noodle casseroles—lubricated by cream of mushroom soup and occasionally topped with breadcrumbs or crushed potato chips—are a Minnesota staple. Love them or hate them, they are an economical meal choice for anyone on a budget who is also tasked with feeding a small army.

My parents would roll me out in a reclining wheelchair—which they had also rented for the recovery—and park me by the head of the table. I had to rotate slightly to the side so that I could eat everything while lying down, and occasionally I needed extra help. Dinners during this time were uproarious affairs, with lots of laughter and witty banter between family members and friends.

We often get stuck in this idea that the activities we do in the community are what define us, are what make our days meaningful. And while hobbies, engagement, and social contributions are all indeed valuable, I do believe that it's the company of good friends—and the laughter that so often ensues—that captures the essence of a good life. I believe love truly *is* all you need.

IN THE MIDDLE of October, I was finally able to return to school for my senior year. I was glad to be upright once more and involved in all the school activities I'd missed—most especially orchestra, of course.

As winter approached that year, my mother and I started experiencing more conflict. No doubt hormones had a lot to do with it. Looking back, it's almost comical that we both failed to recognize the collision of menopause and puberty, but it was not funny at the time. Our fights were frequent and bitter, and they escalated quickly. And they all centered on where, and how, I was going to attend college.

I wasn't planning to major in music in college or even to pursue it professionally, as the only "music career" on my radar was that of a classical violinist in a symphony orchestra. Although I still loved my violin, devoting four to eight hours to practicing every day sounded very grueling, especially since I needed to do all that extra reworking of my fingerings and bowings.

During high school I'd become quite a fierce competitor in the debate club; political science was the preferred major of *that* posse. Maybe I'd be a lawyer, a judge, a professor—I had no idea, really—adulthood felt so far away. My most pressing concern was *location, location, location!*

My mom wanted me to stay in Duluth to attend one of the local colleges. I wanted to go to school in San Diego—the fabled land of sunshine and beaches where my older brother, Ben, had briefly lived after high school.

My mom wanted me to hire personal care assistants to come to my dorm room and help with my daily physical needs. I wanted to care for *myself*, without any outside assistance.

My goal was to experience what I considered to be "real" independence. I still loved my aide Mary, but I was ready to be done with having a caretaker shadowing me. Shedding the aide was a rite of passage in my mind; for my mom, it put me in the path of an oncoming train.

Both of us adamantly refused to give in.

My poor dad was in the middle of everything. He was always willing to lend a sympathetic ear after one of our blowouts. But he was no fool either. He wouldn't choose sides—the best I ever got was him saying, in a resigned voice, "OK, I'll talk to her about it."

At some point I had to decide where I was going to apply to college.

As much as I daydreamed of sunny California, the idea of actually going against my parents' wishes to that extent felt too daunting. I was worried they might just refuse to bring me there or disown me or something. I wasn't willing to risk permanently damaging our relationship. And, if I'm honest, I was secretly afraid of living that far away.

But just because I was giving up the California fight did not mean I was surrendering all hopes of moving away from home for college. And I'd be damned if I had a personal care attendant there to help me.

My parents weren't convinced that I could take care of myself without assistance, but they weren't tyrants, either. So after a number of NATO-level negotiations, they agreed that I could attend college without an aide if—and this was a big "if"—I could prove that I was able to shower, dress myself, and use the bathroom without their help.

I started doing everything by myself to practice. It took me significantly more time and effort than I expected, but I did not complain to my parents, lest they revoke their offer. Meanwhile, my beloved aide Mary was out for several months recovering from surgery, so I used that chance to practice at school too. I missed Mary, of course, but I wanted to be independent in college more than anything.

Within a month or two it became clear that I could manage my daily care—just barely, but hey! If it appeased the Parental Units, that's all that mattered. Plus, I wrongly assumed I'd get faster over time.

My mom's first choice of colleges was the University of Minnesota Duluth (UMD), which I wouldn't even deign to consider (ugly!). It was a small campus located in a woodsy part of town (boring!). And the buildings were all connected by long hallways so the students didn't have to go outside in the winter (wait...convenient?!).

Yes, even though it was a completely wheelchair-accessible campus, I had made up my mind: I wasn't going to go to school in my hometown.

After many long, fraught discussions, my mom finally conceded—I could move as far away as the Minneapolis–Saint Paul metro area, in the center of the state. Her rationale was that she could get to me within three hours if I was injured or if my wheelchair broke.

Eventually my parents and I agreed on Macalester College in Saint Paul. It had a great financial aid package for families like us who were lower income, which meant I would accrue very little debt. Plus, the entire campus was only a few blocks long, so my mom felt better knowing I wouldn't be navigating a sprawling network of buildings on my own during the snowy winters.

When we finally toured Macalester's campus during the spring of my senior year, I had to admit that it was pretty. The campus had lots of old brick buildings, and there were huge leafy trees and flowers everywhere. The student leading the campus tour had a nerdy, sarcastic sense of humor, much like my friends in Duluth. Even though it wasn't the coastal cityscape setting I'd imagined, I could picture myself fitting in there.

As we were guided around the campus, I felt the smallest flutter of excitement, which was a relief after so much strife. It was as good a compromise as we were going to find.

NOW THAT I'M older, I can understand how difficult it must be for the parent of a disabled teenager who is getting ready to leave the nest. For my mom, after so many years of providing me with loving physical and emotional care, the last thing she wanted was for me to get into a dangerous or unsupportive situation in college. She was especially afraid of her being too far away to get to me quickly in case of an emergency.

As much as I tried to downplay her fears, they were valid. And though I would have never admitted it at the time, sometimes her worst nightmares were indeed realized.

One day, when it was twenty degrees below zero outside, my wheelchair batteries failed as I was heading back to the dorms after class. (You don't know the real meaning of winter until you've spent one in Minnesota.) There I was, stranded on the sidewalk, with rapidly increasing odds of frostbite.

Luckily, I had my cell phone with me, so I called campus police. A pair of officers pushed my heavy wheelchair down the block, back to the safety of my dorm room. I was keenly aware, however, how differently that scenario could have gone if I'd forgotten to grab my phone that day.

Other consequences of not having a personal care attendant on campus were more mundane but had just as much impact. Perhaps the biggest issue was the time it took to get ready in the morning, without help showering or getting dressed. Using the bathroom could take up to forty-five minutes by itself, sometimes even longer during "that time of the month."

This not only meant that a lot of hours were lost to other, more scholarly activities, but my personal care routine took a lot of energy too. I had less energy to spare, because most of my reserves went to basic hygiene. It was also strangely isolating, knowing that my roommates were off doing fun college things while I lingered in the bathroom. But this was the independent life I'd fought for, so I didn't complain to anyone.

I have good memories from college too, like the time my roommates and I got to see The Decemberists perform at a small club. The wheelchair seating area was right by the stage, and we all danced and sang along to every word. We didn't get to meet the band afterward, but at the end of the night, their violinist at the time, Petra Haden, made eye contact and silently slid a tambourine to the edge of the stage as a souvenir. My roommates and I played that tambourine with gusto every weekend. It's one of the few mementos I have kept for all these years.

Another fond memory was a short-term program offered in January during junior year, when I decided to stay on campus, without my roommates, to attend class. My parents protested at first. It was risky for me to be without any assistance whatsoever, but I insisted I could handle the dangers.

For those three glorious weeks, I felt like James Bond on a solo mission. I attended class all day, then in the evenings went on stealthy, solitary trips to coffee shops to read books and drink mochas, or to visit friends off campus for game nights. Or, best of all, one night I caught the bus to Minneapolis to take myself on a date to the Dakota jazz club. I sat all alone in the dimly lit room at a small, round table near the stage. Just me and an espresso martini, listening to the fabulous jazz trio sparkle onstage—a certain kind of heaven. It would be too exhausting to live alone all the time, but I'm grateful I got to experience a taste of freedom then.

As it turned out, my time at Macalester College would be the only independent years of my life.

Even if it wasn't practical for me to live without personal care assistance, I still don't regret my decision to attend college by myself. My mom and I were *both* right: It was a little dangerous, but I deserved the right to try new things and test my limits. Setting sail, making mistakes, learning from them, and finding a new way—these are all important rites of passage, which are too often denied to disabled youth. After all, who among us hasn't looked back at our past self with a wry smile and thought, *What the hell did I know?!*

10
Medical Mayhem

ONE SUNNY SUMMER afternoon during college, a few of my friends, including Elliot, went skinny-dipping back in Duluth. This would be no small feat for me. The secluded swimming hole we wanted to reach was down a large rocky hill that my wheelchair couldn't navigate. I stripped down, wrapped my naked body in a towel, and proceeded to be passed down the hill by my three friends, who were positioned at descending heights along the hillside, like a sack of potatoes on a conveyor belt.

The four of us swam around for a while—with me wading in the shallow water—and then warmed ourselves on some large, flat rocks. For some reason, the topic of teeth came up on that lazy, sunny afternoon. Although it wasn't a *huge* self-esteem issue for me, I've never been fond of my teeth. I referred to them as Stonehenge because they were, and still are, so crooked.

"I think they are beautiful," Elliot said, as he smiled down at me from the rock above. And then he did something that caught me completely off guard: He slipped his finger inside my mouth. "Just like you." In an instant, electricity was pulsing through my entire body. He moved his finger over my teeth and then removed his finger like nothing had happened. But in such small moments, lives are changed.

I'd never really seen myself as sexually desirable. I mean, I thought that I was pretty in my own ways—I had nice eyes and hair and my breasts were OK, though a little on the small side. But even if I saw the beautiful parts of myself, I'd spent my young adult life wondering if another person would ever be able to recognize that beauty within me. More important, I'd never been told I was beautiful by someone I loved before.

By the time Elliot graduated high school, he openly identified as bisexual. Since I'd first met him, my feelings for him had never waned, though I obviously had developed other crushes during college. But so far all my romantic feelings for boys remained unreturned. Even if there was chemistry between us, it would inevitably lead to an awkward conversation where said boy would assert that we should "just be friends"—the three dreaded words of an unrequited lover. This relationship felt different somehow.

Six months later, I was at Elliot's dorm for a party. A bunch of his goofy friends were there, drinking heavily. The night went by in a blur, but I do remember one thing: Elliot and I ended up having sex. This was clearly not the ideal circumstance for one to lose their virginity, but even the next day as I awoke to the blood-soaked sheets and the realization that we hadn't used a condom, I was secretly thrilled. I'd been pining for him for years, and every pent-up emotion had finally been expressed.

His friends who had also crashed at their apartment were still there, so we didn't get a chance to talk about what had happened the night before. I left feeling confused and hopeful, and slightly panicked: I had to procure a morning-after pill. One of my college roommates volunteered for Planned Parenthood, so I knew what I had to do. I called the clinic and made an emergency appointment.

I hadn't told anyone about my encounter with Elliot yet; it was embarrassing we'd had sex without a condom. I should have known better. Besides, making sure I didn't get pregnant was the most pressing issue on my mind that day.

A year earlier, during a follow-up appointment for my spinal fusion, Doctor Lonstein had told me I wouldn't be able to carry a baby to term.

"Not even on bed rest?" I'd asked, aware of several women with OI who had survived pregnancy and were now enjoying motherhood.

"Unfortunately, no," he said. "With brittle bones, pregnancy is risky no matter what, but in your case it's simply not safe. Your scoliosis was already affecting your lung capacity before we operated. Even though it shouldn't get any worse now, your capacity has been compromised."

Then he gestured at an X-ray of my spine that he'd been examining earlier in our appointment. "By the end of pregnancy, a baby takes about 20 percent of a mother's oxygen, and I just don't think it would be smart to assume you have that much to spare."

Besides the medical concerns, I had no idea what sex meant for our relationship. Were we still just friends, or were we transforming into something more?

It was Friday afternoon when I entered the clinic. I didn't have to wait long before being called back to an exam room. "What can I help you with today?" the pleasant-sounding nurse asked me.

"Well, last night I had unprotected sex and I need to get a plan B pill."

"I understand," said the nurse. She seemed unperturbed by the idea that someone who looked like me could have sex. To be honest, I hadn't been expecting that. It felt good to be addressed as an adult woman capable of making her own decisions about her body. "Have you ever used this medication before? It can have some side effects, so I want to make sure you're prepared."

"What kind of side effects?" I asked, suddenly feeling a little less confident and much less adult.

"Well, some of the side effects are nausea or vomiting, dizziness, headache, breast tenderness, cramps. Those should pass within a few days. But the key side effect to be aware of is that your menstruation might be heavier than normal for a bit." She continued, "This happens pretty often and should clear up within a week, so don't be alarmed if you have extra heavy bleeding. But if your period becomes extreme, I'd follow up with your doctor, or at least give us a call."

I thanked her for the information, and she gave me a prescription that I could fill that afternoon at the nearest Walgreens. I left feeling scared, but without any other viable options. I knew for sure that I couldn't safely become pregnant, and I wanted to avoid an actual abortion at all costs. This felt like my only clear choice. I wanted to call my mom, but I knew she would have disapproved of my rash decision-making the night before. Instead, I swallowed my fear along with the little white pill.

The next six weeks were a whirlwind I will never forget.

Elliot and I both came home from college in mid-May, and it turned out that whatever had happened between us earlier that month was *not* a one-night stand. On a camping trip, under an overhang of rocks by Lake Superior, in my childhood bedroom—we were always finding ourselves in places to be physical. It was freeing and confusing at the same time. After years of wanting to be with Elliot, I finally was—but frustratingly, I had no idea what that meant.

Were we dating? Was this just a summer fling?

All the while, something else was brewing under the surface. I'd barely even noticed in the midst of this emotional turmoil, but the nurse had been right. The plan B pill I took did mess up my period, big-time. In fact, it had never fully ended since that week in early May. Essentially six weeks of bleeding nonstop. When I think back, I'm not sure why I wasn't more alarmed, or why I never made an appointment with my doctor. Maybe I was too distracted to worry. But finally, this imbalance in my body triggered a tipping of the scales that could not be ignored.

Elliot and I were camping during the annual Midsummer festival at Mesaba Co-op Park; it had become one of our traditions. We had a tent all to ourselves up on a secluded hillside. We'd spent the night playing fiddle duets and dancing and drinking wine and whiskey in coffee cups up at the big dance hall, ending the evening singing folk tunes around the bonfire, as always.

Only this year we stayed awake later than usual, wrapped in each other's arms. He was on top of me as we kissed in the tent, a heady rush of excitement and the tension building... When all of a sudden, I couldn't get enough air.

"Hold on," I said, panicked. "I can't breathe!" For no apparent reason, I had suddenly begun gasping for air. I could feel my body getting out of control as my heart raced faster and faster. I tried to calm myself down as Elliot sat by me, but nothing was working. "I think I have to go to the hospital," I managed to wheeze out. We both knew Elliot was in no condition to drive.

"I don't want to call 9-1-1," I said, distressed at the thought of waking up the entire campground.

"Don't worry about the noise," said Elliot. "Everyone will understand."

Reluctantly, I found my phone and dialed, praying that the call from this secluded campground, way out in the woods, would go through. Mercifully, someone answered.

"Please state the nature of your emergency," said a matter-of-fact operator.

"I am having trouble breathing. I just can't get enough air." My inhalations were fast and shallow as I fought to keep from giving in to the panic.

"We can send an ambulance out to you. Where are you located?"

"Are you sure that's necessary? I'm at a campground and I don't want the sirens to wake everyone up."

"Ma'am, this sounds like an emergency, and you need to get to a hospital so you can get checked out. I can tell the ambulance to keep its sirens off, but I think it's important to send one. Now, where are you located?"

By this time, talking felt impossible, so I handed the phone to

Elliot so that he could give directions. Shortly thereafter, he hung up the phone.

"They'll be here soon. Try to stay calm," he said, as he started helping me cover up a little.

Sure enough, a few minutes later we heard gravel crunching beneath the wheels of the ambulance as it silently pulled up the long driveway and parked at the bottom of the hill, its bright lights flashing in the dark night.

I cringed as I heard voices—people were definitely going to hear the commotion. A couple of EMTs brought a stretcher up to the tent, and Elliot directed them on how to lift me out. They carefully walked me down and put the stretcher in the ambulance to start getting me stabilized.

Elliot crawled into the ambulance and sat next to the stretcher. "Can you spell your name for us, please?" they asked me. I shot a pleading look in Elliot's direction. I needed to focus on breathing, not talking. "G-A-E-L-Y-N-N White, like the color," he said, knowing that this was exactly how I introduced myself to strangers. He smiled at me, and my heart melted a little.

"Date of birth?" They continued their questioning. "January 21st, 1984?" Elliot asked me, and I nodded. I was getting hooked up to monitors and oxygen as they asked us what happened. Being questioned by these authority figures was more than a little embarrassing; it was quite evident by our lack of clothing and the smell of alcohol on our breath what we'd been doing.

Without stating the obvious, Elliot told them that we were lying in the tent, when all of a sudden I couldn't breathe.

"Any asthma, heart disease?" they asked me.

I shook my head no.

"Well, we'll get you in and they can run some tests. The oxygen should start kicking in soon and hopefully you'll feel better."

It was true, I was already starting to breathe a little easier, though my heart was still racing and I was still feeling shaken up.

"All right, sir, we're going to have to ask you to exit the vehicle now."

"What?!" I asked, the panic setting in again.

"It appears that he has been drinking, and he's not family. It's a liability to bring him. We have to get you to the hospital."

There was nothing we could do, so with a quick squeeze of my hand, he escorted himself out. The doors were closed swiftly behind him. I was on my way to the hospital, away from home and all alone.

I spent the next eighteen hours in a hospital room in a small town in northern Minnesota.

No one there could figure out what caused my breathing issues the previous evening. Once I'd been stabilized, none of my stats looked *too* out of whack. Yes, my oxygen levels were on the low side and my heart rate was on the high side, but the staff didn't seem particularly alarmed.

The doctor on duty guessed it was a respiratory infection, but he decided not to administer antibiotics. My parents came to retrieve me the next day. I was discharged with no clear diagnosis and no follow-up plan. It seemed like a blip on the screen of my summer vacation, but this couldn't have been further from the truth.

Two weeks later, it happened again.

This time I was hanging out with my girlfriends from high school (The Van Girls, of course), who were all home from college. We were watching a movie and laughing hysterically, when suddenly I couldn't breathe. My mom drove me to the ER in Duluth. There, they admitted me to the hospital for observation, and hopefully some answers.

Once again I was experiencing low oxygen levels and an elevated heart rate for no apparent reason. Aside from supplemental oxygen and a chest X-ray, nothing else was being done. I felt like I was just taking up space, lying in a dreary hospital room while my parents took turns sitting with me.

The next day was uneventful, and during a lull in the afternoon, my parents left me alone to get lunch in the cafeteria. The doctor wasn't due to stop by for another hour or two, so I happily turned on the TV.

A couple of minutes later, the by-now-all-too-familiar sensation of constriction started creeping into my chest, and within a few seconds, it left me desperately gasping for a full breath. I pressed the call button on the side of the hospital bed, growing more anxious with each passing moment. A male nurse sauntered in with a cheery expression, until he saw the terror in my eyes. "What's wrong?" he asked, rushing over to my bedside.

"I can't breathe again," I croaked, as an alarm on my monitor started blaring.

"Hold on, I'm gonna get some help," he said, as he rushed toward the door and waved another nurse into my hospital room.

A young female nurse came over, and they started looking at my monitors. "Her oxygen's 83 percent, her pulse is 185." Even I knew that those numbers were bad news. They turned back to me, and the female nurse sat next to me and held my hand in an effort to calm me. But the situation in my body was getting more desperate, and I felt myself pee my pants, which was not normal for me in any circumstance.

"I'm sorry," I said to the poor nurse, who was now sitting in a puddle of my urine.

"It's OK," she said reassuringly. "We just need to have you focus on your breathing right now. Deep, slow breaths."

"What's going on?" I panted. "What's wrong with me?" I felt like my heart was going to explode, like I was suffocating, like I was breathing into a plastic bag.

They glanced at each other and then back at me, uncertainty clearly showing in their eyes. The male nurse asked me, "Where are your parents? They were here not too long ago, right?"

"Yes," I said between quick, shallow breaths. "They went to get lunch in the cafeteria."

"Do you want me to go get them?" he asked, cautiously.

Racing thoughts flooded my mind. *Was I dying?* I had no idea, but it certainly felt like the closest thing I'd come to dying. If I was dying, I desperately wanted to see my parents. The thought of never seeing them again brought me close to tears, in the midst of all the terror. "Yes," I said, and the nurse started to head to the door.

But then a competing thought struck me. I needed to focus! Maybe there was still a chance I could pull through this if I put all my strength into getting control of my breathing. If my parents came into my hospital room and found me in this condition, they'd either panic or break down. Either response would take my mind off the task at hand, and I could tell a very narrow window was closing ahead of me. "Wait!" I called after him. "Never mind. I don't want them to see me like this."

"Are you sure?"

I nodded. "Am I going to die?" I looked up at the female nurse holding my hand.

"I don't know," she said truthfully. Just then I felt a surge of determination. If I could just make it another couple of minutes, at least then I would have a shot at recovery.

"You can get my parents," I told the nurse, changing my mind yet again. And then I looked straight ahead, silently repeating to myself, *Don't die. Don't die. Breathe. Breathe.* I have no idea how long I sat there, the task of gulping in breaths of air consuming my entire being.

Slowly at first, my breathing began to even out. My heartbeat eased up a bit and my breaths grew a little deeper. The worst had passed, at least for the moment. Just then, the nurse arrived with my clearly concerned parents, and I felt a wave of relief. *I made it. I'm still here.*

11

The Lost Summer

THE NEXT DAY, the nurse on duty consulted with my parents and me.

"OK, so what have the doctors tried so far?"

My parents and I looked at each other, practically shrugging.

"Nothing. They've just been monitoring me," I said.

"Is your heart rate usually this elevated?" he asked. Ever since that spike the night before, it had been hovering around one hundred thirty beats per minute.

"No," I said. "Not until I first had trouble breathing a couple of weeks ago."

He shook his head. "That's just not normal for someone your age. I'm going to get you switched over to the ICU."

In an unsettling way, I was happy to hear this—maybe I would finally get some answers.

Once I'd been transferred to the ICU, the nurses there hooked me up to a BiPAP machine, with supplemental oxygen.

A BiPAP is almost like a step down from a ventilator. It forces air into your lungs through a heavy face mask over your mouth and nose and a few seconds later sucks it out again. The nurses hoped that the extra deep, ultra even mechanical breaths would help to stabilize me. Then they inserted an IV into my left arm and gave me a drip that contained some sort of sedative. I don't remember much after that.

But those days in the hospital would be seared into my parents' memories forever. They had been looking forward to finally getting some answers from a specialist, but to their horror, when the doctor assigned to my case walked into my hospital room, he literally gasped. It was clear he hadn't read my chart closely enough to expect this genetic oddity awaiting him. He stood there frozen for a moment, staring conspicuously at my bendy limbs, curvy spine, large head, and short stature.

The doctor regained his composure and introduced himself to my parents as I lay unconscious, breathing mechanically in the corner.

Then he—rather unceremoniously—cut to the chase.

"Does your daughter have a living will?" he asked.

"A living will?" my mom snapped. "She's only twenty-one. No, she doesn't have a living will!"

"I'm so sorry," the doctor responded, "but there's nothing I can do for her."

Apparently at this point, my dad broke down and started crying. "I just don't know how I'll ever be able to say goodbye," he said, turning into a puddle before my mother and the doctor.

Lucky for me, my mom had a very different response.

"Gaelynn was perfectly healthy less than a month ago. She has a *bone* disorder—her lungs have always been *fine*. I'm getting a second opinion." And with that, my mom got to work.

I had no idea this conversation happened until many weeks later, because at the time I was unconscious. Despite the medically induced haze of that hospital stay, I have faint memories of family members sitting by my bed, holding my hand. At one point, I remember my mom holding a phone up to my ear so that one of my friends could say hello. My friend told me that her whole synagogue had prayed for me that week and that her mom's hippie friends were sending positive energy too.

Even though I still had no idea what was wrong with me—and it didn't faze me as much now, since I was all drugged up—I nonetheless felt a warm, steady sense of comfort knowing so many people were sending good wishes. Hopefully, their pleas would make it through to the right ears.

I do, however, have one distinct memory from the ICU. One afternoon, my parents came in to let me know that I had a special visitor.

"Should we send him in?" they asked.

They left the room, and in walked Elliot. We locked eyes as he passed through the doorway. I can still see his face—his expression was a mixture of sadness, relief, gentleness, and hope. It's hard to explain how happy I was to see him. It was as if a hand reached inside my chest and gripped my heart, squeezing until it took my breath away.

There's something unique about the intensity of the first time you fall in love. Now, twenty years later, I'm happily married to my husband, Paul. Of course, I still experience those moments where it sweeps over me—the realization of just how much you love someone who is living and breathing and mortal. But the first time you experience that beautiful and bittersweet truth, it bowls you over.

I don't remember what we talked about or whether he sat by my bed or if he held my hand. Truthfully, all I remember is how I felt. Besides, our visit didn't last long. I had been so overwhelmed and happy to see him that it threw all my vitals in a tizzy. My heart rate started to soar and my breathing became erratic. Soon enough, alarms were blaring and the nurses politely had to ask Elliot to escort himself out.

Needless to say, that was the only time Elliot was allowed to visit me in the hospital.

MEANWHILE, MY MOM was on the hunt for answers. She told me later that she was absolutely furious with the pulmonologist who had told her I was going to die. "He just walked in, took one look at you, and practically blurted it out. You could tell he didn't have anything invested in you making it. I couldn't rest until I knew all our options were exhausted."

First, she called the hospital where I'd had my spinal fusion. My mom hoped Doctor Lonstein would suggest a more proactive approach, as he had treated many people with my disability before. She had an educated hunch that the same could not be said of the dismissive doctor at the hospital in Duluth.

Doctor Lonstein's longtime nurse answered the phone, and my mom explained the situation. The nurse took notes and promised to pass the message on to Doctor Lonstein as soon as possible.

Within hours, my mother got a call back.

"Doctor Lonstein is recommending you get in contact with a pulmonologist he trusts down here. Tonight. Like, right after we get off the phone. His name is Dr. Paul Kubic. Here's his number."

"Thank you so much. I don't know what we'd do without you."

"Don't mention it. Please keep us posted, OK? Doctor Lonstein has a soft spot for Gaelynn."

My mom breathed a sigh of relief. Finally, she had someone with her in my corner, ready to fight.

Less than an hour later, my mom was on the phone with Dr. Kubic.

"So, walk me through what they've tried so far."

"Nothing," my mom replied.

"Nothing? Surely they've tried prednisone. That is typically the first step for any patient displaying these symptoms."

"No, they really haven't done anything except give her oxygen."

There was a slight pause on the other end of the line while Dr. Kubic gathered his thoughts.

"Well, I'm going to consult with a different pulmonologist up in Duluth and see if we can get him to prescribe prednisone. We can see how that works and go from there."

At the very end of the day, a young, soft-spoken doctor from a rival hospital in Duluth was at my bedside, examining me. Sure enough, this pulmonologist agreed with Doctor Kubic's recommendation and prescribed me prednisone. He also ordered an ambulance for the next morning, to bring me down to the Minneapolis hospital where Doctor Kubic was based. I took the medicine and settled in for the night, praying that I'd feel even slightly better in the morning. Well, was I in for a surprise!

The next morning, not only could I breathe again, but my oxygen had stabilized and my heart rate was normal. Why hadn't my first doctor tried the medicine right when I came in?

All of us—my parents, my family, and the hospital staff—were ecstatic to see such a dramatic improvement overnight. It felt nothing short of a miracle. Even though I seemed much better, I was still instructed to take the two-and-a-half-hour ambulance ride to Minneapolis so that they could investigate further. Although none of us wanted to think about it, there was still a chance my situation could deteriorate again.

A couple of hours later, my dad and I boarded the ambulance. Instead of lying listless in the hospital bed, my breathing controlled by a BiPAP, I was sitting upright in the gurney without so much as supplemental oxygen. Back in true form, I was feeling perky and bantering with the EMTs as I held a brightly colored GET WELL SOON balloon that my aunt had given me that morning. My dad, still nervous, kept reminding me to save my breath. But I couldn't help the enthusiastic chatter, after so many days of feeling like I was hanging on by a thread.

THE DIFFERENCE BETWEEN the hospital in Minneapolis and the hospital in Duluth couldn't have been more noticeable. Right away, the Minneapolis hospital assembled a team of five doctors to work on me, and this group immediately asked for my input. They listened intently and were even open to my ideas. It felt so good to be taken seriously, to have my perspective taken into account.

Back in Duluth, nurses had to intervene repeatedly to help me get adequate care. For example, at around 3 a.m. the night before I left for Minneapolis, one nurse came into my room and cautiously told me, "I'm not a doctor, so take what I am about to say with a grain of salt. But my son has asthma, and when you have these breathing attacks it looks an awful lot like asthma to me. When you get down there, I'd push to get some breathing tests, so you'll know if that's part of the problem. But you didn't hear that from me," she said, with a twinkle in her eye. I thanked her for her advice, and she scuttled away. Those nurses felt like guardian angels.

When I told Doctor Kubic what the nurse in Duluth had suggested, he agreed to order respiratory-function tests for the next day. In the meantime, he ordered nebulizers to be administered every five hours, as well as a bunch of blood work. The blood work revealed that I was severely anemic, most likely due to the six weeks of bleeding I'd had after taking the plan B pill, which I'd confessed at some point to both my mom and my doctor. I was placed on iron supplements immediately.

Sure enough, the breathing tests the next day indicated that I had asthma. The doctor prescribed an albuterol rescue inhaler, which I carry with me to this day.

The breathing tests also showed that I had reduced lung capacity, as expected, because of my small chest cavity and severe scoliosis. But it was much worse than they'd imagined. I could only take in about one-third the amount of air as a regularly sized person my age. I'm small, of course, but my capacity is significantly reduced even if you take my short stature into account. Essentially, my lungs have no reserve when things go wrong.

After the tests, Doctor Kubic discussed their results. "What happened is still somewhat baffling to us, because you never had any traces of infection or symptoms of a virus. Our best educated guess is that it was the perfect storm. Anemia can, over time, make it difficult for red blood cells to carry the oxygen you need to survive. And your body really can't operate on any less oxygen than it's doing already. Maybe this stress caused the asthma attacks, or maybe some irritant triggered it and sent the whole system out of balance."

I sheepishly admitted that in May I'd started smoking clove cigarettes occasionally, and his eyes flashed in alarm.

"This is very serious, so please listen. You, of all people, absolutely should *not* smoke if you want to avoid having this happen again someday. Your lungs simply can't handle it."

I took his words to heart. There was no way in hell I wanted to experience that feeling of suffocating ever again. And with that, he sent me home with a remarkably clean bill of health.

AFTER I GOT back from the hospital, Elliot and I continued our romantic escapades. Nonetheless, the energy had shifted somehow from the beginning of the summer. For one, we were both clearly scared that I'd end up unable to breathe again, so every time we kissed or fooled around, he was constantly checking to see if I was OK.

Although I appreciated his concern, it underscored a new kind of anxiety I'd never dealt with before—the feeling that a serious medical catastrophe was lurking around every corner.

But there was more to it than that. I'd realized in the hospital how much I cared for him, and it didn't feel right to keep hooking up with him if we weren't going to define our relationship. At the same time, I could sense that Elliot was withdrawing a little more with each passing day. I knew he had something on his mind, and I waited nervously for things to unravel.

The inevitable finally happened one afternoon not long before we were due to return to college, I a senior and he a sophomore. That day, we'd packed a picnic lunch and brought along a bottle of

Elliot's homemade dandelion wine. We set out in my van for a destination farther up the north shore of Lake Superior. Elliot wanted to show me a cave-like overhang along the beach that would make a perfect private shelter for enjoying each other's company.

When we got there, Elliot laid a blanket out on the pebbles, lifted me out of my wheelchair, and set my seat cushion next to me in case I needed something to lean on.

For at least an hour, we ate, drank, talked, and laughed. Things seemed blissfully normal again. I was reminded how supremely comfortable it felt to be in this friendship we did so well. . Eventually, and not unexpectedly, things became physical.

"Are you OK?" he asked me for the third time as we started to make love.

"Yes," I whispered, but inside I felt a heavy sadness. I knew I couldn't keep living in this liminal space between friend and romantic partner.

Once we were fully clothed again, I finally got up enough courage to ask him.

"I'm wondering how you view this relationship. Do you think before we both go back to school we should define it? I think that might be a good idea."

Elliot looked pained and sat silently for a few beats too long. "I don't think I'm able to do that." He sighed and continued with a steady gaze. "I'm really sorry, Gaelynn, but there's something I need to talk to you about. First, though, I want you to know that I care about you so much, and nothing I'm about to say changes that. But I think I'm gay. No, I *know* I'm gay. I'm just coming to terms with it. We can't continue like this."

I sat motionless on the rocks, taking in the news. I'm not sure why I wasn't angry at him for his less-than-sensitive timing in delivering the news, but for some reason, I wasn't.

But I *was* profoundly sad. I'd always hoped that maybe, just maybe, we could nurture our own version of happily ever after. But it wasn't meant to be.

Like a balloon deflating, reality set in. I wasn't going to end up with Elliot after all.

Tears sprang up in my eyes.

"Do you think we can still be friends?" I asked, beginning to cry in earnest now.

"Of course!" Elliot shot back, irritated that I would ask such a silly question. "You're one of my best friends, and I love you. But this isn't fair to either of us."

I knew he was right. Our romantic relationship had to end.

Nevertheless, I was devastated.

12
Picking Up the Pieces

WHEN I STARTED senior year at Macalester College, I made a point of moving on from Elliot. In general, my strategy involved making out with random boys at bars.

Every Thursday night, my roommate and I would go to Plums, a college bar in our neighborhood. We'd sit and have one drink together, and then we'd split up on the dance floor to find boys who would dance—and make out—with us.

I enjoyed testing out my newfound sexual prowess while songs like "Billie Jean" and "Toxic" blared from the speakers. Flirting became like a game to me—a human version of catch-and-release. While I still didn't feel great about how things had gone down with Elliot, I did feel more confident than I had before our summer fling. That, at least, was a positive.

My roommate and I had no intention of taking any of these boys home with us. Instead, we would make the trek back to our apartment side by side, comparing notes and laughing hysterically. We were definitely not trying to meet our life partners at Plums. Case in point: One night my dance partner kept smacking my forehead with the brim of his visor whenever he went in for a kiss. Yes—a visor, indoors.

But those nights at Plums were the highlight of an otherwise dismal year.

I wish I could say that I was able to process my summer's medical saga gracefully. After all, I was happy to be alive, and I'd been looking forward to my senior year at Macalester.

I desperately wanted to put my near-death experience—and Elliot—behind me, but I hadn't realized the emotional damage my respiratory crisis had inflicted on me.

I've since discovered that there's a name for this particular kind of suffering: medical trauma. I've also learned that medical trauma affects *many*, if not most, people with disabilities.

In general, medical trauma refers to physiological and psychological responses to pain, injury, serious illness, medical procedures, and invasive or frightening treatment experiences. It's not surprising that I had anxiety from nearly suffocating several times over the summer—it was a terrifying experience. But I think there was more to the trauma than that.

When you're disabled, there's another manifestation of medical trauma that follows you around: a deep distrust of medical professionals, especially doctors. It is horrifying to realize that sometimes, by virtue of your disability, you are seen as less valuable, perhaps not even worth saving, by doctors who are supposed to care for you.

I've often wondered why that pulmonologist told my parents I was going to die before trying a *single* meaningful medical intervention. What preconceived notions about disabilities did he have that made it so easy to write me off as a lost cause before trying any basic treatments, like prednisone or albuterol? Did he assume my quality of life was poor? Did he predict that I'd have a shorter life span, or that whatever years I had left would somehow be less beautiful or fulfilling? Any other patient in my position would have received prednisone. I was only twenty-one years old—happy, healthy, active—and I was certainly anticipating a bright future. Did his biases prevent him from seeing me as a full person?

I also wonder what his professors taught him about disability in medical school. Did they emphasize that disabled people are just as valuable, vibrant, complex, and lovable as any other human being? That they have contributed—and will continue to contribute—to society in meaningful ways? Or were disabled people in his coursework portrayed as one dimensional: as diagnoses, as statistics, as potential complications, as case studies, as cadavers?

The betrayal I experienced, even if unintentional, made me acutely aware of the fact that from now on, to ensure my own survival in the hospital, I or a loved one had to make a call: *Is this doctor writing me off because of my disability?* If the answer was yes, then it was necessary to get a second opinion—to fight like hell for proper care. I'm so glad my mom had the courage, resilience, and self-direction to do that when I was sedated.

Practically every disabled person I know carries with them medical trauma stemming from an experience in their past. Sometimes it's finding out a doctor had been ill equipped to handle their case, but instead of getting a second opinion, the doctor forged ahead, with disastrous consequences. Sometimes it's a doctor's obsession with *fixing* the disabled patient, when all that patient wants is to live a meaningful life as they are. Sometimes it's a doctor dismissing a person's symptoms when they really point to an undiagnosed chronic illness.

In particularly disturbing scenarios, patients are denied care entirely without their consent, simply because their quality of life is deemed too low to justify intervention. This pernicious reasoning can be used during national health emergencies to justify treatment rationing. When times get tough, disabled people are typically the last in line for medical care, and they know it.

This general lack of security, trust, and good faith is damaging to disabled patients and their families because they feel the burden—real or imagined—of defending their own, disabled lives. They are not trained medical professionals, but if they want to survive the medical system they have to be able to make sense of their treatment plans. They must ring the alarm when something doesn't seem logical regarding their diagnosis. They listen to their gut, seeking out and learning from the stories of people who share their disabilities. This quest is exhausting, confusing, and yields mixed results. Sometimes anxiety *does* muddy the waters. But what other options do they have?

For me, accepting what a doctor had to say on faith would have landed me dead in 2005.

If we want to *truly* transform this situation, there will have to be a greater focus on teaching medical professionals about the value of disability. In truth, disability is a *natural* part of the human experience—it's been around forever, and it does not *have* to imply lower quality of life. Instead, each person should have the freedom to decide what "a good life" looks like to them. That's why doctors should *actually listen* to their disabled patients whenever they speak up.

When I was born, a doctor from Shriners Hospital in Minneapolis reached out to my mom and said, "We can make your daughter walk—just let us take her to our clinic to operate on her." My mother had the foresight to push back. "She's just a baby, and her disability isn't life threatening. I can't make that decision for her without her consent." It turned out that I decided not to get the surgeries later on; by that point, I did not feel that my happiness was tied to the ability to walk.

I know other disabled people, however, who were *not* given the choice as children about what kind of body they wanted to inhabit. Some endured many surgeries because of someone else's dream that they might be *normal*. What would the world look like if normal just meant happy?

SIX WEEKS INTO my senior year at Macalester, I could tell that my all-too-recent brush with death had done a number on my mental health—my anxiety and depression were out of control. Since my health scare, I had become obsessed with my heart rate and breathing, checking it every few minutes with a pulse oximeter that I'd picked up at Walgreens. I knew my compulsive thoughts and behavior weren't healthy, but I didn't know how to escape them. I felt trapped and ashamed.

My focus was shot, and my sleep schedule was abysmal. On my best days, I could act like any other college student who was drowning on the inside. But on my worst days, the fear of having another breathing attack made me so nervous that all I could do was bury myself in blankets to keep from crawling out of my skin. It didn't help that none of my Macalester friends had been there when it happened. Although they tried to sympathize, it was painfully clear that the concept of almost dying was purely a hypothetical one to them. I felt incredibly isolated.

By the end of October, I had skipped so many of my classes that my only two options were failing my courses or withdrawing from college. I chose the latter and moved home just ten days later. Partly, I wanted to be closer to my parents, who had gone through the whole hospital ordeal with me. They supported my decision, so long as I went to counseling for my anxiety.

I agreed to the terms and said goodbye to the school I'd called home for over three years.

I felt incredibly self-conscious about dropping out of school, like I'd let the anxiety get the better of me. But I told myself that this was merely a temporary measure, that my time in Duluth would be brief. I would get my mental health under control and then move back to Saint Paul so that I could graduate from Macalester College and finally put this strange emotional saga behind me.

13

Open Mic Night

ABOUT A WEEK after I moved home, my brother Greg called up my parents to inform them that he, too, was withdrawing from his college classes and planned to return to Duluth. One should never underestimate the influence of older siblings on the decision-making of the younger ones!

My parents reopened their doors to both of us, relinquishing their dreams of an empty nest. They wisely required both of us to enroll in college courses while we lived at home. The irony was not lost on me: despite the high school drama to avoid it, I had finally ended up at UMD after all.

As children, Greg and I had been great playmates, but as teenagers, we had bickered constantly. Our years apart during college, however, had quelled the angst. I was glad Greg was back in Duluth to keep me company. We still poked fun at each other, but in a good-spirited way. Plus, he was the one who talked me into going to my first open mic.

Greg had a great voice, played guitar well, and had written about a dozen of his own songs over the years. As a teen, he'd learned that his guitar was a surefire way to pick up chicks; henceforth he was rarely seen without it. Greg wasn't shy by any means, but having me there next to him onstage made performing seem less intimidating. Every Monday, we'd drive down to the venue and sign up for a three-song set. I would improvise on my violin and sometimes sing harmonies. We even practiced at home during the week, to build up our repertoire. All those hours of singing duets as children paid off. Dare I say, we sounded pretty good!

These Monday night open mics were hosted at the same English pub where I'd first learned to fiddle with Elliot a few summers earlier. It felt good to be back there, making music once again.

At that point, anxiety still heavily interfered with my life. It was hard to enjoy anything, and I felt trapped inside my own fear-racked mind, with no escape hatch. Anxiety poured gasoline on every uncomfortable sensation. The smallest of triggers, such as getting even a little out of breath from physical exertion, or a slightly elevated heart rate, sent me into a doom-filled mental spiral. I was secretly convinced that another bout of respiratory failure was just around the corner.

Eventually, thanks to a very insightful and compassionate therapist, I learned that I was experiencing symptoms of post-traumatic stress disorder. She assured me that my uncontrollable thoughts were to be expected—practically normal, given their harrowing origin. Who *wouldn't* be triggered after an experience like mine, heart racing and unable to breathe in the hospital?

Playing music with Greg was a great escape during that first year back in Duluth, because it gave me a brief respite from my compulsive thoughts. It was nearly impossible to be obsessed with my heart rate when I was concentrating on which verse came next. No matter how anxious I'd been feeling that day, by the time I left those open mics, I was always at least a little happier.

I enjoyed open mics so much that I started going to the Old Time Jam on Thursday nights again. I hadn't been to one of those since high school, with Elliot, and I'd forgotten how much I'd missed the boisterous camaraderie of the old folkies.

On one such evening, I met a banjo player and guitarist named Andy Gabel. As usual, the ragtag bunch of us gathered around the large round table toward the back of the bar with our instruments in front of us. The tunes were chosen one at a time around the table. Whenever one song ended, it was the next person's turn to pick.

Sometimes I'd know the tune, other times I'd stumble through it until my fingers caught on or improvise harmonies to provide the band with a fuller sound. We'd play for almost an hour, take a break for more beer and a stretch, and then do another forty-five minutes or so before heading home. It was during a break that Andy introduced himself to me.

"Hey, I'm Andy," he said, still clutching his guitar. "I go to UMD too. I've noticed you in the halls a few times."

Andy was tall, with shaggy blond hair and striking blue eyes. He had broad shoulders, strong eyebrows, and a very fit, muscular build. I had never seen him at UMD before, but that wasn't surprising. I drove at top speed down the corridors, usually late for my next class.

"You sound really good on that violin," he said, a little nervously.

"Thanks!" I replied. "Sometimes I feel like I'm barely keeping up."

"Me too. I'm still pretty new here," he said. "Hey, wasn't that you, playing those harmonies?"

"Yes, I like improvising," I said. "But I didn't think anyone could hear them!" I had always banked on anonymity at these fiddle jams, which is why I didn't mind butchering tunes I didn't know.

"Don't worry. They sound nice!"

There was an awkward pause while he worked up the courage to continue the conversation. "Hey, since you have such a good ear, I was wondering. Do you think you could learn a tune by just hearing me play it for you?"

"Maybe?" I ventured. "But not on the first time through or anything."

I have a pretty good ear, but I don't *actually* have perfect pitch.

Nevertheless, he persisted. "Can we try it out on this tune? It's called 'Blackberry Blossom.'"

He sat down in a chair against the wall and readied his guitar.

"Now?" I asked, feeling ambushed.

"We still have a few minutes until the break ends," Andy said. "See if you can find the melody."

Andy was clearly excited at the possibility of us playing "Blackberry Blossom" together.

"OK, so this tune is in G major, and it starts like this," he said, slowly plucking the strings of his guitar. He played quietly, almost furtively, so as not to attract attention to the two of us. As he played, I gazed steadily at his fingers and tried to let the melody sink in. The first part of the tune was catchy indeed, with an upbeat, bouncy feel. The second half was a bit lost on me, but I could hear some potential harmonies.

"Do you want to try it now?" Andy asked me eagerly, after he'd played it one time through.

"I can try, but it might take a while," I said hesitantly, trying to temper his enthusiasm.

I felt anything but confident. But with laser-beam focus on the melody he was playing, my fingers began to match his after only a few times through.

"Wow, I can't believe you learned that so fast!" Andy said, clearly delighted. "Wanna trade off? You take the melody, and I'll play the chords. Next *I'll* take the lead, and you can try harmonies."

We made it through "Blackberry Blossom" a few more times. With each pass, both our mutual confidence and our smiles grew. The experience of "clicking" with someone while making music is joyful and heartwarming—as in, a literal warmth radiates from your chest cavity. It's a form of love at first sight, but it's not lustful. It's like being thrown a life raft: Just like that, you make contact and are found—rescued, even—out there in the vast sea of humanity.

The break was over, and the other musicians began to gather around the table. Andy and I beamed at each other. By the end of the night, we had decided to form a band.

Shortly thereafter, Andy and I started having weekly practices. Andy would bring his guitar to my place, and we'd play through a list of tunes we had compiled while sharing a six-pack of beer. Band practices were easygoing affairs with plenty of conversation and laughter between songs. We named our fledgling duo Gabel and Gaelynn. I mostly improvised backup fiddle parts and lent vocal harmonies to his folk and bluegrass tunes. And I whistled on a couple of numbers too.

There were also, at Andy's insistence, a few tunes where I sang the lead. I started with "Little Boxes" by the 1960s folk singer Malvina Reynolds—a tune that was later made famous by the show *Weeds*. Singing lead was terrifying and exhilarating at first. Due to nerves, I could never remember the words exactly; even now, I ad-lib the different house colors listed off in the chorus.

We had our first proper show at the now-familiar English pub and played there often after that. They were noisy gigs where we were mostly just providing background ambience, but there were always at least a handful of people listening intently—besides my parents, even! In time, we branched out to other venues around town. We loved playing together—we even carried our instruments around with us at UMD so that we could sneak in a few extra tunes in the hallways.

Those first few months of playing music with Andy were some of the best in my life. So much so, in fact, that I called him from a party—slightly tipsy—in May. We had been playing for about three months at that point, and we'd just had our first showcase at Homegrown Music Festival, which is a notch in the belt of any Duluth outfit. It was packed! I couldn't imagine stopping now.

"Andy," I said wistfully, "I really love playing music with you."

"Me too," he replied. "Homegrown was amazing."

"Yes, it was! I'm so sad that I have to go back to Macalester in the fall," I lamented. That had been my plan all along. But now the thought of leaving had me close to (slightly drunken) tears.

"You don't *have* to go back, you know," Andy replied, with an encouraging tone. "You could always decide to graduate from college in Duluth. Then we could keep playing together!"

How had I never thought of that before?

I had been so focused on getting back to my "normal" life at Macalester College that I'd failed to grasp the obvious: Music is what would make me happy, not the school listed on my diploma.

"You're right, aren't you?" I exclaimed, overjoyed by this revelation. "I can graduate from UMD instead. Andy, I'm gonna stay in Duluth!"

I knew I wouldn't be finishing college at Macalester, but I was sure it was the right decision.

I have never doubted it since.

14

The Quiet Guy with the Nice Eyes

I MET MY husband, Paul, in the summer of 2005 during open mic night at my usual haunt, the English pub downtown. It started like a typical Monday evening. Andy and I were scheduled to do our three songs at eight o'clock, and when our slot arrived, a couple of friendly bartenders hoisted my two-hundred-sixty-pound wheelchair up to the stage area since there was no ramp. At that point I didn't realize that inaccessibility was a *systemic* problem, not just a fluke of a few venues.

I improvised on my violin and sang a few carefully rehearsed harmonies to complement Andy's guitar parts and singing. We played one of his original songs and two well-worn folk tunes.

A few of my friends had come to watch me play, including two of my closest cousins, Rachael and Carolyn. Once I was done playing, I joined their table by the door and ordered a black and tan.

We had barely started on the latest gossip when a group of three guys came in through the swinging doors. We invited them to sit with us, and they ordered a pitcher of beer.

One of them was an acquaintance. The second boy was tall and lanky with curly brown hair. He was talkative and funny, and his wide, frequent smiles added to his charisma. The third boy was shorter and quieter and seemed to be taking in his surroundings. I was drawn to the tall boy with the easy charm, but sparks almost immediately started flying between him and my cousin Rachael.

"Let me see your hand," he told her as he reached out and wrote some nonsense like PEN 15 with a permanent marker. She blushed. Romance was evidently blossoming before my eyes.

Slightly dejected but always resilient, I looked around and noticed again the quiet guy at the end of the table. "Hi!" I said, as I drove over to where he sat. "What's your name again?"

"It's Paul. I'm his roommate," he said, motioning toward the tall boy, who was now sitting right next to my cousin Rachael. "You're Gaelynn, right?" I nodded, and we were off! That night I got to know him better by directing a round of twenty questions his way, all of which Paul answered dutifully. Later he would affectionately give me the nickname of Question Quigley.

Over the course of my interrogation, I learned that Paul was a senior at UMD and that he was majoring in history. He had been a custodian for work-study during most of college and he was thinking of applying for a full-time position with Facilities Management after he graduated.

His main hobby was fishing, which I couldn't pretend to love as much as he did. We did have some overlapping interests, however, such as camping, cooking, reading books, and gardening. As the evening wore on, I found his understated but thoughtful personality increasingly appealing. And Paul was attractive too. He had a pair of kind blue eyes, a friendly, well-proportioned face with a nicely defined, clean-shaven jawline, and a short mop of golden-brown hair. By the end of the night, I had all but forgotten the tall one. My heart was now invested in Paul Andrew Tressler.

MY COUSIN RACHAEL and the tall boy got serious pretty quickly. This was great news for me, because now I had a direct line to Paul. I made Rachael invite me to any and all activities where Paul might be present, and to her credit, she complied with only minor eye rolls.

My first big break came in July, when the tall boy and his friends planned a camping and biking trip along the shores of Lake Superior. My cousin Rachael dutifully invited me to tag along.

I'd recently purchased a bike trailer for outdoor adventuring called the Chariot, and I was excited to try it out. I could ride snugly inside it while being pulled by a bicycle, and it even came with attachments for cross-country skiing for the winter months.

Everyone met at my parents' house so that I could be loaded into the bike trailer—it felt strange to leave my electric wheelchair behind for the night. Rachael had convinced her sister Carolyn to come with us so that I'd have enough help at the campsite, away from my wheelchair.

I was (not-so-secretly) over the moon when Paul offered to pull my bike trailer to the campsite.

It was a gloriously sunny day, and I basked in the glow of Paul as he propelled us along quietly.

It took us a couple of hours of biking to get to our campsite, which was really just a rocky beach. We ate sandwiches upon our arrival and then started a fire. My cousins Rachael and Carolyn lifted me out of the Chariot. I sat on the pebbles, leaning on Carolyn's arm for support. My posture was permanently atrocious, especially without my wheelchair.

The sun set as the waves splashed nearby. We passed around copious amounts of boxed wine, which led to animated conversations late into the night. Paul grew increasingly talkative, in part due to the wine. He was goofy and liked to joke, but there was still something reserved and serious about him. I stayed near him so that I could learn more about my enigmatic crush.

The fire burnt itself down to embers, and we spread out the sleeping bags we'd hauled with us. I, of course, picked a spot by Paul.

Paul and I ended up having our first, rather drunken heart-to-heart that night. I asked Paul if he wanted to have kids—I'm not known for subtlety. He said he wasn't sure. I told him that I wanted to raise kids, but that I would need to adopt.

"What do *you* think of adoption?" I asked, all casual-like.

"I think adoption's cool," he said, unperturbed by the topic. "If there are kids out there who need families, then adoption is just as valid as having your own—maybe even more so."

I was secretly giddy to hear this—I had always worried that my inability to have children would be an issue in my marriage.

No, we weren't even dating yet, but that didn't hinder the husband-vetting process. With Paul, I put the cart so far ahead of me that it took seven years for the horse to catch up with it.

We eventually fell asleep side by side on the rocks.

Too few hours later, the group awoke—sore from the rocks, but surrounded by natural beauty. We packed up and began the long ride back to Duluth. Paul and I hadn't even kissed or held hands, but already I was imagining our wedding day.

Of course, Paul wasn't aware of my true matrimonial intentions. Before we started actually dating, we spent several months hanging out with friends at group activities like movies, campfires, barbecues, and weeknight concerts at our favorite bars downtown.

Around August, Paul and I started spending time by ourselves.

Even though I was thoroughly smitten with him, our relationship remained platonic into the fall. I was never exactly sure when Paul developed his first twinge of romantic feelings for me, so I asked him about it not long ago. He thought about it for a minute, then grinned:

"It was after we had watched that movie at your parents' house," he said. I had long forgotten about that night. "We sat next to each other on the couch, and then I lifted you in your chair so that you could see me out. When we said goodbye, you went in for a hug. You kissed me on my shirt, right in the middle of my stomach, because you were so short. It was cute. Then you parked your chair up against the screen door so that you could watch me walk to my car."

I had worn him down with my charm at last!

But even then, it would be months until we started dating. Our first kiss was late one night on a camping trip with our friends. I was in heaven when I awoke the next morning. Finally, a romantic relationship was on the horizon! But on the ride home, when it was just the two of us, he sheepishly made a confession. "I'm sorry. I'm not looking for a relationship. I shouldn't have let that happen. I just want to be friends." I was utterly crushed, but I still wanted to see him.

From then on, whenever we were alone, Paul and I inevitably ended up making out. But without fail, a few hours later, he'd reiterate that he just wanted to be friends. After a few more rounds of this bewildering behavior, I'd had enough. I took some time away from him to nurse my wounds.

Then, in mid-November, he called me to ask if we could hang out. It had been a few weeks since our last encounter, and I'd resisted calling him. But of course, I still had feelings for him, so I said yes.

We had a fun afternoon at his house, catching up and taking pictures together on his new MacBook. Eventually, as I'd feared, we started kissing. But this time I wasn't going to give in.

"Look, Paul, I obviously really like you. But I can't keep doing this—it's too stressful."

He nodded, silent.

"I'm confused," I continued. "We keep finding ourselves in this position, so you must have feelings for me, right?"

"Yes, I do."

"Then what's going on? Why can't we just *date* if we like each other?"

There was a long pause; we sat next to each other on his bed.

Paul looked massively uncomfortable, but he finally explained what was holding him back.

"You're right, I have feelings for you," he said. "And it's not fair to keep doing this to you. I guess…" he trailed off, suddenly looking self-conscious.

"What is it?" I prodded. "I just want to understand."

"Well, I mean—all my life I never really imagined the kind of person I would date. It's not like I have a type or anything."

Paul took a deep breath and continued. "But I never pictured dating someone who—who would *stand out* so much."

I took a moment to consider this before responding.

"So it's about the disability?" I asked. My heart suddenly felt heavy. I had always suspected that my disability was the reason that my crushes, save Elliot, hadn't claimed to reciprocate my feelings, no matter how much chemistry I'd felt between us.

"Kind of," he said truthfully. "But it's not *you*, or the disability itself. I'm just worried about how other people will react to our relationship."

I gave him a quizzical look.

"I'm not ashamed of your disability," he explained. "I'm just used to blending into the background. If we start dating, that is something people are going to notice."

Finally, it made sense. Paul was much more introverted than I was, and I'd never considered how dating someone so conspicuous would throw him into the spotlight. His hesitation was understandable, but could he get past it?

This was a very delicate, and important, conversation for us to have, so I thought through my next words carefully. "I can understand how we might stand out as a girl who uses a wheelchair dating a nondisabled guy, but do you think it's actually a *bad* thing?" I asked.

"No!" he replied quickly. "I don't think it's bad. It's just unusual."

Gaining confidence, I continued. "Well, if it's unusual, that's just because people never see it in their day-to-day lives. It takes people like you and me to have those relationships so society can realize that they're not bad, or even very different. Once people start seeing it more regularly, it will become normal. But they have to *see it somewhere* first."

He sat pensively for a moment. "You're right," he said eventually. "I suppose most people, once they get used to us, will be fine with it." I could feel his energy shift as he processed out loud.

"Plus, if any of my friends *do* judge us," he continued, "I suppose they aren't the people I want to hang out with anyway."

I nodded in agreement. And then I ventured to ask, "So what does this mean for us?"

"It means I'm OK with it! With having a relationship. Let's do it!" he said. He went in for a kiss.

A small, creeping doubt wormed its way into my mind. "Wait," I stopped him. "Are you sure? You're not going to change your mind later?" I didn't want to get my hopes up yet again.

"No! I'm sure," he said.

"You promise?" I asked.

"Promise."

He held out his pinky to swear his truthfulness the old-fashioned way.

Then we kissed, and the rest is history.

AS AN "INTERABLED" couple—in which one partner has a disability and one does not—Paul and I experience a day-to-day reality that is markedly different from most other couples our age. Since practically everyone will need personal care if they live long enough, I joke that we fast-forwarded our relationship by four decades.

When we started dating, however, I almost never asked Paul for help.

It was important to me to be as independent as possible around Paul so that he did not feel like my caregiver.

At least that is how things started out. Until one evening, when I found myself in desperate need of assistance.

Five months or so into our relationship, I'd been asked to give a joint talk at UMD with another disabled musician named Billy McLaughlin. He had developed an issue in his hands that made it impossible to strum his guitar the typical way. But instead of quitting, he figured out a new way to play left-handed. He held the guitar upright in front of him and tapped the strings instead of strumming them (sort of like a dulcimer), and the sonic effect was really quite mesmerizing.

That afternoon, Billy and I were supposed to give a talk to some music students about how we reinvented our instruments to work with our bodies. But all Billy wanted to do was play! He saw my violin, which I'd brought just in case, and asked if we could try jamming on one of his songs. I happily obliged, and soon we were giving an impromptu performance for the students.

When the hour was up, Billy asked if I'd come out and join him on one song during his public concert that night. This was going to be a big audience of attentive music aficionados. I'd only played bar gigs, so I was terrified. But of course, I said yes.

Paul was thrilled for me. We went home so that I could get dressed up for the concert.

A few hours later, we were waiting in the darkness backstage, watching Billy begin his set. I was going to join him on the sixth song. My entire body was on high alert, swimming in adrenaline. Suddenly, I *really* had to pee.

"Now?!" Paul asked incredulously.

"Yes," I said, squirming.

"Do you have enough time?"

"I think so, if we hurry!" I replied. We let the stage manager know and ducked out to find a bathroom. Paul, as usual, helped open the bathroom door and then waited outside the stall. The clock was ticking; I started getting nervous about missing my cue.

"Are you almost done?" Paul asked with an edge of urgency.

"No!" I had several minutes of labor ahead of me. "What do I do?" I asked, panicking now.

"I can help you, if you want," Paul offered.

I felt conflicted. This was not my idea of romance.

But ultimately, time was not on my side. "Are you sure?"

"I'm the one that offered. Can I come in?" he asked.

"Sure," I replied and took a deep breath. Paul came crawling in from under the stall door. To my immense relief, he helped me without making it weird, and I made it back with plenty of time to spare.

After that fateful concert, I started to ask Paul for assistance more often. It just made life easier. Daily tasks like getting dressed in the morning and using the bathroom by myself took forever. When Paul helped me get ready, it meant he didn't have to sit around and wait for me. It still felt a little awkward for me at first, but it quickly became a part of our routine.

I understand now why I had resisted asking Paul for help. American culture, for better *and* worse, prizes individualism and self-sufficiency—we've all heard messages like "pull yourself up by your bootstraps," "do it yourself," and "live on your own terms." But if you examine these notions of "independence" more closely, you will often find a fear of vulnerability lurking just below the surface. This fear of needing support can be really damaging. How often do people suffer in silence because they refuse to ask for help?

Although I've always valued freedom and independence, I no longer consider them all-or-nothing propositions. It's OK to be independent sometimes and need help at other times. Or to need support in certain ways, while in turn offering your unique version of support to others. We rely on each other to survive—it's *interdependence* that allows us to truly thrive. The sooner we accept this truth on a collective level, the sooner we can drop the shame around needing help. The sooner we get the help we need, the more we can focus on the people we love.

15

The Public Forum

I GOT MY first taste of advocacy through a UMD student organization called Access for All, which promoted disability awareness on campus. Its faculty adviser was someone I hadn't seen in over a decade—Nancy, my favorite American Sign Language interpreter at Access Theater. During my senior year of college, I served as one of the group's three co-leaders.

Toward the end of that fall semester, students interested in learning ASL found out that the university was planning budget cuts that included drastically reducing the number of ASL course offerings. Access for All became invested in opposing these cuts.

My motivation came from my Deaf friend and mentor Jeff, who had had a great impact on me during my Access Theater days and beyond. He demonstrated first-hand the importance of ASL in my community. By this time retired, Jeff volunteered as a tutor in the Continuing Education ASL classes, so that more people in the Duluth area could learn this useful language.

The ASL classes had always been popular, but they were considered elective courses and didn't have guaranteed funding. The administration planned to reduce the number of beginner-level classes by about half and cut the higher levels entirely.

We asked Nancy why there wasn't a Deaf Studies minor at the university. "About fifteen years ago there was another set of students just like you who tried to push for a Deaf Studies minor," she told us. "They just didn't reach critical mass, and the issue eventually fell off the radar."

Nancy told us that to get a minor approved, we'd have to demonstrate that it was something the community really wanted and that UMD students would actually enroll.

As far as I was concerned, the gauntlet had been thrown.

We started a petition demanding that, instead of cuts, the university make a Deaf Studies minor.

Not only did we believe it would be a boon to the Deaf community if more folks knew ASL, but we thought it would be a great minor for students majoring in education.

We circulated a petition among students, faculty, and staff, and in one month we collected over fourteen hundred signatures.

Next, we hosted a public forum on campus to raise community awareness. We invited speakers from the Deaf community to explain why a minor was important. A state senator and a state representative agreed to say a few words of support. The three of us co-chairs also prepared our own remarks.

We invited seven of the highest-level university administrators to attend the forum but received nary a peep in response. In our multiple follow-up letters and voicemails, we gave them the option to speak if desired or just to attend as special guests. We always included scanned copies of the petition with our letters so that they could see our community support. The day before the forum took place, the local newspaper ran an article about it. Yet the administrators still hadn't even acknowledged that the event was happening. This was discouraging, because our hope was to negotiate with them, not shame them into submission.

Nonetheless, we didn't let their silence stop us; the event could still have an impact without them. The night before the forum, to my surprise, I received a call from the vice chancellor.

"Hello, Gaelynn. Thanks for taking my call," he said, with an air of formality. "I am contacting you on behalf of the university administration. We read the article in today's paper, and we have concerns about the public forum." He paused briefly. "We're hoping you'd consider canceling it."

My heart started pounding, and I could feel myself starting to shake. It wasn't just nerves—it was something else. I was *mad*.

After all those emails and voicemails and copies of the petitions, the administration seriously waited until the day before our big event to address it, to finally deign to call me? I found this dismissive and presumptuous, rude and unfair.

I felt myself getting dangerously close to the edge of emotional outburst, but something inside advised me to keep my cool—to reason with him, despite my anger.

"I'm sorry, I don't think we can cancel it now," I said, as calmly as I could manage. "It's tomorrow. Everything's already set up."

"I see. That's understandable," he replied, clearly disappointed. Then he threw in, almost as a frustrated aside, "It's just that—it feels like you're trying to make the administration look bad."

What? I thought angrily. *Then why didn't anybody freaking talk to us?*

I steadied myself for a moment, realizing that this was do or die.

If I ever believed that humans could solve conflict through dialogue rather than fighting, that we are capable of leveling with each other respectfully, then this was the time to try it.

Even though my heart was thumping furiously in my chest, I forced myself not to raise my voice.

"We're not trying to make you look bad, and I'm sorry if it feels that way to you. We really did want your involvement in this process," I said honestly.

"Well, it feels like you're going over our heads by making it a public event," he said.

"But we tried to involve you! We just never heard anything back," I said. Then an idea occurred to me, and I went over to my computer to pull up my emails. I began to lay it out, as patiently and respectfully—yet firmly—as possible. "Do you remember getting that email with the petition attached on October 12th? We sent paper copies to your offices as well."

He paused briefly. "Yes, I remember." But I wasn't done yet.

"And then we sent another letter and another copy of the petition on October 27th. Do you remember getting that one?"

"Yes," he admitted, perhaps seeing where this was going.

"And then we sent you a third letter on November 14th."

"Yes," he replied sheepishly, and sighed. But still I continued:

"We really did want to discuss our proposal with you. But since you never responded, we decided to go ahead with the forum to try and raise awareness anyway."

And then something completely unexpected happened. He said, "I think I owe you an apology. We really underestimated you."

The humanity—his humility—in that moment made my breath catch. "Thank you. That means a lot." And I meant it. But I wanted him to know that there was more the administration could do than apologize.

"We'd really like you to come tomorrow," I said. "It's not too late to add you to the list of speakers. We're really not trying to make anyone look like the bad guy here. We are honestly just excited about the possibility of a Deaf Studies minor. If you come, I think you'll see that it's worth pursuing—and that there's a lot of support for it."

"We'll be there, at least some of us," he said. "And sure, you can add in a spot for one of us at the end of the program," he said. "Thank you for talking with me. Again, I apologize that we didn't take you more seriously at the beginning. See you tomorrow night."

I hung up the phone, my head still spinning from our unlikely exchange. Even back then, it was not lost on me how differently that conversation could have gone if I'd let my outrage take over — or if he'd let his. I quietly thanked whatever spirit had intervened during our interaction.

The next night, Paul dropped me off early so that we could finish setting up the room. To our absolute amazement, four of the seven administrators we'd invited attended the public forum. We made a point to welcome them and tried to convey our genuine enthusiasm for the evening rather than any adversarial energy.

The room was packed. Almost four hundred people showed up in support of the Deaf Studies minor.

I was so overwhelmed by the turnout that I had a hard time keeping it together during my speech. People really did care! After our remarks, it was time for the attendees to speak. I was thrilled to see how many community members came onstage to speak at the podium. The room was abuzz with positive energy.

One of the community members who came forward that night was Jeff. He told the audience how his decision to learn ASL after two decades of lip-reading had opened up a whole new world for him. A Deaf Studies minor, he said, could open the same door for many others. Then he ended with the characteristic sense of humor I so admired. "A minor is a good start," he said. "But why stop there? I want to see a Deaf Studies major in Duluth. In fact, it should have a whole building!" The audience started to clap and cheer, and I was a puddle of tears.

As we were about to wrap up the event, one of the university administrators rose from his seat in the front row and slowly made his way to the stage. I sat frozen in anticipation. After all this work, all the outpouring of support we had received, would the administration just utter empty platitudes? I felt a twinge of cynicism.

"Thank you for inviting us here today to listen and to learn," the administrator began. "It has been both educational and moving to see the support for American Sign Language at this university and in the broader Duluth community. And I want to let you know that we have heard you—that we are listening. While I can't make any guarantees from this podium tonight, I can promise you this: We will seriously consider the feasibility of a Deaf Studies minor, and we will commit to working with the students who organized this forum to get a proposal in front of the Board of Regents. It is our honest hope that the Deaf Studies minor will become a reality."

The room erupted in applause, and relief and surprise washed over me—truthfully, I hadn't expected that response. Paul, who was sitting next to me, gave me a kiss and said, "I am so proud of you!" Then Jeff came over and gave me a big bear hug. The rest of the night was a glowy, joyful haze.

It turned out the administrator's assurance wasn't just empty talk.

About a week later, Nancy gleefully informed the Access for All leadership team that the administration wanted us to submit a proposal for the Deaf Studies minor. I had no idea we'd actually be involved in the creation of the program! We quickly got to work, researching similar programs around the country. We created program requirements and course descriptions, then handed in our proposal to the administration.

It took several months to hear anything back from the Board of Regents, but just before graduation we found out that the minor had been approved.

Starting that fall, students would be able to enroll in the Deaf Studies minor.

It's been almost twenty years since I graduated, and—as of this writing—the Deaf Studies minor is still going strong. To this day, it is one of my proudest accomplishments—that our little cohort of students was able to bring about lasting change at UMD. There is no plaque commemorating Access for All's grassroots effort—by now I doubt that anyone even wonders how the Deaf Studies minor came to exist. Nonetheless, it warms my heart to know that some people out there can communicate with ASL because we refused to give up.

This experience is why—even after all this time—I still believe that a small group of committed individuals truly can change their corner of the world.

That respectful dialogue, perseverance, and collective action can rule the day.

And that once in a while, everybody wins.

16

Hatching The Murder of Crows

BY THE TIME I graduated from college, I was firmly embedded in the Duluth music scene. Andy and I played shows regularly, and we even recorded a live album for friends and family. I had also developed a bit of a reputation for hopping in as a guest violinist during other people's shows, as my good ear for improvising became known among my music friends.

Then a couple years after college, Andy moved out West. At first I felt like a musical orphan, but within the year I had joined two other ensembles in his absence. Both were folk duos, heavy on violin parts and vocal harmonies.

At this point I still didn't think of music as a potential career path—thus my degree in political science. Right out of college, I served as an AmeriCorps VISTA member and then worked at a number of nonprofits. Music was just something I did for fun.

One night in 2011, my latest band was opening for my favorite Duluth musician, Charlie Parr, at a fundraiser. Charlie is a much-loved American roots guitarist and songwriter. He has long hair, round glasses, and an unruly beard, and always keeps his resonator guitar close by. I loved all his songs.

My bandmate was a friend from college; she was the songwriter, lead singer, and guitarist. As always, I improvised on my fiddle and sang the backup harmonies. But my friend knew how much I loved Charlie's music—how I dreamed of playing with him someday.

That night I was enjoying a glass of wine after our set when she started goading me to jam with him onstage.

"I can't ask to play with him," I protested. "He'll think it's pushy!"

"No, he won't!" she said, with a hint of mischief. "What's the worst that could happen?"

"But I'm too nervous!"

"Just take a deep breath," she instructed, playfully taking the wine goblet from my hand, "and ask him. One, two, three. Go!"

She had picked a good moment to push me toward the stage. Charlie was taking a short break, messing with a tuner hooked to his guitar. I approached him timidly, feeling a tight knot form in my stomach.

"Charlie, you sound great!" I squeaked.

"Hey, there, Gaelynn! Thanks. It's good to see you!"

I took a pause and worked up the courage. "Hey, so, if you ever want a fiddle during your set, I'd be happy to play backup sometime." I hated imposing myself on people. But it was true, I had so often daydreamed of jamming with him.

"Sure," he said, with no hint of hesitation. "Wanna bring your fiddle up for my next set?"

"Now? Yes! I'll go get it!"

I rushed back to where my girlfriend was standing, and we giggled as she helped me get my violin. Charlie and the sound person got my equipment all plugged in, and within minutes I was playing harmonies alongside someone whose music I'd loved for years.

By now, jamming with someone—improvising harmonies and seeking out countermelodies on my violin—was my main specialty. Still, most of Charlie's tunes were a lot faster than my usual repertoire, and my bow was absolutely flying across the strings to keep up. I could feel my heart thumping and my lungs gulping in air, but somehow my fingers seemed to know exactly where to land amidst the frenzy. By the end of the set my body was spent, but I'd never felt so energized.

As he wrapped up his cables, Charlie said, "Hopefully we can play together again sometime."

My heart nearly exploded.

WEEKS LATER, I was out of town with my parents. We were visiting my dad's extended family in rural Wisconsin. Cell phones barely worked out there, so texts could only ping through when the stars aligned. Around eleven at night, my phone beeped. I retreated to the back bedroom to read the message.

In the other room, cousins, aunts, uncles, and grandparents were having six simultaneous conversations layered on top of one another, the typical mode of communication for my dad's side of the family. I reveled in the silence for a moment, then checked my texts. There was a message from a number I didn't recognize: "Hi, this is Alan from Low. Please give me a call back at this number. Thanks."

Alan Sparhawk was the guitarist and songwriter in Low, the much-revered indie rock band from Duluth. He had formed the band in 1994 with his late wife, Mimi Parker, who played the drums and sang angelic harmonies. Low's sparse, dirgelike sound and bittersweet lyrics really resonated with people; the band had gained a sizable following around the world and toured often. Low is often credited with inspiring a whole new musical genre, dubbed *slowcore*.

This had to be a prank! Why would Alan Sparhawk be texting *me*?

Of course I knew who Low was—it was hard not to if you lived in Duluth. But up to that point I'd only heard their Christmas album.

I was convinced it wasn't really Alan texting me, but I had to be sure. I dialed the unfamiliar number. It rang and rang, and finally a message played: *The number you have dialed has a voicemail that has not been set up yet. Please try again later.*

Disappointed, I decided to drop it for the moment and get back to my family.

The next day, I awoke to another text message from Alan. "Hello, I got your number from a Duluth sound engineer. I hope that's OK. I saw you jamming with Charlie Parr at the farmers' market. I'd like to do a project with you."

Indeed, a few weeks earlier Charlie and I had jammed for a second time at the farmers' market that I managed with my best friend, Leah. He had been the musical guest that week, and I'd brought my fiddle with me just in case there was another chance to play with him. Sure enough, when he saw me, Charlie asked, "Did you bring your fiddle with you?" *Why, yes!* I happily joined him for a few tunes that afternoon, but I hadn't realized Alan was there, listening.

About a week after his mysterious texts, Alan and I met up at a local diner. For someone who didn't know much about Low, except that everyone in my hometown loved them, I did an embarrassingly small amount of research ahead of our first meeting—none. I realized just how foolish this was when I shook his hand and, to my horror, the only words that tumbled out were, "I really love your Christmas album."

Alan looked like his music: intense, with a hint of melancholy. He was tall and very thin, dressed mostly in black, with a hard jawline, piercing blue eyes, and curly blond hair. He spoke in quiet tones, but there was a slight edge running underneath. Was it caginess? Mistrust? Shyness? Insecurity? Or was he simply deliberate with his words? I wasn't sure.

"You got my attention when you were playing with Charlie," he said, sitting across from me at a booth in the diner. "You can really improvise."

"Thanks," I said nervously.

"No, I'm serious," he said firmly. "Most people can't do that. Especially not string players."

I appreciated his compliment, but his energy was a bit unnerving to me. I could practically feel his stern gaze drilling into my brain. He was dark and moody and intense, and difficult to read.

"Anyway, after I heard you, I couldn't stop thinking about this project I have coming up," he continued. "I'm doing an instrumental score for a movie that's playing in Duluth over Halloween weekend. But I don't want to do it alone. I'm interested in this idea of strings, layers of strings over suspenseful guitar. Have you ever used a looping pedal?"

I had no idea what a looping pedal was, and told him as much.

Unfazed, he explained patiently, "A looping pedal is a real-time recording device. It records you as you play, then plays it back on repeat, in a loop. You can record multiple layers."

This sounded intimidating. The most gear I'd ever used onstage was a microphone.

I must have looked concerned, because he reassured me: "I'll operate the pedal for you. You can just do what you do best, play harmonies to the loops."

I only vaguely understood what he was talking about, but I very much wanted to say yes. Based on his reputation alone, making music with Alan was not an opportunity to be missed.

The only thing was, I hated horror movies. I imagined trying to force my way through this gig on Halloween, but who was I kidding? I'd have to confess, even if it meant forgoing the opportunity.

"Is it a scary movie?" I asked, "I can't really handle those."

"It's a Lon Chaney film called *The Penalty,* from the 1920s. It's considered a psychological thriller, I suppose, but it's nothing like the stuff they're making today. I don't like horror either."

"Well then, yes!" I exclaimed, "I can do that for sure."

"There is one last thing worth mentioning, though," he paused, unsure of how to proceed. "The villain is missing his legs. I'm not sure how you feel about that. It's a pretty big part of the plot."

Does that mean he'd just asked me to do this film because I had a disability? I tried not to dwell on it.

I'm not a huge fan of films with a disabled villain—it's been heavily overdone in both movies and literature. These roles usually aren't the most nuanced, imaginative, or edifying portrayals of the world's largest minority, and they do little to combat the negative stereotypes disabled people face daily. Even worse, until recently almost all of the disabled characters in films have been played by nondisabled actors.

I didn't have these thoughts so neatly laid out in my mind that afternoon at the diner, but since then I've learned a lot about disability representation in our culture. If someone were to ask me now to do a live score for *The Penalty*, I'd probably push for us to pick a different movie. But at the time, I was so relieved that it wasn't a slasher film that I pushed the villain issue out of my mind. I said yes, and we scheduled our first rehearsal.

PLAYING WITH ALAN Sparhawk was a crash course in experimentation, listening, and musical confidence that proved to be completely invaluable. Quite simply, he changed my life.

To get ready for our live soundtrack gig, he came over to the small house I owned with Paul. I watched attentively as he set up his gear in the living room for our first rehearsal. He took out a green metal device, about the size and shape of a shoe box, with a bunch of buttons and dials. This, he explained, would be the pedal that operated my loops. I had no idea how it worked or how I was going to connect it to my violin. But he'd clearly thought this through.

"This lapel mic should pick up enough sound from your violin for now," he said, taping the small microphone to the body of my instrument. "I'll start looking for a more permanent solution."

Alan used one cable to connect the new microphone with the looping pedal. He ran a second cable from the looping pedal into an amp he'd brought from home. I suddenly had an electric violin, and our first rehearsal could begin.

Alan set up his laptop so that we could watch the film and riff. He had the great idea of coming up with a few distinct musical themes that we could revisit and build on as the movie progressed.

Making up melody lines was new for me. Up to this point, I had always played along to other people's music; I'd never ventured into writing my own. But I started to pull fragments of melody out of the ether and work it out on my fingerboard, then play it back to him. "What about this?"

He'd have me repeat it several times while he determined what chords supported the new tune. Piece by piece we built the whole soundtrack this way, taking notes and recording voice memos along the way lest we forget them between rehearsals. It was exciting to be building something together from scratch.

Alan was the king of musical multitasking, at least as far as I was concerned. He could play his own instrument while operating my looping pedal, layering my violin parts in real time as I improvised. I simply harmonized with what I was hearing, weaving and winding above and below the increasingly intricate sonic landscape.

The deep, dark, warm sound of Alan's electric baritone guitar paired really well with the violin. His carefully placed chords formed a bedrock on which the violin could explore.

As I grew comfortable playing with the loops, I started to experiment. Maybe a high pass of shimmering tremolo to accent the melody line below? Or some plucking to create additional texture? Nothing was off limits; all I had to do was listen closely and play what moved me.

Whenever Alan heard something he thought worth capturing, he simply pressed the record button. This is one place his musical genius really shone through—he had such a good ear for creating abstract sonic sculptures.

The looping pedal he used didn't save anything, so at the end of each piece all the loops were erased. It was such a freeing exercise—I could build my sandcastles dangerously close to shore, then gleefully watch the waves wash them away.

We rehearsed five or six times like this ahead of the show.

The Penalty was a success. More important, we had a great time making music together. After the film ended, Alan turned to me and said, "Well, that was fun. We should book more shows."

So we decided to form a band. After some deliberation, we named our new band The Murder of Crows. Alan had recently watched a documentary on crows, and I had always loved them. Plus, even though *murder* is just another name for a flock, it was edgy enough to be legit.

Playing with Alan required me to be braver in my musical decisions and play more boldly. Rather than simply providing supporting harmonies and ornamentation, my violin was now the centerpiece of our instrumental numbers. This pushed me into a radically different headspace—instead of following a leader, I was often the one charting a song's course. Nonetheless, I had to remain attentive to Alan's harmonies and thematic shifts. The improvisational dance of our instruments made me feel fully alive and present in a whole new way. Occasionally these alchemical moments moved me to tears in the middle of rehearsal. I believe this profound musical shift with Alan is what unlocked the door to songwriting.

WHEN I STARTED playing music with The Murder of Crows, I had a job I loved, working as a receptionist at the Boys and Girls Club.

Every weekday, a paratransit driver, usually a gentleman in his seventies, swung by the house to pick me up. It wasn't the most glamorous way to get around town, but it gave me more independence than always relying on Paul for rides to work.

Some days the driver and I would chat, and some days I'd use the time for reflection. But one afternoon, something new happened. All of a sudden, song lyrics, with the melody attached, popped into my head. It was like magic.

I was surprised, even confused. It was the first time a song had ever come to me. By this point, I had been playing violin for seventeen years, and I had never once spontaneously conjured up song lyrics. Nor did I even desire such a thing. My identity as a violinist was so firmly established in my mind that songwriting hadn't registered on my list of musical aspirations.

Still, my brain was clearly downloading a song (*writing* feels far too active a word). What was I supposed to do? All I could think of was to sing it over and over and over to myself so that I wouldn't forget it during the drive.

When we finally got to the Boys and Girls Club, which was located on the second floor of a hockey practice facility, I zoomed up to my desk to let them know I was there. Terrified that I would lose the thread of my song, I cut all small talk short and blurted out, "I have to make a really important phone call. Sorry about this! I'll be right back."

I grabbed a notepad and a pencil before making my exit. I needed to go where kids couldn't find me, and fast. I beelined it to an empty hockey rink downstairs. I paced (rolled) up and down the sideline, singing to myself and scribbling. It was a messy affair, crossing things out when a word didn't rhyme or a phrase didn't fit with the cadence.

After twenty minutes of electrified writing, I'd come up with two verses, complete with a melody:

I don't know the words for the song I want to sing you
I don't have a name for what I want to bring you
I don't understand what you've seen or all that you
have done
But if I could bring you peace today, my battle would
be won.

You're weighted down with worry, you doubt what
you are worth
You question if you'll ever know your place upon this earth
But if you saw what I see, this perfect person standing
next to me,
If you could kindly let yourself be, your battle would
be won.

Gradually, the heady writing buzz started fading, and I knew that I'd made as much progress as I could that day without getting fired. I sang the verses into my phone's voice memo app, then tore off the note page of new lyrics and stored it safely in my purse.

That night I happened to have a practice with Alan. Our first official show as The Murder of Crows was the following evening. I really wanted to sing my new song for him, but I was petrified. What if he hated it? I hadn't even shown Paul yet!

I felt awkward, preemptively embarrassed—I had no idea what I was doing writing song lyrics.

But the note page was burning a hole in my focus. Finally, during a break between two instrumental numbers, I confessed that I'd written a song earlier that afternoon.

"Why don't you sing it for me?" he asked, setting his guitar down on his lap, expectantly.

A cement block landed in the pit of my stomach.

Why is it that the things we want the most are so terrifying?

I set my violin on the couch and rummaged through my purse until I found the lyrics.

Unfolding the paper, I tried steadying myself. It was like looking over the edge of an abyss. I pushed ahead anyway, trembling as I sang the two verses to Alan. When I was done, I could hardly bring myself to make eye contact with him. When I did, he looked relaxed and pensive.

"Nice work," he said, his tone encouraging. "But it needs a third verse. Do you think you can finish it by tomorrow?"

"Yes, but why tomorrow?"

"It's good," he said frankly. "We should play it at our show."

"Tomorrow night?!" I squeaked incredulously.

"Yeah, why not?" he asked casually. "Gotta start somewhere!"

So that is how I went from flying a kite to piloting a plane in the span of twenty-four hours.

Our show the next night was busier than usual. All the chairs were full in the front, and there were clusters of people listening in the back. More than a few dedicated Low fans were curious to see Alan's newest project. It was exciting to be playing for such a big, attentive crowd—the energy in the room was hushed, palpable.

I was in my improvisational element and loving it. But then came the moment I'd been inwardly dreading. Toward the end of the set, Alan whispered, "Let's do your song now," and motioned with his eyebrows for me to introduce the new piece to the audience.

I reached for my revised lyrics that were resting on the small table next to me; I didn't have them memorized yet. I had finished the third verse just a few hours earlier, once again at work.

> *We don't know the outcomes, how this story will unfold*
> *We only have a moment, and it is not ours to hold*
> *A place to fall, a time to land, we grow by grace and a tender hand*
> *The beauty of this hidden plan is our battle has been won.*

I had texted the newest lyrics to Alan that afternoon. He expressed his approval with a one-word reply: *Perfect*.

I inched toward the vocal mic, my body tense. I spoke to the audience nervously. "I just wrote this song, and I've never written a song before. I hope it doesn't suck."

Alan, in his characteristic deadpan, said, "That's terrible—do the introduction again," to the great amusement of the audience.

I giggled, his humorous interjection loosening me up a bit, and tried again, with gusto:

"I just wrote a new song, and I hope you enjoy it."

The audience cheered supportively.

With that, I started to sing.

17

Solo Mission

AFTER I FINISHED "Grace and a Tender Hand" (the name of my new song), several more came in quick succession. Some thundered into my brain nearly fully formed, when I least expected it. Others trickled in much more slowly, almost painfully, popping in as tiny fragments of lyrics and melody and bouncing off the walls of my mind nonstop for days.

I knew I was onto something when the first song fragments wouldn't leave me alone. Eventually another small sliver of the verse would emerge from the mist. Piece by piece, the song would grow until I finally understood it enough to finish it during a traditional writing session with pen and paper.

One afternoon I was visiting my parents' house, and my mom could tell that I was tired. "Why don't you lie down and take a little nap in the office?" she urged me. Her office was my old bedroom, and it still contained my old twin bed, now used by guests.

I climbed out of my chair and into my childhood bed, snuggling underneath the colorful patchwork quilt, relishing the sheer luxury of napping in the middle of the day—something I rarely did. Then a lyric and melody blasted into my brain: *Bird, why do you sing? Fate has clipped your wings...*

I'd already learned the hard way that when a song comes to me, it won't stay around long, so I have to write it down immediately. With a little dramatic groaning heard by no one, I lifted my head from the well-worn feather pillow and reached for my phone so that I could sing it into the voice memo app.

As I did this, something interesting happened: A second melody and lyric line appeared.

But it wasn't the second line of the song. It was a completely separate section. Right away, I could hear how the two melodies would complement each other when sung simultaneously.

With that realization, I felt a massive surge of energy. I quickly opened my phone's notes app to start tapping out the lyrics for the second section:

You make me feel like a bird in the sky
Fly round and round and I can't fall down.
You make me feel, make me feel so free
Like I just came awake, not afraid to be.

The song was about playing with Alan and his magical looping pedal—it truly felt like soaring. Nonetheless, I was a little uncertain about my new circumstances.

On one hand, the possibilities with our new band, The Murder of Crows, felt endless. Creatively, I was more charged with artistic energy than ever before—songwriting and looping had both dramatically expanded my musical horizons. What's more, Alan was a well-respected, seasoned musician, and he seemed to be genuinely excited about and invested in our band. If he was willing to shepherd our project forward, with all the skills and knowledge and support he had amassed over the years, who knew what musical adventures might await our fledgling duo?

On the other hand, I had a sneaking suspicion that there was a glass ceiling located somewhere just above me that I couldn't see yet. My disability was extremely visible—I wasn't exactly the picture of the sexy female musical pop star. I had always secretly wondered if my disability made me too "unmarketable" or "uncool" to be taken seriously as a professional musician. Perhaps, I had thought, I was still destined for a life of musical obscurity in Duluth.

But for once, I decided not to let the unknown bother me. I wanted to sing my heart out either way.

I was excited to show my new song to Alan. I could even hear how I wanted him to loop my violin at the beginning of the song. This was a big deal for me—I'd never heard my loops in my head in advance before. Up to that point, everything on my violin had been improvisation.

The interlocking parts meant, by default, that the song had to be sung as a duet. I was aware of the fact that this tune, bouncy and bright, wasn't the typical mood of our sets as The Murder of Crows, and I couldn't have written a more off-brand song for Alan Sparhawk's vibes if I'd tried.

At our next rehearsal, I showed him my new song and asked him to record the violin loops that I'd heard in my head. Alan listened patiently, then he started strumming out a guitar part to complement the loops. Then, as instructed, he sang the first part, a single phrase that repeated multiple times throughout the song: *Bird, why do you sing? Fate has clipped your wings.*

I soon joined in. The two parts lined up exactly as I'd imagined. Alan looked just a tiny bit uncomfortable as we practiced our cheerful duet—admittedly it was a bit sing-songy—but if he had any reservations, he kept them to himself that day. Later Alan told me that the tune got stuck in his head quite often. We named it "Bird Song," and we'd go on to sing it at every show.

THAT SUMMER, WE recorded a seven-track album of mostly atmospheric instrumentals in my living room. Alan had a small run of fifty CDs printed up locally. He even took the time to stencil a black outline of a crow onto every single one of our blue handmade album covers.

A month or two into rehearsals, Alan announced that he wanted to help me figure out a way to use the looping pedal by myself. "We just need to find a pedal that can fit in your wheelchair," he said, as he examined the available space on the left side of my seat cushion. "Then someday you'll be playing shows by yourself."

I seriously doubted his prediction—the idea of performing solo terrified me! Besides, I was having so much fun with our newfound collaboration, I didn't feel a pressing desire to branch out. But I decided not to voice these qualms, because Alan seemed invested in the idea (excited, even, which was uncharacteristic of him). I privately hoped that he'd forget about it.

But to my surprise and secret horror, Alan showed up a couple of weeks later with a small amplifier and a blue box containing a Memory Man looping pedal. The pedal was about the size of a large postcard and about as thick as one of the later Harry Potter books. The dimensions were a big reason he chose that model; it was small enough to fit on the left side of my seat cushion, leaving space for me to pivot my violin in front of me.

"You mean, you're just gonna leave this stuff here?" I asked.

"Yeah, you can keep the gear," he said. "It'll get you on your way."

"Wow, thank you!" I said, taken aback. I was already feeling quite grateful for his mentorship over the past few months, but this show of generosity caught me completely by surprise. I wanted to hug him, but I was pretty sure that would make him uncomfortable.

"No problem," he said, his gaze meeting mine momentarily, then shifting away to a spot on the floor. "Here, I'll show you how it works."

He gave me a little demonstration of these new toys, trying to keep it as simple as possible.

"The button on the left—you hold that down to record," Alan explained. "Be sure to press it down firmly the whole time you're recording. It stops the loop whenever you release the pressure."

This proved to be difficult, but not impossible. Annoyingly, my leg wasn't strong enough to maintain constant pressure on the button; I'd get tired and my knee would shift slightly, ending the loop prematurely. But I knew that with practice I could get it.

"Next up, the button on the right is to erase the loop," he said. "It's just like my green pedal—you can't save any loops on here."

Simple, I thought.

"Moving on, the top row of rotating knobs are for effects," he said enthusiastically. "I'm not really sure what yours do yet."

He tested each knob out and identified echo, decay, and a few other ones my brain refused to understand, let alone remember. Try as he might, I just wasn't comprehending their functions.

Not to be defeated, Alan asked Paul for some mailing labels and a permanent marker. He stuck two labels across the top of the pedal and marked the ideal position of each knob with a small arrow, all aiming in different directions at the top of the pedal.

"There you go," he said triumphantly. "It's like a cheat sheet until you're able to do some experimenting. This will get you started."

ALAN'S GIFTS REMAINED untouched for over a week. I had left everything set up on a wooden chair in our living room—the looping pedal was beckoning me, taunting me, to try it out. I'd eye it with suspicion, a mix of curiosity and dread. Eventually, musical inquisitiveness got the better of me.

One weeknight after my usual shift at the Boys and Girls Club, I had some time at home alone. My personal care attendant, who helped me cook and get ready for bed while Paul was at his custodian job, was about to leave for the evening. Before she departed, I asked her to set my violin on the couch so that I could reach it. I had an hour to myself before Paul got home from work.

I finally felt ready to tackle the looping pedal. I plugged it into my violin tentatively and switched on the amp, which hummed to life. I positioned the pedal under my left leg, adjusting it until I could finally reach the button I was supposed to push. I then attempted, awkwardly, to record a few measures of melody to loop. Frustratingly, it was almost impossible to get the timing right.

Rhythm has never been my strong suit, and it turned out that looping hinged on keeping time. I tried to count out a simple, stable rhythm in my head (one-two-three-four, one-two-three-four), but I was nervous about missing the beat. This made my leg twitch, which invariably caused the loop to cut out one beat before I intended (one-two-three-four, one-two-three *shit!*). It seemed that all I could manage was sloppy, irregularly timed loops.

But my years of classical training had taught me something that came in handy. When trying to conquer a difficult passage, you just play it repeatedly, until your brain and body finally fall in line. So I kept at it, trying and failing and failing again.

Suddenly, like magic, I got the counting right! The first loop—which was really just a bunch of rhythmic D's strung together—was timed correctly (one-two-three-four, one-two-three-four). The simple rhythm was repeating in an endless, steady chain.

I could finally add a second loop. This was easier than creating the first one because the rhythm was already set in stone. For this layer, I bounced between F-sharp and A. Next I added a low A, to provide the bass line. I had just created a three-part happy rhythm, in the key of D major.

Then I let my creative instinct take over. I listened to the simple loop until I had an idea for a melody line. I hit Record, then added it into the mix. Next I added a harmony part, one that moved in tandem with the melody. Then for some extra flourish, I added a line of plucking at the end. Just like with a painting, you can go too far, so I made myself stop there.

I listened to my creation on repeat for several minutes. A warm, fuzzy ball of excitement filled my chest—it sounded like a symphony, but it was just me and my violin! I could barely contain myself. I had to show Alan. I pulled out my phone and took a video of the amp, with the mini symphony of music pouring out. I texted it to him. It was nearly midnight, but I couldn't help myself. When Paul got home, the loop was still playing, my triumphant first creation.

DO NOT BE deceived, that was *not* the glorious moment where I achieved mastery over my looping pedal. On the contrary—my progress was extremely slow. It took me over a year of practicing until I could reliably create loops that were both in time and musically interesting.

In truth, looping was one of the most frustratingly difficult skill sets I have ever tried to acquire. More often than not, I wanted to blow my pedal up. But on those rare moments when I could get everything to work, the loops sounded sublime. The potential was there, just out of my grasp.

I knew that I needed motivation to keep practicing. Most musicians (including me, usually) dream of gigs where an audience is enthralled, listening intently. After all, it can be a little boring or disheartening to play your heart out onstage if no one is even paying attention.

But, in this case, providing background music was perfect.

My looping wasn't yet good enough to withstand scrutiny, but I knew that if I didn't put myself under at least some pressure, I'd never bother to truly master the pedal. Luckily, I found the perfect place to experiment and work out the kinks: a local pizza shop!

The owners of said pizza shop were more than happy to accommodate my request for a background music gig. Every Tuesday night, I serenaded their customers for two hours. I was paid a handsome sum of fifty dollars, a free ten-inch pizza, and a complimentary glass of wine. It was a pretty sweet deal for a brand-new solo artist who was still lacking in her looping skills and wavering in her onstage confidence.

At first, no one even looked over—which, of course, was perfectly fine with me. But with each new gig, my skills slowly improved, and the music got more interesting. My repertoire expanded to include my original songs, which I had finally figured out how to loop.

The attendance wasn't ever particularly *robust*, but nonetheless a regular group of family members, friends, and local music lovers began to coalesce. They had caught on to the gig, and it became a weekly routine for us all: music and a slice (or three) at the pizza shop on Tuesday nights.

ONCE I WAS comfortable singing and looping alone, I wanted to try making a solo album.

Up to that point, I had recorded three albums in the context of a group. But a band album isn't a true reflection of my artistic mind, not completely, at least. Recording a solo album, however, felt risky, revealing, and terribly permanent. What if it sucked or lacked creative vision? I'd have no one to blame but myself.

My first recording session took place at a beautiful cathedral that had been deconsecrated and turned into a recording studio. The only other person present that day was the recording engineer, a quiet guy named Jake Larson who was about my age. I was so nervous that afternoon that I'd even asked Paul to leave. Jake wore a red bandanna and a poker face and wasn't much for small talk, which was fine with me because I was in no mood to chat. My internal pressure was high. I couldn't shake the idea that I had to get a *perfect* take of each song.

I was live-looping all the music, so I ended up recording three takes of each song and picking my favorite. Most were traditional Celtic or Old-Time fiddle tunes, but I included one original song for good measure. To save money, I planned to record the whole album in a single afternoon. And sure enough, after a grueling four-hour session, we had all the tracks we needed.

There's only so much editing you can do with live-looping, but Jake and I did some basic mixing over email. I wanted the fade-ins and fade-outs to be just right. I'd listen and send him my notes, and he'd send me updated versions of each track to approve. The last step, perhaps the most important, was choosing the song order. In the end, we were both happy with the album.

Since I didn't have the backing of a record label, I crowdfunded the production costs through GoFundMe. With the generous help of family members, friends, and local music lovers, my debut album, *All the Roads That Lead Us Home*, was released in November 2015.

By commercial standards, the release was nothing big—it didn't top any music charts or get national airplay. But the album *did* receive a glowing review in our local newspaper, and I played a jam-packed album-release concert at the same pizza shop where I used to rehearse every Tuesday night. To me, it was the beginning of a new era. The spotlight no longer scared me the way it had before. I was gaining confidence and honing my voice.

18

Safe Harbor

PAUL AND I had purchased a cute little bungalow in a working-class neighborhood in Duluth during the second year of our relationship. At that early stage, we weren't ready to talk about getting engaged, let alone marriage, but finding a wheelchair-accessible rental house was so challenging that it made buying a house feel like the next logical step for us as a couple.

Purchasing a house is a fairly large commitment, and it seemed likely that Paul and I would get married eventually. But whenever the topic of nuptials came up, Paul got squeamish. He assured me it didn't have to do with me. Paul is an introverted person, and the idea of standing up in front of a couple hundred people during a ceremony in which he is at the center of attention filled him with dread.

Paul always maintained that getting married wouldn't meaningfully change our relationship. "Marriage, no marriage—our love is the same love either way," he would say. Maybe that was OK for *him*, but I, on the other hand, wanted to get engaged, wear a sparkly ring, plan a wedding, have a reception. I wanted to experience all of it!

By 2013, Paul and I had been dating for nearly seven years, so try as I might to maintain a Zen attitude toward our perpetually unwed state, I was indeed starting to get impatient for Paul to pop the question. I started making subtle hints—more like strongly worded requests—about engagement rings, and he promised he'd start looking into it.

An unexpected result was that diamond-mining practices and

human rights violations soon became frequent topics of conversation. I appreciated that he was taking these important issues to heart, but I couldn't tell if his research was just a delaying tactic to quiet me down.

Months passed. Life was good, we were happy, but we still weren't engaged. With all my might, I valiantly suppressed the urge to take him by the shoulders and shake some sense into him.

I finally cracked when we received an invitation in the mail for my cousin's wedding. More specifically, her second wedding. Since Paul and I had started dating.

The fact that my cousin had experienced twice as many engagements as I had in the past seven years was indeed quite irksome. And yet here *we* were, seemingly idle.

It was a Saturday morning and I was in the bathroom washing my face when Paul had the audacity to mention my cousin's big day. I felt a flash of irritation, precisely the kind of moment when biting one's tongue is advised.

Of course, I did no such thing. Instead, I blurted out something extremely snarky, like, "Are you going to wait until her *third* marriage to propose?"

It was, admittedly, a low blow.

"*What?!*" Paul responded, equal parts surprised and hurt.

"I'm sorry," I said. "That was mean. I am just getting impatient. We've been together so long. When will *we* be the ones getting married?"

"Fair enough. I understand," he said. "But I can't do anything about it right now. Can we just try to enjoy our day off together? Hey, let's go up the North Shore! We'll get breakfast in Two Harbors."

My mood lifted immediately. "Yeah," I said. "Sorry about being crabby. I'm probably just hungry."

Paul assured me things were fine, and we prepared for our impromptu weekend adventure. Two Harbors is a small town about twenty miles farther up the shore of Lake Superior. Paul and I loved visiting there, and over the years it had become our spot.

We had spent many lovely nights at the town's municipal campground, which was right on the shoreline. We'd watch the moon rise over Lake Superior at night and then go to bed to the sound of honking geese and the clanking of the ore boats unloading at the docks nearby.

It was a bright, sunny day as we drove up the familiar shoreline. The first stop was at our favorite greasy spoon for a breakfast of hash browns, eggs, and bacon. Then we hiked on a paved bike path that ran through the woods and up to the town's picturesque lighthouse. It was late May, the first really warm day of spring—perfect weather for meandering through the forest.

I enjoyed the sights on our nature walk: copious amounts of just-blossomed wildflowers and an occasional white-tailed deer. Partway down the bike path, we discovered a dirt trail that led right to the rocky shoreline. There was a wrought-iron bench just off the trail, facing the water. "Wanna check this out?" Paul asked. "Can your chair make it?"

"I think so," I said. I navigated the narrow trail as Paul pushed the handlebars. We reached the bench, and Paul lifted me over so that we could sit next to each other.

Being up close like this is when the true majesty of Lake Superior begins to sink in. The massive boulders that made up the shoreline were the size of horses, probably larger. They spread out in front of us in a jagged horizon, as if tossed there haphazardly by the gods. Icy blue water splashed against the rocks, spraying white foam at the site of impact.

We sat for a while in silence, enjoying the gorgeous view. Then Paul reached for his wallet, seeming to fumble for a credit card or a receipt. Instead, he pulled out a small slip of paper.

I recognized it. It was a "coupon" from a booklet I'd made him years earlier as a gift for Valentine's Day. These handmade coupons were valid for things like movie nights, home-cooked meals, massages, campfires, and other fun date-night activities.

"I'd like to redeem this," he said as he handed it to me.

This one was the last coupon in the book. It read, "Good for a lifetime of love and affection. Expiration Date: Never." I was touched that he'd saved the coupon all these years, but I wondered why Paul had chosen this moment to redeem it.

Until, that is, he started getting down on one knee, in front of our bench. He took a black velvet box out of his pocket and opened it to reveal a delicate gold ring with a brilliant diamond in the center.

"Gaelynn, will you marry me?" he asked.

Tears welled up in my eyes, and I felt a wave of love for this kind man, whose clear blue eyes looked up at me expectantly.

"What? Really? Yes, of course!" I said, as I started to blubber.

Paul looked relieved. He put the ring on my finger and kissed me. Then he quickly scrambled back onto the bench, so as not to attract the attention of any wayfaring strangers. I giggled.

Paul shies away from public displays of affection, which is probably why his proposal had been made in the woods, at least partially shielded from the gaze of other humans.

I confessed to feeling sheepish for my childish outburst that morning, but Paul told me not to worry.

"I'm just glad I didn't have to pull the ring out of the closet to stop the argument!" he exclaimed.

We both laughed.

"By the way," he said, switching gears. "You'll be happy to know that your ring contains a certified blood-free diamond. I finally found a jeweler in Duluth that could guarantee it!"

And just like that, we were finally engaged. I was glad Paul hadn't compromised his values on account of my wanting a sparkly ring. After all, his integrity is one of his handsomest features.

19

An Unexpected Roadblock

THE MOMENT WE got engaged, my inner wedding planner was released from captivity. First, I bought my wedding dress with my cousin Rachael, who was also my maid of honor. I didn't want Paul to see the dress before the big day, but I knew I would show him the second I got back from the store if I took it to our house, so we dropped it off at my mom's place on the way home. Still, Paul could tell by my expression that something was up as soon as we came through the door. "You bought a dress, didn't you?" he asked intuitively.

I confessed, but somehow managed not to tell him exactly what it looked like. By the following week, I had already chosen a date, booked the church, secured a reception venue, and lined up catering. I love planning events—especially fun ones like this—and Paul was happy to let me handle the logistics. He was busy worrying about saying his vows in front of all our friends and family—all eyes on him, at the front of the church.

One afternoon shortly after our engagement, I went to Starbucks in downtown Duluth to do some wedding planning while enjoying my favorite beverage—a small mocha with no whipped cream and half the chocolate.

I took a sip of the sweet, creamy coffee goodness and dialed Alan's number. I usually texted, but this felt too important. Surprisingly, he answered, and I told him about our engagement.

"Congratulations, both to you and Paul," Alan said warmly.

"Thanks," I said. "But that's actually only part of the reason I'm calling," I said, a little apprehensively. "I have to ask you something. We were hoping that you'd be willing to play—"

He inhaled sharply, and I could practically see his body tense up on the other end of the line.

"Oh, no, you don't want us for that."

"What do you mean?" I asked, caught off guard. I hadn't even finished asking the question yet!

"Please don't ask Low to play during the ceremony," he said. "We get asked to do that all the time. It always ends up so stressful."

I swallowed a guffaw. Did he really think I would want such moody music at my wedding?

"Oh, I didn't mean Low! And I'm not talking about the ceremony," I assured him. "We were hoping The Black-Eyed Snakes could play during the reception." This was another side project that Alan fronted—a raucous blues outfit that played noisy local shows a few times a year. Paul and I both loved their sound.

"The Snakes? Yeah, that sounds fun!" he said, his voice instantly enthusiastic. "Do you have a date picked out yet?"

"Yes, it's December 21st," I told him. "I thought Low might be home from touring for Christmas."

"Yeah, we are," he said. "I'll put it on the calendar. Thanks for asking us... And congratulations again. Tell Paul hey."

I hung up the phone, beaming. The wedding plans were coming along perfectly.

Or so I thought.

THAT YEAR, MY life felt like a steam engine that was threatening to veer off the rails. I had a clerical job I didn't really like, but it paid the bills, barely. In the summer, I released two albums with two different musical projects, and both of the bands booked a mountain of shows to promote their respective new albums. I was playing constantly while trying to balance my day job. By the fall, I was massively drained and frazzled. Something needed to give, but I refused to admit it.

Instead, I simply tried to muscle through the stress, despite a growing sense that this wasn't how I wanted to live. But if you ignore gut feelings for too long, your body eventually sends you a message that you *can't* ignore. And that's exactly what happened. In my case, it was the bleeding.

Early that October, my period came as scheduled and then decided not to leave. This wasn't normal bleeding either; I was soaking through extra-heavy pads within the hour. When the bleeding still hadn't stopped ten days later, I decided I had to see a doctor.

Years earlier—shortly after I started dating Paul—I went to a gynecologist to get on birth control. After what had happened with Elliot, I didn't ever want to take a plan B pill again. But when the doctor was doing his intake interview, he let his biases slip big-time when he asked, "I'm assuming you want me to prescribe this birth control to mitigate your menstrual cramps?"

I was offended that he made this assumption so easily, so I corrected him, a tad defiantly.

"No, it's because I don't want to get pregnant."

"Oh, I see." The thin, gray-haired man paused awkwardly. "So you're sexually active?"

"Yes," I said, secretly wanting to whop him one.

"OK, I can prescribe that," he said. "You know, if you're interested in avoiding pregnancy altogether, we could discuss a hysterectomy sometime in the future. That's always an option."

I struggled to process this. I knew that my lungs were too small to carry a baby to term. Still, I didn't think that a gynecologist I'd never seen before was clued in to my full medical history.

In any case, would he have casually suggested surgical sterilization to a nondisabled person in her early thirties? I sincerely doubted it. I was annoyed, but I wasn't up for arguing.

"I'll let you know," I responded, making a mental note never to see that particular doctor ever again.

But now I was experiencing unexplained bleeding just months before my wedding. As much as I was dreading the possibility of another tactless gynecologist, I knew that I needed to see someone. I called a friend of mine who's a nurse and asked her for a recommendation. I wanted to make sure she knew exactly what I was hoping to avoid, so I relayed my infuriating encounter from years earlier. She recommended Dr. Mark Widstrom and assured me that he was open-minded and smart and would treat me like a whole person rather than a less-than medical anomaly. I booked an appointment, hoping to get some straightforward answers.

I liked Doctor Widstrom immediately. He was kind, seemed very intelligent, and took time to listen to me as I explained my symptoms.

But I wasn't prepared for what he had to say after my exam.

"I have some difficult news for you, Gaelynn," he began, with a serious expression and a calm, metered tone. "As you know, we weren't able to do a full pelvic exam because of the position of your hips; your hip bone is blocking us from seeing what we need to in order to rule out cancer. So I'm recommending we do a hysterectomy."

A *what*? I felt ambushed by his news.

On top of the fact that the month before my wedding was the *worst* possible timing for a major surgery, I couldn't help but doubt the true intentions behind his recommendation.

I struggled to find the right words. "If this is the only reasonable course of action, then of course I'll do it, but I just have to ask..." My pulse quickened and my voice was shaky. "You're not recommending that I get a hysterectomy because I have a disability, right?"

"What? No!" he quickly exclaimed, looking both surprised at my suggestion and a bit betrayed.

I immediately regretted saying anything. It was clear that Doctor Widstrom was nothing like the other gynecologist who had flippantly suggested surgical sterilization seven years earlier.

Nonetheless, the intersection of sexuality and disability is fraught. Society's prejudices had been clear to me even as a teenager: Sex and pregnancy weren't "for" people with disabilities like me, and the idea of being a good romantic partner and of parenting with a disability was stretching the imagination a bit too far.

"I feel bad even asking, but I am not sure how much training you had on disabilities in med school," I said. "I have read that it's not uncommon for hysterectomies to be a go-to procedure for disabled women. And historically, disabled people have been discouraged from having kids."

That turned out to be a bit of an understatement on my part. Disabled people weren't just *discouraged* from having kids—as I would later learn, disabled people in the United States were subjected to systematic sterilization for many decades. Eugenicists, who gained significant traction in the early 1900s, claimed that the health of the nation could be improved by forbidding "weaker" elements from reproducing, while encouraging "the strong." Involuntary sterilization became a brutal tool of eugenics, rooted in the idea that some people aren't "fit" to have children.

Thirty-two states went on to pass eugenics laws. As a result, forced sterilization occurred with alarming frequency in the US from the early 1900s until the late 1970s—and the 1927 Supreme Court ruling in *Buck v. Bell*, which upheld involuntary sterilization, still hasn't been overturned. Disabled people were often the primary targets of eugenics laws, but these policies were also used against women of color, immigrants, prisoners, and women living in poverty. Even if unwanted surgeries aren't as commonly foisted on disabled people as they were in the past, the harmful messaging and legacy of eugenics remain to this day.

I told him about my birth control incident, hoping he would understand why I'd felt compelled to ask. He took in what I had to say without arguing, making excuses, or getting defensive.

Instead, his eyes locked onto mine and he said in a steady, earnest voice, "I would never recommend a surgery like this if I didn't think it wasn't absolutely necessary."

"Are you sure we can't wait?" I asked. "I'm getting married!" I was practically pleading with him.

"I know, this is really bad timing," he said sympathetically. "But it would be irresponsible of me to send you away without making sure whatever is causing the bleeding isn't cancer."

This was hard to accept, even if it made sense. "But there's good news," he continued. "If everything looks OK when we get in there, we'll be able to leave your ovaries and just take out the uterus. That should prevent early menopause."

Ugh. Avoiding early menopause seemed like a pretty crappy consolation prize. My heart sank.

Recovering from surgery was absolutely *not* on my wedding prep to-do list. But my gut told me that Doctor Widstrom was right.

"OK," I said, resigned to my fate. "Let's do this."

We scheduled the surgery for early November, a mere six weeks before our wedding.

THE WEEKS LEADING up to the surgery were strange. I was still making wedding plans, but now there was a big question mark hanging over the whole event—a subtle *if*, no longer *when*.

And although I had known for years that I wouldn't be able to carry a baby to term, I felt a surprising amount of sadness about the hysterectomy. It meant that the door to pregnancy was closing for good. Growing up, I had always envisioned myself becoming a parent, one way or another. While adoption was still an option in theory, it was filled with a daunting set of unknowns.

From what I'd heard, adoption was a long, grueling, expensive process, with or without a disability. If Paul and I did decide to adopt, would we be able to afford it? We'd also have to prove that we could care for a child. Would an adoption agency consider us eligible, in light of my own need for physical care? Of course, I felt more than capable of tending to a child's needs emotionally and intellectually, but I wouldn't exactly be able to haul a kid out of a burning building.

What's more, did Paul and I even *want* to adopt? We'd tossed the idea around before, but never seriously. It would change our lives so drastically! What if our marriage suffered for it?

And if we ultimately didn't end up adopting, would we regret it? That question also haunted me.

It didn't help that many of my close friends and relations had young families at the time. Most of their children were under the age of five, and that chapter of parenting seems to be (from the outside, at least) equal parts torture and tenderness. They were exhausted and frustrated, and unfortunately it showed. On more than one occasion, they blurted out biting statements like *You wouldn't understand—you've never been a parent* or *We can't just do whatever we want like you and Paul, because we have kids.*

Their remarks felt insensitive, passive-aggressive, and more than a little hurtful, in light of my upcoming surgery. I tried to remember that these exhausted new parents weren't in their right minds. They probably needed sleep, therapy, or antidepressants—or all three.

Nonetheless, I felt isolated at a time when I really could have used a little compassion.

A few friends of mine have since faced their own hysterectomies, struggled to get pregnant, or experienced the heartache of miscarriage. They, too, had to process their mostly unacknowledged grief in a society that seems to idolize parenthood.

Our cultural messaging can cause a person to feel defective or less-than because they'll never get to experience the often-touted "miracle of childbirth" or know a "deeper love than they ever imagined possible." Sometimes these sentiments are so pervasive that they don't stand out—until you have an open wound that's trying to heal.

Eventually I learned to accept the possibility that Paul and I might choose not to become parents. But that didn't mean the life we were building together, with its unique struggles and joys, was any less meaningful. Children or not, Paul and I could still use our life's energy to contribute to the world around us and to support the people we love.

There's no shame in being childless. We are all traveling down different paths, equally valuable and worthwhile.

THE DATE OF the surgery barreled toward me quickly. I got most of our wedding affairs in order—I paid the vendors, applied for the marriage license, coordinated volunteers to handle decorations, and sent the invitations. The dreaded operation day soon arrived, and once again I drifted away on the operating table.

When I awoke, Doctor Widstrom explained that the surgery had gone great. In an almost-too-vivid description, he said that my uterus had practically leapt out of my body. To my immense relief, he told me that everything looked totally normal. We had to await the pathology results before declaring the official all-clear, but Doctor Widstrom assured me that there was little cause for concern. Paul sat by my bed, nodding attentively. This was his first time in the hospital with me.

As Doctor Widstrom wrapped up the post-op consultation, he told us, "I'm leaving town tonight, but my nurses can get messages to me. If you get worse instead of better, go to the ER."

I was discharged from the hospital the next afternoon. At home, my body seemed to be healing up quite nicely. I felt a little less tender and a bit more like myself with each passing day.

But on the fourth morning, I woke up with a fever. I had to wrap myself in a quilt to keep from shivering. Paul drove me to the hospital.

I was readmitted with a postoperative bladder infection. The doctor on call ordered antibiotics and fluids, both through an IV.

When a nurse came in to administer the antibiotics, I peppered her with questions. "You know I only weigh seventy-three pounds, right?" I asked. "Is the dose you're giving me the correct amount for someone my size?"

"Yep," she said confidently. "It's been adjusted for your weight."

Just then a thought occurred to me. "What about the IV fluids? I don't drink as much water as other people, because I'm so small. Probably only half as much, on a daily basis."

"The fluids are a maintenance dose," she assured me. "Your body will be able to process them."

Not wanting to look too suspicious of medical professionals, I decided to drop it.

But as the day wore on, I felt worse, not better. There was pain all over my body, and I was bloated and uncomfortable. My skin, in particular, was sore to the touch. The doctor decided to keep me there overnight.

Thankfully, the nurses let Paul stay in the room with me. The residual trauma from my respiratory incident years earlier was once again making its presence known, and I was too anxious to be left alone in a hospital without a familiar face nearby. I fell asleep that night amidst blinking lights and beeps, with Paul scrunched up next to me in a small reclining chair.

By the end of the next day, I felt absolutely horrible. I was in immense pain. And now my heart rate was elevated, my oxygen level was beginning to dip, and I was having heart palpitations. All this made me exceedingly nervous—was my worst medical nightmare coming back to haunt me for a second time? I felt so awful that I began wondering if I'd even be around for the wedding. All I could do was lie there, trying to calm my agitated body while anxious thoughts swirled in my mind. Paul stayed with me every moment, sitting next to the bed and holding my hand. I was incredibly grateful for his comforting presence amidst the chaos.

Later that afternoon, a nurse came in to check my vitals. On her way out the door, she crossed below the bottom of my hospital bed and said quietly to herself, "Eighty-eight pounds."

My ears pricked up. "What's eighty-eight pounds?" I asked.

"You!" she said. "The hospital bed has a built-in scale."

A bolt of terror shot through me.

"But I'm *not* eighty-eight pounds!" I exclaimed. "I'm only seventy-three!"

Several frustrating hours later, I finally had my answer. Thanks to the infection, my bladder hadn't been emptying properly. Dumping large quantities of IV fluids into my veins had obviously not helped the situation—I had gained fifteen pounds of water weight in just two days. My skin hurt because it was literally being stretched out.

This deluge of fluids had also messed up my body's electrolyte balance, causing my heart to beat irregularly. Left undiagnosed, things would have started getting dangerous pretty quickly. Luckily, the nurse on duty had a habit of talking to herself. If she hadn't, who knows whether they'd have figured it out in time?

The fluids had to be flushed out, and fast. First the doctor inserted a catheter. Then he prescribed diuretics along with intravenous magnesium to balance out my electrolytes.

The next day, I felt like a new person. I was going to make it to the wedding day, and I was even more convinced that Paul was the person I wanted by my side for life.

A FEW DAYS after I got home from the hospital, I started thinking in the shower about how meaningful it was that Paul had stayed by my side throughout the ordeal. He had remained calm, patient, and comforting the entire time, even when things got scary. My recent foray at the hospital surely hadn't been the kinds of adventures Paul had been expecting when we started dating seven years earlier. Nonetheless he had handled it with grace.

Suddenly, under the warm running water, a few lines with a melody attached popped into my head:

> *Our love's a complex vintage wine*
> *All rotted leaves and lemon rind*
> *I'd spit you out, but now you're mine.*

I loved how the metaphor, as abstract as it was, captured the essence of our partnership. Our relationship was beautiful and romantic in many ways, but it wasn't typical or carefree. It had depth and character, and both of us were committed to seeing it through.

For a full two weeks those lines were all I could hear. This tiny snippet of a song bounced around my head nonstop. It was starting to feel a bit like torture, until finally the clouds broke and another line came. I remembered how it felt as Paul held my hand in that hospital bed:

We walked the pier and back again
It was the most scared I've ever been
You held my hand until the end.
And I love you.
And I love you.

Mercifully, the third verse came shortly after that, and soon, "Someday We'll Linger in the Sun" was completed—the song that would change my life three years later.

20

Merry Matrimony

SIX WEEKS AFTER my surgery, our winter solstice wedding finally arrived. I remember sitting nervously with my bridesmaids in an empty coatroom as we waited for the ceremony to begin. The room was tucked away at the back of my parents' church, the same one where they'd been married over thirty years earlier.

I was wearing the wedding dress I'd surreptitiously purchased with my cousin Rachael, though today it hardly resembled the original. A friend had lovingly altered the dress for me, shortening the skirt's layers by several feet so that it fit me just right. The bridal party's festive bouquets had been arranged by another friend and included holly berries, ivy, pine cones, and beautiful red and white roses. Paul and I hadn't seen each other yet that day, which heightened our anticipation.

The associate pastor came into the coatroom, telling us that it was time to line up. Elliot began playing "Silent Night" on his violin, and one by one my seven bridesmaids proceeded to the altar. My sweet little niece and nephews, incredibly serious about their responsibility, carefully carried the wedding bands and presented them to the best man. Then Elliot switched melodies and began playing one of my favorite fiddle tunes. My dad, dressed in a tux, linked his arm with mine. I tried not to cry, since the ceremony hadn't even officially started yet.

As I slowly made my way down the aisle, I recognized so many of the people I loved surrounding me. I caught sight of Paul, looking truly handsome and just a little nervous in his new black suit, green tie, and white poinsettia boutonniere. When I reached the front of the church, I turned and hugged my dad, who was visibly holding back tears. I rolled my wheelchair up the ramp leading to the altar. My dad had built it especially for the occasion. He had even picked matching carpet for its surface so that it blended in with the rest of the flooring in the sanctuary.

A pair of ministers officiated the ceremony together, alternating Bible readings and sharing their own reflections. When it was time for our vows, Paul handed me a small embroidered handkerchief to wipe my eyes, and I made it through. Then one of the ministers led us through the exchange of rings. The butterflies returned—we were almost married! I slipped a titanium band onto Paul's finger, and Paul clasped a slim gold wedding band onto mine.

Wait, *clasped*?

Yes. Because of my disability, the joints in my fingers are too enlarged for a ring to slide on easily. But when Paul was shopping for my engagement ring, the jeweler showed him a nifty gold band that pops open and slides closed via a tiny button on the band. The only problem? It's called... an *arthritic shank*. The jewelry industry could certainly stand to rethink the name for this useful ring modification. After all, nothing says *I love you, darling* like an arthritic shank!

Unbeknownst to everyone, Paul and I had a festive trick planned for the end of the ceremony. Before the wedding, we tied a sprig of mistletoe to some fishing line and connected it to the end of a very long pole. Then we entrusted it to the best man, who was now waiting for his cue. When the pastors called out in unison, "It is our privilege to present to you the newly married couple!" the best man dangled the pole above our heads, and our first kiss as husband and wife took place underneath the mistletoe. Laughter erupted, and Elliot played *Joy to the World* as we descended from the altar. Our family and friends clapped as we passed them in the aisle, beaming.

The rest of the wedding night was a beautiful blur. We had dinner with friends and family in the church basement, our meal catered by the owners of the restaurant that had provided food for my parents' plays back when they first launched the dinner theater. Then the reception continued at a bar downtown, which the venue owner had kindly allowed us to use for free.

Several friends had volunteered to decorate the place that morning, and they'd transformed it into an impressively festive reception space. They hung more strings of Christmas lights than I could count, draped all the high-top tables with white tablecloths, and set out dozens of poinsettia-themed centerpieces, which had been assembled by my hardworking aunties.

The reception started with a family-friendly folk dance, accompanied by familiar fiddle tunes. Later, Alan Sparhawk and his raucous blues band took the stage, blasting the throngs of dancers with music to close out the party. The venue opened to the public at ten o'clock, and by the end of the night it was packed. I knew most of the people from town, but there were certainly more than a handful of folks surprised to find themselves dancing alongside a woman dressed in white and rocking out in a wheelchair with her new husband.

We left the venue around two in the morning, as big, fat snowflakes fell from the sky. We headed to our room at a nearby hotel for the night and (eventually) fell into a blissful sleep. When we awoke the next day, the sun streaming through the windows, we looked at each other and grinned. "That was the best night ever!" we said, practically in unison. And, in truth, it was.

21

The Infamous Phone Call

AFTER PAUL AND I got married, one of the first calls I made was to the county Public Health and Human Services office. I needed a caseworker to guide me through the Medicaid eligibility changes that had been triggered by the wedding. This was my least favorite aspect of getting married, but it had to be dealt with.

For me, being on Medicaid was (and still is) a necessary part of life. In addition to covering my surgeries, medicines, and wheelchairs, Medicaid also paid for personal care attendants (PCAs) to help me bathe, dress, and use the bathroom. Every weekday evening, PCAs came to our house to help me get ready for bed while Paul worked his late-night custodial shift at the university. I needed assistance to stay safe and live independently.

For most Americans, paying for PCAs out of pocket isn't feasible—five hours of basic PCA services a day can cost thousands of dollars per month. Unfortunately, no private health insurance companies cover PCA services, so Medicaid is the only option for all but the wealthiest of disabled Americans.

There are barriers in place that keep most people from qualifying for Medicaid due to disability. For one, a person must prove that they're significantly disabled and that their income doesn't exceed the threshold established by the program guidelines. The most common way to qualify is proof of Supplemental Security Income (SSI). SSI is the federal program that sends out monthly payments to low-income disabled people whose daily functioning is seriously affected by disability.

If you are born with a significant disability and your family does not earn too much, as was the case for me, it is relatively straightforward to qualify for SSI. For those not born disabled, applying for SSI is often a long, difficult process with a ton of paperwork. Worse still, most people's applications get rejected at least once. One of my good friends from college developed multiple sclerosis, and she had to apply for SSI three times. Her application process was a yearslong affair, and it really took a toll on her.

Those who do manage to qualify for SSI—and thus Medicaid—must stay under a certain income threshold to keep their benefits. This threshold is really low—in many states, disabled people can't earn more than twelve hundred dollars per month. Ironically, having a decent job can threaten a disabled person's care. Medicaid income limits keep the disabled poor, barring them from participating fully in the American dream.

And if a disabled person gets married, their spouse's income counts toward the income limit, which makes it almost impossible to receive SSI and Medicaid if both spouses are working. These outdated, penalizing income guidelines have been huge barriers for every disabled person I've ever known when they get married. There's even a name for it: the Marriage Penalty. Disabled couples often can't enjoy the same lawfully wedded bliss as their fellow Americans because of Medicaid eligibility. They are essentially treated as second-class citizens by the government.

When I was a baby, my dad applied for and received SSI and Medicaid. Medicaid paid for my hospital bills, and SSI helped keep my low-income family afloat financially. My mom worked mostly part-time so that she could help me whenever I broke a bone. Every six months, my dad had to send in a renewal packet and proper documentation to prove to the county and the state that I was still disabled and that the family was still poor enough to qualify for Medicaid.

When I turned eighteen, the SSI payments started going to me directly. And unfortunately, so did the biannual paperwork. After college I had low-paying jobs, so I never crossed the earnings threshold that would have disqualified me from receiving Medicaid.

But I knew that as soon as the ink had dried on our marriage license, everything would change. I would no longer qualify for SSI—or Medicaid—because of Paul's income (at the time he made thirty thousand dollars per year as a custodian at UMD). Fair or not, the government would soon start adding his pay to mine when calculating our family's total income, and this amount would put us well over the threshold.

If I lived in a different state, I would not have even considered getting married, because I can't afford to lose access to Medicaid. But Minnesota has a great public healthcare program called Medical Assistance for Employed Persons with Disabilities (MA-EPD)—a Medicaid alternative that was created for disabled workers who aren't eligible for SSI. The best part of this program is that there are no income or asset limits. So long as a disabled person stays employed or self-employed, they will continue to qualify for healthcare. While this is great news for disabled Minnesotans who can work, this obviously isn't available for *all* disabled people, as not everyone can maintain a job.

To be eligible for MA-EPD, I first had to get "certified" as disabled by a State Medical Review Team. After that process was completed, I could then enroll in the healthcare program. On MA-EPD, I would pay a sliding-scale premium each month based on my income (luckily, this healthcare program doesn't factor a spouse's income into its premiums).

But I had to act quickly—otherwise, I'd lose my healthcare benefits after January 31, only a month away. I wouldn't be able to work with my PCAs, see the doctor, or get a new wheelchair until I was enrolled. And getting certified as disabled was not a simple process.

After Christmas, I faxed a mountain of hospital records and forms to the State Medical Review Team. To my relief, in early January I received confirmation that I had been certified disabled. This designation would last for seven years, and then I'd have to get recertified. Now, at least, I could apply for MA-EPD. I gathered up the required paperwork—my tax return, our bank statements, our most recent pay stubs, and a statement from Paul's retirement fund—to send with my enrollment packet.

A few weeks after I sent it all in, I received a letter back from the county. I ripped it open and to my dismay, the big, fat word DENIED stared back at me.

Why in the world would my application be rejected? I thought I'd followed the instructions to the letter! Confused, I picked up the phone and dialed the county's Public Health and Human Services office.

After a few minutes of hold music, I finally got through to a person.

"Hello," I said. "I am hoping to talk with someone about a denial letter I just received in the mail."

"Case number?" the woman on the other end of the line responded, matter-of-factly.

I read off the digits to her. "I recently got married, so I lost my SSI," I explained. "I was certified disabled by the state so that I could apply for MA-EPD. However, for some reason the letter I just received says that I was denied for Medicaid. But that's not even the program I was applying for—I need MA-EPD."

Several excruciating moments of silence followed. She finally spoke. "I looked through your case notes, and it appears that the only program you could even be eligible for is called MA-X."

"What's that?" I asked, starting to feel uneasy. "I've never heard of it."

"'MA-X' is a special designation for disabled people who aren't qualified for SSI, but who still need Medicaid to pay for things like personal care services. Your wages combined with your husband's puts you over the income guidelines for MA-X. That's why you got the denial letter."

None of this made any sense to me, and my unease turned to panic. "But I only wanted to be considered for MA-EPD, not MA-X. I am *employed*, and MA-EPD doesn't have any income limits."

"Unfortunately, you don't qualify for that program since you're not eligible for SSI anymore."

Now my head was swimming. What she was saying went against everything I'd ever read about MA-EPD: You didn't *have* to be eligible for SSI if you were certified disabled—that was the point! I wanted to remain levelheaded, but I could feel myself sliding toward hysteria.

"I don't understand," I said. "I'm *certain* that I qualify for MA-EPD. I read about it before applying. I got the state medical review because the last case worker told me to do it!"

"Well, they were wrong," she said, her tone sounding slightly irritated.

Frustration welled inside my chest. I wished a different case worker had taken my call.

"OK, so if for some reason I *don't* qualify for MA-EPD—which I still don't see why not—you said that the only other option is MA-X, right? But you just told me we make too much right now. So, hypothetically, how much less would we have to earn to qualify for MA-X?"

"Combined, you'd have to earn less than fourteen hundred dollars per month."

My heart fell, a heavy stone taking its place. "But that's less than my husband earns at his job, without even factoring in my paycheck! We could never live on that. We have a mortgage!"

"Well," she said, with a definite edge to her voice now, "those are the guidelines."

I let out a deep, heavy sigh of resignation. I'd been sending in those damn health-care renewal packets every six months for the past decade—tracking down pay stubs and bank statements and whatever else. But I'd done it, every time. Even though I had always hated the hoops, I'd never let them beat me before.

For the first time in my adult life, I saw no viable options ahead of me. I was at a loss.

"Well," I said slowly. "If I'm not eligible for either program, then what would you suggest I do?"

With no preamble whatsoever, she responded, "I would suggest you get a divorce."

I felt the hot, prickling sensation of anger creeping up into my cheeks. Of course, I'd known for years that the system was broken, even if I personally hadn't run into any insurmountable problems in the past. But now, an actual case worker had just told me—a newlywed—to get a divorce. And she told me that over the phone, with no sign of compassion. Complete indifference. She may as well have suggested I order a pizza.

My mind and body were buzzing with rage. I felt subhuman, totally helpless, stripped of any power or choice. I had no reasonable options, and the woman tasked with assisting me didn't seem to care. I felt like I'd been reduced to a caged animal. And when animals are backed into a corner with no reasonable chance of escape, they use the one tool they have left: They bite.

"What the *fuck* are you talking about?!" I screamed into the phone, my anger finally spilling out of me. "I can't believe you would even fucking suggest that to me! We just got married last month—*three fucking weeks ago!*"

"Try to calm down," the case worker said, trying to shush me.

Paul ran over from the other end of the house, thinking I'd fallen out of my wheelchair. "Gaelynn, what's wrong?!" he called frantically. When he saw me screaming on the phone like a woman possessed, he looked a little scared.

My shouts continued to fill the air. *"I did all the paperwork the last case worker sent me, and for what?"*

I could hear her stammering on the other end of the line, but I honestly didn't care.

"Why didn't someone warn me I wouldn't be eligible?" I yelled. *"Why the fuck didn't anyone tell me not to get married at all?!"*

Finally my emotional hell storm started to blow itself out. I was still mad—*fuming*—but at least I had control over my vocal cords. I quieted down, but I didn't apologize for my outburst.

"Are you still there?" I asked, feeling somewhat human again.

"Yes," she said awkwardly. "I am just reading through the regulations one more time. The rulebook the state publishes, maybe there's something in here..." She trailed off, distracted by her reading.

"Here it is! I found it!" she cried. "I have good news: It turns out you *are* eligible...for MA-EPD!"

Are you fucking kidding me?

"Wait, are you completely sure?" I ask warily, afraid she might still manage to ruin my life.

"Yes! Let me read it to you," she said, now almost cheerful. Sure enough, she read the exact guidelines I had seen myself, earlier. I had done everything correctly. She had just misread the rules.

A tidal wave of relief washed over me. I felt like laughing and crying at the same time. But truthfully, I was too emotionally spent to do either. I just was glad my healthcare plan didn't necessitate a divorce.

We ended the call on an even keel, our tone friendly. *She's only human,* I thought, as I hung up.

My profanity-laden outburst was certainly uncharacteristic of me, and it wasn't my proudest moment. But did I feel *bad* for yelling at her? No. Because what if I hadn't lost my temper? What if my fury hadn't compelled her to do some double-checking? What if I had accepted her answer at face value, hung up the phone, and broken the horrible news to Paul?

How many disabled people have needlessly gotten divorced because they've received inaccurate information from the people who are supposed to be supporting them?

I tell this story frequently now, because it perfectly illustrates the bitter reality that many disabled people face: being at the mercy of arbitrary rules administered by people who don't seem to care. This is the most egregious incident I've faced, but I've gotten my fair share of bad advice and felt the sting of dismissal—even blatant disrespect—from "helping professionals" over the years. And I know that I'm not the only one. A gross imbalance of power, coupled with mind-numbing bureaucracy, creates this unfortunately common scenario.

Getting health care shouldn't require mountains of paperwork, and no one should ever have to choose between Medicaid and marrying the person they love. It's simply *not* radical to believe that every person, regardless of disability status, deserves good health care. I hope I live to see it happen—health care as a human right, not a heartache.

22

Gig Economy

I'M NOT SURE if I would have decided to pursue music as a career if it hadn't been for a late-night conversation with my best friend, Leah. We were talking about what we would do with our time if we knew we only had one year—or even five years—left to live. As a child, I had always had big dreams for myself (interpreting French at the United Nations, for example), and yet here I was struggling to pay bills in a series of low-paying clerical jobs that were at best only mildly interesting to me.

Was there a way to connect my work to my passion?

Leah, for example, loved animals more than anyone I knew, and she was currently teaching horseback riding. "I wish I could charge people money for the things I *like* to do," I said to her wistfully one night over wine. "You're able to make a living with horses. I'm so jealous!"

"Well," she mused. "You like music. Why not look there?"

"Yeah, I guess," I responded. "But I can't make ends meet by playing shows around Duluth."

"Sure, but have you ever thought about violin lessons?"

Leah's suggestion sparked a new pathway in my brain. *No, I hadn't.*

"*Could* I do that?" I asked, more to myself than to her. "I use such a different technique playing the violin—I wonder if I could teach a student who holds the violin up on their shoulder."

"I'm sure you could figure it out!" she said enthusiastically. "You'd be a good teacher."

Though she didn't know it, Leah planted a seed that evening that would grow into a rewarding teaching career. Several months later, I started giving my first lessons out of my home to a few acquaintances. I worked out the kinks when it came to explaining how to hold the instrument and the bow—pictures, diagrams, and videos were extremely useful in this regard. Aside from that, the differences in technique were pretty easy to navigate. After all, playing an instrument really comes down to creating beautiful sounds, practicing, and learning new tunes.

Early on, I decided I would only teach traditional fiddle music—I didn't feel equipped to tackle classical violin, as I hadn't played classically in years. I also decided to take only beginners and intermediate students. Advanced students would need a higher level of subtlety than I could offer in terms of bowing technique, since I played my instrument more like a cello than a violin. I certainly didn't want to be responsible for someone's botched audition to Juilliard!

Once I felt more confident in my ability to teach, I started advertising my lessons. I loved both the freedom and the challenge of self-employment. I relished setting my own hours, and I enjoyed figuring out how to attract new students. Most of all, I loved being able to make music every day of the week. I taught lessons each weekday, in the afternoons and early evenings. Then several nights a week and most weekends, I performed shows at local venues.

After a few months, I moved my lessons to a bright, sunny office suite that was part of a hip new coworking space. The room had white walls accented with thick timber beams. The offices boasted big windows that overlooked the harbor of Lake Superior. I could never have afforded such a beautiful place on my own, but luckily a seasoned life coach, who liked to see her clients in the morning, was looking to split the rent with a part-time entrepreneur. The later office hours and the location were both perfect for me, so I eagerly signed the lease. Within the year, I was teaching fifteen to twenty students every week in this idyllic setting. My fiddle students ranged in age from six to sixty-five—I loved the variety in their energy levels, skill sets, and personalities.

My teaching philosophy had two main tenets:

(1) Don't make practicing a power struggle or a barrier to entry.

When I was younger, my parents never forced me to practice outside of school, so, for the first three years, I didn't really practice. Playing violin was just something I did for fun with my friends. When music started becoming more central to my identity and I started connecting with the songs I was playing, my desire to practice blossomed all on its own.

I've heard far too many stories about music lessons becoming a battle of wills between parents and child—to the extent that the moment the kid is allowed to quit taking lessons, their instrument goes into a closet, never to reemerge. Some things maybe *are* worth fighting over, such as math homework or cleaning a messy bedroom, but music is a sacred expression of play and creativity. It's far too precious to risk destroying a child's lifelong love of music over the idea that they must practice a certain amount each day.

This isn't to say that I didn't encourage practicing. For my younger students, I would offer a sticker if they came to their lesson with a note signed by their parents saying they'd played their designated material nine times throughout the week. It was a pretty low bar, but it did the trick. Never once did I dispense a coveted sticker for less, no matter how compelling the reason (and there were many impassioned pleas for unearned stickers).

The adult students weren't motivated by stickers, but they had their own hang-ups around practicing—namely, guilt. They would set some imaginary bar for themselves, and if they got too busy to practice they'd contemplate stopping their lessons right away. I always tried to talk them out of quitting. Even if they never touched their violin outside of our weekly lessons, which was unlikely, they were still playing the violin nearly fifty times per year. And while they weren't learning as fast as they would have with added practice, they were still gaining skills and familiarity with their instrument. Any music is better than no music! Here, too, I'd seen the aftermath: Once a student stops playing, it's harder to pick it up again.

(2) *Never suggest anyone quit, no matter how badly they play.*

It is absolutely *not* the instructor's job to foretell someone else's musical future. I'm exceedingly grateful that my first orchestra teacher, Mrs. Sommerfeld, didn't turn me away because she couldn't imagine me succeeding at the violin. I squeaked along with everyone else those first few years. The violin is an unforgiving musical partner at the beginning, sounding more like an out-of-tune cat howl than an instrument. Over time, students will either get better at it, or they'll decide they hate it all on their own. I don't need to weigh in.

I had one student—a woman in her mid-fifties—whose playing was so painful to hear that I had to try and hide my wincing. When we started lessons together, she held her bow like a baseball bat and played it like a hacksaw. Every time she played a tune, she'd swear a lot, and then laugh heartily. If anyone seemed like a lost cause, it was her. But again, it wasn't my place to dissuade her from her instrument of choice, and she was clearly enjoying herself. I just kept encouraging her to hold her bow more delicately. A few months in, she finally started making progress, and listening to her play no longer made me want to crawl out of my skin. But even if she had never improved, I would have continued with our lessons. Music is good for you no matter what—it has intrinsic value far beyond performance.

This fact was brought to life with startling clarity through one of my adult students, a woman in her mid-sixties. She had gray hair and a friendly, round face and had recently retired from a busy career in nursing. She had built herself a tiny house out in the country using a one-car garage as the bones. It didn't have running water or an indoor bathroom, but she loved the quiet and simplicity her little sanctuary provided.

As a student, she was every music teacher's dream. She practiced almost every day, simply because she loved to play. She was enamored with Scandinavian fiddle music in particular. She was always bringing in new Swedish and Norwegian fiddle tunes for us to try out. She even built her own fiddle using a kit with the help of an experienced violin maker. I always enjoyed hearing her interesting life updates during our weekly sessions.

One day before her lesson began, I asked how her night had gone. She answered me honestly. "I was actually having a pretty crummy day, so when I got back to the house, I poured myself a glass of red wine and played my violin outside on the back deck. I played for a couple of hours, and I felt a lot better afterward."

Her answer was a clarion reminder that has stuck with me ever since. Of course I knew from experience that playing violin could boost my mood, but by this point, it had become my job. My music always had a purpose: I taught lessons, I had band practice, I played shows. But when was the last time I had taken out my violin for the sheer joy of it? I honestly couldn't remember.

If teaching taught *me* anything, it was that music is so much more than most professionals give it credit for. It's bigger than proper technique, it's bigger than giving good concerts, and it's certainly bigger than hefty album sales or name recognition. Music is a fundamental tool for human expression. It connects us to our emotions and to beauty itself. Music is for everyone, not just the virtuosos or the PhDs or the music critics. Music has been part of humanity's existence since before the written word, and it will continue to sustain us long after sites like Spotify go offline. When I get bogged down by the typical frustrations of a working artist, or if my mind slips into comparison mode, I remind myself that the true value of music isn't tied to capitalism or financial success. Music is a pure, even holy, activity to be pursued with reverence. I hope this is something I always remember.

23

Debut in DC

IT WAS LATE February 2016, and life was going along quite swimmingly as a fiddle teacher by day and a gigging musician by night. Then—on that random Wednesday afternoon in between fiddle lessons—I received the life-altering phone call from NPR Music telling me that I'd won the Tiny Desk Contest. The following days and weeks morphed into a surreal dreamscape.

For one thing, the contest's producer and cocreator, Bob Boilen, told me that I had to keep the news a secret for a week so that I wouldn't ruin NPR Music's big announcement—a whole, agonizing week! Thankfully, they let me tell my parents, Paul, Alan, and Leah, but no one else.

I wanted to shout the news from the stage at my show that Friday night. After my set, an older gentleman came up to chat. "How's the music biz treating you?" he asked me.

I wanted to burst and spill the good news, but I simply smiled and replied, "It's going great!" Soon enough, the world would know.

The hours ticked by slowly, each insufferably long minute inching me ever closer to my new, unknown fate. Everyone else around me carried on like it was just a normal week.

This must be how psychics feel all the time, I thought with amusement.

A few days after the phone call, I developed the nagging worry that maybe NPR Music had only selected my video because of my disability, not because of my music. The painful confusion I'd experienced after I was rejected from that elite string ensemble a dozen years earlier came back. I couldn't shake my internal doubts, so I expressed my concern during one of our prep calls. Bob was quick to quell my fears.

"Gaelynn, I am actually glad you brought this up," he said. "I had a feeling you might be thinking this. I just want you to know that our judges took their jobs very seriously. Your *song* is why you won. But in case you still have doubts, you should know that two of our judges didn't even look at their screens while they were listening to the entries. One of these judges told us that when your song came on, they were so drawn in that they had to stop what they were doing to run over to their computer to find out who was playing. It was truly the music that captivated them."

That made me feel better, but it's what came next that really put my mind at ease. "I want you to feel good about everything that happens next week," Bob said. "Now, I can't control the stories other news outlets write about you, but I can control how NPR Music frames the story. So you tell me: How do you want us to talk about your disability? We will do whatever makes you most comfortable." My heart softened; I felt supported in a way I didn't know I'd needed. I was so grateful that Bob had my back.

SUDDENLY, IT WAS the day before the contest announcement. We did a dry run of the interview I would have with the hosts from *All Things Considered*. I was extremely nervous about it all, but I knew I was in good hands.

I felt restless and jumpy that evening. I stayed awake late, endlessly tweaking my website in anticipation of the traffic it would receive the next day. I finally crawled into bed around three in the morning for a few hours of fitful shut-eye.

When I awoke on March 3, 2016, I was absolutely bombarded with voice mails, emails, and social media notifications in response to the initial press release. After the radio interview aired, even more messages started pouring in. Many of the messages were from friends and family, but some of the congratulatory notes came from strangers.

The support from folks in my home state was especially touching. People were just brimming with joy that a musician from Minnesota was being highlighted out of all the entries from around the country. We Minnesotans are, after all, proud of our musical legacy—Bob Dylan, Prince, Soul Asylum, Semisonic, Low—but often we feel a bit like the underdog. I hadn't really stopped to think that I was representing my state in some small way. The whole experience was emotional, humbling, and extremely heartwarming.

The prize for winning the contest was filming an official Tiny Desk Concert at NPR Music's headquarters in DC. The concert would be posted on NPR Music's YouTube channel, as well as on their website. After that, I'd do a four-city tour with NPR Music staff over the next couple of months.

As Paul and I prepared for the trip to DC, Bob asked if I was interested in bringing Alan out with me to play at the end of my set. "Don't feel pressured," he said. "We just didn't realize that the two of you worked together until we had chosen you as the winner and started doing more research into your background. We love Low's music, so it would be a treat for us to hear you two play together. But this is *your* day, so only bring him if that feels good to you."

Truthfully, the thought had already crossed my mind. Alan was such an important musical mentor to me during my first years of looping and songwriting. The Murder of Crows had been a training ground for my musical development, and it only felt right to include him now. So even though I knew these kinds of performances were old hat to Alan, I decided to ask him to join me in DC. My plan was to do the first two songs solo, then bring him out as a surprise guest. He happily agreed.

Arriving at the tiny Duluth airport a few days later, Paul and I made a rather ridiculous sight. We had never flown anywhere together before, so we packed as if we were car camping. In addition to our checked luggage, my wheelchair, and my violin, we carried loose pillows, hats, and even my mini Orange practice amp, just in case. Alan met us at the gate. He was clearly a veteran traveler, bringing just a sleek carry-on bag and his electric guitar.

The day of the performance, Bob gave us a tour of NPR's headquarters, introducing us to various radio personalities. Unfortunately, I could barely concentrate on who I was meeting—I was so nervous about the concert! I had spent the whole week planning it out, including my outfit. After much deliberation, I settled on a black-and-white polka-dot dress made by the grandmother of two of my young fiddle students. I knew they would be tickled to see me wearing her dress in concert, and it fit me perfectly. I completed the look with a string of gray pearls and a thick black, fabric bow clipped onto the left side of my head.

When his tour concluded, Bob brought us to the NPR Music office to do our sound check. There was his desk, exactly the way it looked in all the Tiny Desk Concert videos. The walls were lined with cluttered shelves of one-of-a-kind kitsch—the signature visual aesthetic of the series.

Alan and I ran through the set. I had been told that the whole thing should last around fifteen minutes, or three songs total. I planned to open the set solo with "Someday We'll Linger in the Sun" and then transition to the traditional fiddle tune "Southwind." After that, Alan would join me for the last number, but I was still undecided about which one to sing. I was trying to choose between our jaunty duet "Bird Song" and a more recent, contemplative song

I'd written, "Moment of Bliss." I asked Bob to help me pick the third and final tune, so Alan and I played them both through. To my surprise, Bob said, "They're each so lovely. I think you should do both of them." Four songs it was.

In the greenroom—a spare office with a couch in it—I touched up my makeup and made small talk with Alan and Paul. Mostly I just tried to gather my thoughts. This was the biggest performance of my life, but I couldn't let the pressure get to my head. I said a silent prayer, asking for my music to be used for the higher good, no matter how the performance went. Then Bob came to get us.

For some reason, I hadn't been expecting the room to be packed for the filming session, but it was. I nervously made my way through the crowd of a couple hundred clapping people and got my violin and looping pedal situated in my wheelchair. Bob Boilen made a brief introduction. I took a deep breath, trying to steady my nerves, and then I pulled my bow across the string.

My hands shook only slightly, and with laser focus I counted out the beat in my head. To my immense relief, the loop was captured correctly on "Someday We'll Linger in the Sun." My body relaxed slightly once I started to sing. I allowed myself to peek out at the room for a moment, scanning a sea of faces. But I was on a mission. I had to stay present with the music.

I did a solo version of "Southwind" next. Then Bob brought Alan out to play. We made quite the pair—Alan sitting next to me, dressed in black, holding his baritone guitar. With his tousled hair, grizzled beard, and yellow-tinted glasses, he looked like a Goth Shaggy from *Scooby-Doo*. My vibe was more akin to Minnie Mouse, in attire and comparative size.

But I was so glad for Alan's steady presence. The experience felt full circle—him beside me for my first-ever performance of an original song, and then joining me on the national stage five years later. The energy in the room was palpable. In the middle of "Moment of Bliss," I realized that most of the audience was crying. I almost started crying myself toward the end of the song—my heart was so full—but I remained centered enough to finish the piece.

Afterward Alan hugged me, Paul gave me a quick kiss—despite the many onlookers—and a few people from the audience came over to say hello. We continued chatting over prosecco during the reception that NPR hosted out on their terrace. I was relieved and bursting with energy. I knew that this concert was the beginning of a new chapter in life.

24

Tiny Desk, Big World

FOR SOMEONE WHO had only played locally, an all-expenses paid, four-city tour felt pretty extravagant. NPR Music arranged our travel and lodging. We didn't even have to worry about food since they catered everything. The first stop was New York, and I could hardly wait. I had long dreamed of performing in this city of nearly mythical proportions.

Paul and I arrived a couple of days early and had the afternoon before the big event to ourselves. It was late April, and the weather happened to be gorgeous. We meandered through the streets to Chinatown delighted by the unfamiliar sights, sounds, smells—not to mention the sheer density of human life—teeming from every building. We stopped for an espresso in Little Italy and longingly read the menus posted on the doorways of the upscale restaurants we couldn't afford. We marveled at the trap doors in the sidewalks and the garbage bags heaped on the side of the road. "No wonder New York City has a rat problem!" we joked to each other, shaking our heads in disbelief.

We spent the whole day outside, traveling as far as our boots—and batteries—would carry us. We were so caught up in our urban reverie that I failed to notice how low my battery was running. My wheelchair came to a halt in a truly inconvenient location: the middle of the Brooklyn Bridge!

Paul had to disengage the motor on my chair and muscle it for what felt like miles across the second half of the bridge. It can roll, but still, two hundred sixty pounds in neutral is a beast. Paul was able to make it with just a few breaks to catch his breath. We stopped at the nearest café to (quite literally) rest and recharge.

FOR MY NEW York City debut that night, I would perform on the show *Ask Me Another,* hosted by Ophira Eisenberg. The show was taped in front of a live audience of about three hundred people before being beamed out via NPR radio. I nervously awaited my cue backstage, watching through a slit in the curtains.

Ophira started off with a couple of silly game-show antics with the audience. After that, she interviewed Bob Boilen. Finally, it was my cue to head up the ramp to the stage, where I would be positioned right next to Bob.

I didn't anticipate how nervous I would become with hundreds of audience members, thousands of radio listeners, and the intent gaze of the unparalleled music aficionado Bob Boilen all focused on me. But as I started my first song, "Watch the World Unfold," sheer panic began to rise.

The physical sensations were alarming: I broke into a sudden, cold sweat, and my bow arm started shaking uncontrollably. My heart rate must have been about a billion beats per minute—I'd never felt so nervous onstage before. The pressure was getting to me, but I had no choice but to start.

To my horror, the first words were croaked out rather than sung:

Pushin' up, pushin' up,
Through the dirt just like a seed

I hadn't taken a deep enough breath, so my oxygen—and sound—was quickly running out.

I couldn't finish the line without gasping for air midsentence.

But you're never quite a flower
You feel more just like a (gasp) *weed.*

I can't believe this is happening, I thought, terrified. I felt like bursting into tears.

My internal dialogue ramped up: *Bob Boilen is going to think I'm a fraud. I didn't deserve to win.*

I contemplated starting over, but I worried I'd be giving too much away. I remembered how in high school my private teacher had made me start the piece from the beginning every time I winced during my lessons. "Don't ever tell the audience when you make a mistake," he always said. "It takes them out of the moment."

I decided to keep playing, but I had to get it together, before my body spiraled out of control. I forced my mind into submission: *Just focus on the next line. OK, now the next.*

Slowly but surely, my breathing steadied and my pulse slowed. By the final chorus, I had mostly recovered my nerves. My next song, "Someday We'll Linger in the Sun," went better, and I finally began to relax onstage. I even managed to enjoy myself during Ophira's interview.

Nonetheless, I felt like I'd missed my opportunity somehow. Usually, I'd assure myself that the audience didn't notice—and generally, that's true. But I had seen it in Bob's eyes. He knew, and that was the hardest part of all.

AFTER THE SHOW, Bob, Paul, and I went out for a drink at a nearby bar, along with a few friends who had surprised me by coming to the show. At one point, Bob and I were chatting amicably, out of earshot from the others. To my chagrin, he brought up my earlier flub onstage.

The mortification returned.

"So you noticed?" I asked.

He confirmed with a serious nod.

"I thought so!" I felt the desperate urge to defend myself, but instead I admitted the truth. "I was so embarrassed. I almost started crying onstage."

"I could tell," Bob said gently. "Don't feel bad. It happens. But I am just wondering: Why didn't you just start over?" he asked.

I told him about my teacher's philosophy—how showing that you messed up makes the audience feel uneasy.

"I'd have to disagree," he pushed back, unexpectedly. "I think starting over when you make a mistake reminds the audience that you're human. It can even endear you to them, if you keep a sense of humor about it." I'd never considered that angle before.

"In fact," he continued, "I'd go so far as to say that mistakes can make the night more memorable to the audience. You don't remember the shows that go perfectly as much as the one time the singer forgot the words to a song and his drummer reminded him. As long as the energy is positive onstage, it's no big deal."

He had a point. "Besides," he said, "I think most people really *didn't* catch your mishap tonight. I have an annoyingly developed eagle eye when it comes to noticing mistakes. That's just a byproduct of going to five hundred live concerts a year."

That was more than I'd even imagined.

"How do you even *enjoy* going to shows if you catch every mistake?"

"I'm not really interested in focusing on the negative," Bob responded. "That's why I've made the decision not to write about music that I think is 'bad.' Sure, I won't lie about my opinion if asked, but I'd rather spend my energy introducing people to the good stuff, the albums that speak to me. There's enough negativity out there already. I don't need to add to it."

That brief conversation with Bob was a balm to my soul—and my wounded ego. It was an honor to get a glimpse into the psyche of such an influential music journalist. I got the sense that Bob Boilen, with his benevolent ethos, was a most precious rarity in the industry.

ON THE FLIGHT home from New York, I was energized—restless, even—by this novel experience of touring. I was seeing the world through a different pair of eyes. I'd never thought I'd be able to travel extensively, but suddenly there was a new path before me, leading a life of travel and adventure! I let myself get lost in the exhilarating thought of touring full-time. I knew there would be a lot to learn, but for some reason I wasn't scared. The prospect of traveling to new cities, performing my music each night, and connecting with people—no matter how briefly—at my shows was hard to resist. I'd been bit by the tour bug, and I definitely wanted more.

But then my spirits fell. I knew I couldn't tour alone. And even if I could finagle a traveling PCA, I really didn't want to be away from Paul for weeks at a time. A few of the touring musicians I knew had seen their marriages seriously rocked, to the point of separation, at least in part because of their extended absences. I would rather stay in Duluth as a fiddle instructor than risk growing apart from the man I loved.

There was only one possible solution: Paul would have to tour with me.

But not under duress. I vowed to myself that I wouldn't pursue touring unless Paul truly wanted to do it with me. And I wouldn't try to pressure or cajole him into buying into my musical fantasy. That wasn't fair to him.

I stared out the window at the clouds below the plane and the bright blue sky overhead. For several minutes I pondered Paul's potential reaction to the idea of touring. *If he says no,* I told myself, *then I will let it go.* After all, I already had a great life as it is. I could accept his answer either way.

Finally, I worked up enough courage to broach the subject. I turned to him. "So, what did you think of that?" I asked timidly.

"The trip?" Paul asked, "It was fun!"

My heart lifted hopefully.

"Do you ever think you'd wanna do this again?" I asked.

"Well we are, aren't we?" he replied, ever logical. "We still have that event in Chicago, and those two shows on the West Coast."

"Yes, I know," I replied. "But I mean, like...do you think you'd ever want to do this full-time?" I ventured, perhaps a bit unsubtly.

Paul suddenly fell silent. He stared at the back of the seat ahead of him, his expression unreadable. I recoiled internally. I'd blown it!

But he was just processing. "I'm not sure," he replied slowly. "It depends on if we could actually make a living or not. I wouldn't go into debt for it, if that's what you mean."

"No, neither would I," I said truthfully. "But you could see yourself doing this for a living if we could make ends meet?" I asked. "Wouldn't you miss your job?"

He paused once and looked out across the aisle thoughtfully.

"I guess I don't really identify with my job in the same way you do," he replied, a calm sincerity in his voice. "I could be happy doing almost anything, as long as the environment didn't suck."

I was flying high, and not just because we were on a plane. I tried to reintroduce reason.

"OK," I probed further, "but what about being gone a lot? Wouldn't you miss being home?" It seemed wise to consider every angle.

"I don't know, it's sort of the same idea," Paul said. "Home is just wherever you are. I don't feel like I need a house to be happy."

At this point, my elated brain had left the stratosphere. Trying to conceal my jubilation, I asked, "So you're saying you'd be willing to consider touring full-time, if we can make the math work?"

To my total delight, he said yes.

25

Hitting the (Bumpy) Road

SO THIS IS WHAT *Alan meant when he said touring is a grind*, I thought, nearly laughing out loud at the harsh, but humorous, realization. At that very moment, I was applying my makeup using a compact mirror and simultaneously munching on a piece of beef jerky for dinner before my set. I was tired and hungry from a long day of driving, but it didn't matter. I had to be onstage in twenty minutes.

The greenroom at this particular venue was inaccessible—up a flight of stairs—so I'd taken over the wheelchair-accessible stall in the ladies' restroom to get ready for the show. It was awkward to be shoved into such a tiny, barely private space with Paul (he had nothing to do other than stand there stoically), but I needed the semblance of a quiet area to prepare to perform.

It was a random weeknight in mid-October 2016. It had only been seven months since winning the Tiny Desk Contest, but already my life was unrecognizable from what it had been before.

SOON AFTER PAUL and I had decided to tour, I found a booking agent. I instructed him to schedule me full-time starting in the fall. United in vision and purpose, Paul and I began to prepare for our new lives as itinerant artists. First, we put our house on the market. Then we liquidated our savings account—a whole five thousand dollars—to buy a used, wheelchair-accessible Ford Econoline.

After that, I rehomed my fiddle students with different teachers, since I knew I couldn't juggle two distinct careers. To our amazement, Paul's supervisors allowed him to take an unpaid six-month leave of absence from his custodial job at the university. This meant we had a safety net: If we hated touring, we'd simply resume our familiar lives of teaching and cleaning.

Luckily, we had a few very supportive and experienced people guiding us through the process. In particular, Martin Atkins mentored me. He and I had first met at the Tiny Desk event in Chicago, during my four-city tour with NPR Music back in April.

Martin Atkins is a British ex-pat drummer in his mid-sixties who is best known for founding the industrial rock supergroup Pigface in the '90s. He wears thick, black-framed glasses, and his wild white hair stands on end like Doc Brown in *Back to the Future*. He drops expletives with unmatched gusto, and he's always sharing hilarious stories from the wild touring days of his youth.

When Martin heard that Paul and I were planning to tour, he gave me a copy of his first book, aptly named *Tour:Smart,* and I quickly devoured all six hundred pages. It covered everything I knew nothing about—from planning tour routes to advertising shows to designing an appealing merch booth.

I kept a running list of questions for Martin as I read, which were mostly about budgeting—we couldn't afford to go broke, no matter how much I wanted to tour. He generously offered to get on a call with me to run the numbers based on my best (and wildly inaccurate) estimates of future ticket sales.

I am not sure Martin realized just how serious we were about touring until that call. I was in the middle of assuring him and myself: If I play fifteen shows a month with at least fifty people in attendance, we'll be able to cover our monthly bills. And that's before factoring merch sales!

"Yes, technically the math works out," Martin interjected. "But there are so many unknowns. Why not try a few shorter tours and see how they go? You can always start small and build up."

"Not really," I snapped, then softened my tone. "It's just that if I want to tour, I need Paul to travel with me."

"I get that," Martin said, "but I still don't see why you'd have to do it full-time right away."

"Paul only gets two weeks' vacation each year. It makes more sense to streamline and do it full-time," I said. "That's why we're selling the house—no mortgage to tie us down!"

"What?!" Martin sputtered. "You're selling your house? Isn't that a little drastic?"

I forgot that I hadn't mentioned that part to him yet.

"Too late now." I laughed nervously. "Someone just put an offer in!"

"That's a bold move," he said, clearly bemused. "When I suggested you try touring, I didn't mean to set fire to your life!"

My call with Martin made me wonder how Alan would take the news. I decided to broach the subject at our next band practice. "Alan, I have something to tell you."

"OK," he said somberly, clearly bracing himself. Before I lost my nerve, I forged ahead, telling him everything we'd been working on.

Alan sat there perfectly still, staring at the wooden floorboards as he listened. When I finished talking, he didn't move.

After an excruciatingly long silence, he finally responded.

"Touring is a grind, man. Are you guys sure about this?" he asked.

"Yes." It was only half a lie. All I knew was that we had to try.

Alan began peppering me with very practical questions to make sure we'd thought things through. He seemed satisfied with my responses and finally relaxed. "I'm sure you guys will be fine," he said. "Just stick together. Now let's jam."

Paul and I handed over our keys on September 26, 2016. Selling the house was bittersweet, but we barely had time to process it. We hit the road for my first tour three days later.

PAUL AND I quickly learned that touring is a career of extremes.

Our first week on the road started with a bang when I performed at a large conference in Chicago. I was overwhelmed by a standing ovation from the two thousand people in the auditorium. Paul sold more CDs after the event than he'd ever sold in his life. People stood in line to talk to me, eagerly asking me to sign their new albums. We took it as a good omen that news of my Tiny Desk Concert had spread far across the land since March.

We shouldn't have.

I didn't realize how *un*glamorous entry-level touring for the average folk musician could be. No one from NPR Music ever sat me down and said, "What you are about to experience on this mini tour with us is not reality for most indie musicians, so do not begin to imagine that this is your new life." Instead, they said, "Congratulations! Here's a glass of prosecco."

Two days after the conference in Chicago, Paul and I set out on an ill-fated adventure that sent me crashing down from the mountaintop. My booking agent had scheduled me for a twelve-city double-bill tour with Jess Klein, an established Americana singer from North Carolina. Each night, we played our own sets and split the ticket sales. Jess was a touring veteran, and my agent hoped that her fan base, paired with my Tiny Desk buzz, would make for a winning combination.

But to my shame and horror, I wasn't much help when it came to packing the house. In truth, I was a brand-new artist whose only fans, so far, were from Duluth or the internet. Yes, the Tiny Desk was a huge boon, but it hadn't made me into an overnight celebrity.

I should have realized just how doomed we were after that first night in Pittsburgh. Fewer than fifteen people came to our show. All of them were eating and drinking, and several were talking quite loudly at the bar. This was not how I envisioned My First Big Musical Tour.

Jess came up from the inaccessible greenroom in the basement to listen to the end of my set and asked me to sit in on two of her songs. Thankfully, the joy of making music with another human blotted out the disappointment I'd felt earlier about our low turnout. We had so much fun singing together that I ended up sitting in with her in every city on the tour.

But the harsh reality of show business kicked in when it was time to settle up. Our contract stated that Jess and I would get 60 percent of ticket sales, after expenses, which included one hundred fifty dollars for the sound guy, a college kid who had enjoyed an easy night of exclusively solo artists. Then we gave the local opener his fifty-dollar agreed-upon fee. Jess and I split the remainder, which amounted to a whopping twelve dollars each.

Never once, in all our planning for this tour, had I envisioned such a ludicrously low payout. It was embarrassing, of course—yet I couldn't help but laugh. I called my dad from the parking lot, giggling as I regaled him with our sorry tale. He chuckled too, then asked, with an audible gleam in his eye, "Why did you drive all the way to Pittsburgh to earn twelve dollars?"

TOGETHER JESS, PAUL, and I trekked through a haphazard lineup of small clubs, dingy bars, and stuffy cafes to entertain audiences of varying sizes, enthusiasm levels, and attention spans. There was no logic to our route, geographically speaking, so the tour involved lots of long drives and quite a bit of backtracking.

The shows were poorly attended overall, and only one of the stages turned out to be accessible. This was especially disconcerting, because I'd written the words GAELYNN USES AN ELECTRIC WHEELCHAIR AND NEEDS A RAMP TO THE STAGE in bright red letters at the top of my stage plot. Theoretically, every venue manager had received this document, but apparently no one looked at my stage plot or cared enough to actually procure a ramp.

Lucky for us, just before we set out, Paul had decided to throw a set of sturdy wooden boards into our already overfilled van, just in case we ever needed a makeshift wheelchair ramp. Unfortunately, nearly every night Paul ended up lugging these unwieldy planks from the parking lot into the venue so that I could get onstage. He didn't complain, but I felt bad about it.

Although the lack of access at the venues was frustrating, I loved performing every night—it gave me an iridescent energy that I couldn't find elsewhere.

Jess was a wonderful role model for me. No matter her mood or the quality of the venue's sound system, she always sang with grace and dignity. I studied her performances like a diligent student—her backstage warm-up routine, the entertaining banter between songs, and how she connected with the audience so authentically. She was the consummate professional.

Playing full-length sets so many days in a row definitely tested my endurance as an artist. But it also provided a chance to hone my skills. As the tour stretched into the second week, I could tell that my playing was getting stronger and my vocal control more refined. I had grown much more comfortable onstage since my flub in New York City six months earlier.

Jess and I always chatted with audience members at the merch table after every show, and it was here where I witnessed many heartwarming interactions between Jess and her longtime fans. She embraced them as she would old friends. It reminded me of how Alan always referred to "his friend in LA" or "his buddies in

Holland"—could it be that, if you kept returning to the same cities, eventually your fans could become your actual friends?

Paul and I really enjoyed traveling cross-country together. It wasn't the lifestyle we had imagined for ourselves, but it suited us. Every day was a new adventure. We marveled at the vistas as we drove through places like upstate New York—hills upon hills, trees upon trees, adorned in fall colors. We talked and laughed and planned over dinners and drinks at the end of the night.

On our rare days off, we slept in and rambled through the streets of new-to-us cities. We both agreed that we preferred this hectic yet deeply creative existence to our day jobs. We knew we had a steep learning curve ahead of us, but we were both energized by the idea of cracking the touring code. As we drove into Duluth after those two weeks with Jess, we were already chomping at the bit for our next departure date.

Interestingly, a couple of days after we got home, Jess posted something on Facebook that made me pause. She wrote:

> *I've always known that touring was exhausting (long drives, irregular schedule, and the sometimes very low pay), but I never noticed just how inaccessible most venues were until I toured with the formidable Gaelynn Lea and her wonderful husband, Paul. It was eye-opening and extremely discouraging to witness how hard they had to work just so she could make it onto the stage. I take accessibility for granted, but Gaelynn doesn't have that luxury. She didn't complain—she played beautifully each night. But it's not right, and something has to change.*

I was secretly grateful to see her post, despite its painful sting. Indeed, things *were* harder than they needed to be! My booking agent had known all along about my disability and my need for ramps, yet clearly there had been a disconnect somewhere—in the end, only one venue on the entire tour had provided a ramp to the stage. I'd tried to take it all in stride, smothering my frustration with positive thinking, simply because touring was still so new and exciting.

But if I was being honest with myself, I *had* felt frustrated about the lack of accessibility. Why weren't venues doing more to become wheelchair accessible? Sure, someone could lift me onstage, because I happened to weigh only seventy-five pounds. But that wasn't a safe (or dignified) solution, and it certainly wouldn't work for every disabled artist. Reading her words gave a voice to the internal discord I'd felt on tour. The lack of access was obvious, even to Jess, and it was wrong.

26

The Tap Tap

IN THE FALL of 2016, I received a request to perform as a guest with a Czech band called The Tap Tap, a pop-rock ensemble composed of disabled and nondisabled performers. Every year, they host a Saint Nicholas Day musical extravaganza in Prague that is televised across the entire Czech Republic. They wanted to feature two of my songs, backed by their band.

They offered to cover airfare for me and Paul, as well as hotels. Tempting as it sounded, I was hesitant to say yes. I had never traveled overseas before, and as a wheelchair user I had a lot of reservations about visiting Europe and its centuries-old architecture.

Years earlier, my high school French teacher had convinced me that I wouldn't be able to keep up on the senior trip to Paris. She told me horror stories: *I'd have to carry a giant converter box for my electric wheelchair! Practically every building would have steps! Transportation would be a total nightmare!* I'd basically already written off The Tap Tap's invitation as impossible.

Still, I mentioned the potential gig to Alan during our next band practice. To my surprise, he encouraged me to do it. "Lots of people use wheelchairs over there," he said. "This band could help you figure things out. You've never been to Europe, right?"

"No, I haven't," I responded wistfully. "But it doesn't actually pay anything. We'll have to cover our food and stuff."

"True," he replied. "You can't do free gigs all the time, but this will be worth it. Prague is really beautiful. You should say yes."

"Really?" I asked, daring to let myself envision this exotic tour.

"Yes. You said early December, right?" he asked, a sparkle in his eye. "Low is doing a Christmas tour in Ireland that month. You could fly over afterward to open for us on a few of the shows. It might make the trip more worth the effort to add in extra gigs."

I was in a state of disbelief. Opening for Low was *huge*. Of course, the band was much loved domestically, but their music was even more popular overseas.

I could hardly wait to email The Tap Tap my answer: yes.

EVEN IF MY concerns were unfounded, I was extremely nervous to fly overseas with my heavy electric wheelchair, so I decided to travel with a folding, manual wheelchair instead. This decision brought with it other logistical problems. My arms simply aren't strong enough to propel a manual wheelchair, so someone would have to push me around during the entire trip. And since Paul couldn't push my chair, carry our luggage, and haul around my violin all at the same time, we would need a third travel companion.

We recruited Leah to join us—after all, I owed her for filming my winning Tiny Desk Contest submission video. The Tap Tap couldn't cover the expenses of an additional person, and Low's budget for openers was a hotel room and just enough to cover meals, but not much else.

I made a budget for all three of us that included meals, trains, extra hotel nights, and airfare—all in all we needed about eight thousand dollars to break even. It was clear that we would incur some debt doing this tour if we didn't get creative. I decided to launch a GoFundMe campaign, promising to mail signed copies of my holiday album to everyone who donated.

The support was heartwarming. We raised all the money we

needed for the trip, and the enthusiastic well-wishes for my first tour abroad only added to our excitement. Passports were acquired, work permits were issued, and bags were packed.

Our departure date arrived. The three of us inexperienced travelers soon found ourselves in an aeroplane over the sea, heading for an unforgettable adventure.

THE FIRST THING I remember about that tour is the jet lag. It was midmorning in Prague when we landed, and by the time we got to our hotel I was really starting to crash. I had not slept much during the flight, and at this point it was five o'clock in the morning to my American brain. To cope with the crushing fatigue, I committed the cardinal sin of international travel and laid down as soon as we checked into the hotel. Forty-five minutes later my alarm roused me from a deep slumber. It was time for band practice.

The Tap Tap had arranged a good-natured guide for us, who walked us to the rehearsal space a few blocks away, located inside a school for students with disabilities. I was surprised to learn that a large percentage of disabled kids in the Czech Republic were still being siloed, at least in part because many of the school buildings were inaccessible. The Tap Tap had permission to hold afternoon rehearsals in this wheelchair-friendly building once the students had left for the day.

I was introduced to the band, a group of about thirty musicians. A sizable number of the band members used electric wheelchairs, similar to the one I'd left at home, if not a bit chunkier. The rest of the group was a mix of less visibly disabled and nondisabled musicians. Instruments included electric guitar, keyboard, and horns, but the majority was percussion.

Everyone shared tentative greetings and shy smiles. It was clear that the language barrier was going to be a big hurdle, since the rehearsal would be conducted mostly in Czech.

I didn't have time to dwell on any awkwardness, though, because Simon, the conductor, jumped straight into the music. He had a very intense, commanding energy—his electric blue eyes were always studying his surroundings, planning his next move. He clearly wasn't interested in wasting time on idle chatter, and he ran the rehearsal as if we were an army marching band.

By this point, my head was swimming because of the jet lag.

"Now for 'Bird Song,'" Simon said, motioning for me to get my violin ready. He counted off in Czech: "Jeden, dva, tři, čtyři," then—nothing.

I was supposed to start the song with my violin, but I'd missed my entrance. Simon's head jerked up in surprise. He shot an annoyed glare at me, his admonishment for my lapse in attention.

Waving away my apology, he raised his arms to restart the song: "Jeden, dva, tři, čtyři." I made my entrance this time around, and we were off.

AFTER THE MIDAFTERNOON rehearsal, we finally got a chance to explore our surroundings. A combination of giddy excitement, disorientation, and bone-weary exhaustion left us all feeling a bit high. Prague was an absolutely gorgeous city. It felt like we'd traveled to another dimension, where past and present coexist. The Gothic architecture loomed above us and gentle hills, speckled with houses, rolled out past the city.

Yet its modern inhabitants were gobsmackingly nonchalant, running about their daily errands amidst the splendor of such ornate buildings. We wandered down cobblestone streets as our guide taught us how to say important Czech phrases like *good day, thank you,* and *another beer, please.*

We saw a veritable castle for the first time, named Vyšehrad, and we walked across the statue-lined Charles Bridge, one of the oldest in the country. Paul, Leah, and I oohed and aahed over the architectural wonders surrounding us. "How old is *that* one?" I'd ask excitedly, pointing at practically every building in sight. Our guide humored me by hazarding a guess, give or take a century. Eventually he started to chuckle. "My wife is French," he told us, "and she likes to say, 'You can always pick out the Americans, because they can't stop asking how old everything is!'"

We all laughed self-deprecatingly at the truth of this observation.

"Don't worry," he said. "I did it too when I first got here. Everyone does, until it becomes home."

THE SECOND NIGHT Simon asked us if we'd like to join him and a handful of band members for a few drinks after rehearsal. We happily agreed. An hour later, a small battalion of wheelchair users took over the bar in our hotel lobby. Simon was much more relaxed outside of rehearsal. Jokes I couldn't understand brought peals of laughter that were instantly relatable.

Though our communication was limited by the language barrier, I gathered that The Tap Tap used music to draw attention to issues affecting the disability community. For example, at one point the city of Prague built a subway station and failed to make it wheelchair accessible. When it became clear that the city was ignoring calls from the disability community to fix it, The Tap Tap hosted a protest concert right at the site of the offending subway stop. This stunt certainly got the city's attention, and to the band's delight, the station was renovated soon after.

The United States was clearly on the right track when it passed the ADA in 1990. There are inconsistencies in enforcing the law, but without it, accessibility is more or less optional. Every place is up for debate, including each new subway station. The lift for disability rights advocates in that environment is enormous, and progress is exceedingly slow.

THE NEXT DAY it was finally showtime. We arrived at the concert hall at noon and waited around in the labyrinth of hallways and dressing rooms backstage. During sound check, I realized just how elaborate this production was going to be. There were laser lights, fog machines, and even a Jumbotron at the back of the stage—its huge screen displayed a close-up of my face while I sang, the band arranged in an arc behind me.

The show went off without a hitch, in part because of the delightful energy emanating from the audience. Since this was an annual production, you could tell they knew what to expect; the show had become an all-ages holiday tradition.

There were a number of onstage cameos scheduled throughout the concert, including a host of winged angels, a red-and-white-garbed Kris Kringle, and a terrifying-looking horned Krampus covered in mangy fur from head to toe. The mayor of Prague even made an appearance to encourage the TV audience to donate to the city's school for disabled children.

My songs were the only part of the show that hadn't been performed in previous years. I started with a solo version of "Someday We'll Linger in the Sun." Then the full band joined me on a group arrangement of my song "I See It Too." The last song of the night was a duet of my own "Bird Song" with the band's lead male vocalist, backed by the band. Simon had arranged the piece himself, with all those drums giving it a distinctly Eastern European flair. The audience of a thousand people gave us a standing ovation.

After the show, the band and I mingled with audience members backstage, still abuzz with adrenaline from the performance. To commemorate the show, Simon asked for a picture with me. We faced each other with broad smiles and sparkling eyes and put both our thumbs up—a cross-Atlantic sign of approval. "Thank you for doing this," he said. "You are a true professional."

Then, as if his inner general simply couldn't resist, he saluted me briskly and winked.

27

Fiddling in the Isles

WHEN MY BOOKING agent found out I was going overseas with Low and The Tap Tap, he offered to line up another show in London too. Wanting to make the most of my time abroad, I agreed.

We flew from Prague to London and took a cab to the show. The venue reminded me of my English-themed bar in Duluth. It had the cozy charm of a pub that was well-loved by its regulars.

A large, inviting wooden bar in the middle of the room took up most of the floorspace, and small tables lined the walls. The stage was a simple elevated platform made of plywood and painted black. There was no ramp, so Paul and Leah lifted me onto the stage.

The venue provided hapless traveling musicians like me with old sound equipment and microphone stands that would have collapsed in a light breeze. But since I was used to playing dive bars, we were able to get my violin sounding all right despite plugging it into a beastly bass amp.

The pub owners were an aging but ever-lively couple who resided above the bar in a small apartment. The wife was a sturdy British woman with a cheerful, round face. Her husband was older—a large Irish man with wiry gray hair.

The set went well, and the concertgoers were enjoying themselves.

I have always loved tweaking the setlist depending on my mood and the energy in the room—like making the perfect mixtape. I carefully arrange the tunes to take the audience on an emotional journey, one that hits all the different tones in the sonic rainbow.

Choosing the last few songs correctly is especially important, because those are the ones people will remember. Since we were heading to Ireland the next day, I decided to end my set with a rendition of "The Parting Glass."

This is a beloved traditional tune that is often sung at bar close, the end of family gatherings, and sometimes even at funerals. But as soon as I started playing, the cynical voice of impostor syndrome whispered in my ear: *You're gonna play Celtic music for actual Irish people? Ha!*

In truth, I was worried about whether this was a good idea. The fiddle tunes I knew were mostly well-worn classics. Would the audience just dismiss me as another American hack job? For my part, I simply wanted to convey the love and reverence I feel for Celtic fiddle music.

What fascinates me most about these tunes are the melodies. They are so memorable and hauntingly beautiful, which is why they've managed to endure—passed down, primarily by ear, from one generation to the next. And so many harmonies can complement fiddle tunes. Celtic music overflows with possibilities when it comes to the looping pedal. You can layer harmonies, countermelodies, and sometimes other fiddle tunes to create a symphony of sound.

I hoped this love of traditional Celtic tunes would be evident to the audiences on this tour, and that my looping would be welcomed as a twist on much-beloved classics—recognizable but sonically fresh. At least that's what I wanted to convey to them. I reminded myself that I couldn't control how my music was received, and that ultimately it didn't really matter. I began to play.

My version of "The Parting Glass" opened with a winding,

abstract loop, in a much slower tempo than is usual for this tune. I started to sing:

> *Of all the money that ere I had*
> *I spent it in good company*

The room grew quiet. I took my time drawing out this haunting, age-old melody, floating the lyrics over a layer of melancholy, swirling violin loops. Then I got to the last lines:

> *So fill to me the Parting Glass*
> *Goodnight and joy be with you all*

To the audience, it seemed the song was nearing its end—but I still had something up my sleeve. "The Parting Glass" is in a complementary key with another upbeat Irish fiddle tune called "The Star of Munster." Together, these tunes make the perfect, albeit unconventional, medley.

As soon as I sang those last words, I began to hammer out a new rhythm on top of the old loop, setting a faster, more driving tone. I played the tune once, then added a syncopated rhythm on top of my previous loops. Now the vibe was as rocking as you are going to find for traditional fiddle music, save for punk bands who amp up their sound with electric guitars and kick drums.

When I started on the final, most raucous pass of "The Star of Munster," I heard a commotion in the back of the room. A man was shouting. Was it an argument? A medical emergency? I kept playing, scanning the audience, discreetly assessing the situation.

It didn't take me long to find the source of the noise. In the back of the crowd, I saw the gentleman pub owner clapping and lurching along to the beat. He was quite simply lost in his own musical reverie. Every few measures, he'd let out a loud "Whoop!" or a full-force, enthusiastic stomp. I'd almost forgotten he was Irish, and I certainly hadn't anticipated his gleeful reaction to hearing cherished tunes from the Emerald Isle in his London-based pub.

The worry I'd harbored about my upcoming shows in Ireland melted away. I couldn't keep from grinning as I ended the song to uproarious applause. It was the owner's cheers that meant the most.

MY FIRST SHOW in Ireland was in a teeny town in County Clare; the concert was being held in a tiny stone church that looked like it was out of a storybook. Adjacent to the church was a small, well-kept graveyard with centuries-old headstones. Inside it was mostly bare, save for a hundred folding chairs arranged in rows with an aisle down the middle. What's more, it was absolutely freezing.

"Sorry about the temperature," our host said, a little bashful about the sparse environs. "There isn't a furnace in the building, but I've turned on the space heaters. It'll be toasty soon."

"That's OK," I said. "Is there a bathroom I can use to get ready?"

"I'm afraid they didn't build these churches with comfort in mind," he answered. "The nearest bathroom is in the pub across the street."

Only slightly thrown, I turned my attention to sound check. It went quickly, seeing as how it took only one big speaker to fill the space with music. Afterward the three of us ventured across the street to use the bathroom. Like the church, the pub had a few stone steps leading to the entrance. Paul carried me, and Leah hoisted the folding chair up the stairs.

As I'd feared, the bathroom wasn't accessible either. Leah stood guard outside the door of the ladies' room while Paul helped me get ready for the show. Once again I found myself hurrying to apply my makeup in a cramped bathroom stall. I stifled a rising frustration — as fun as it was to be traveling overseas, I was growing more aware of how unfair it was to be dealing with lack of access nearly everywhere I went. Show business was never a straightforward affair for a disabled artist, and it was starting to get old.

I'D NEVER ENCOUNTERED such musical audiences before, until performing in Ireland. Folks all across the room tapped their feet and hummed as I played. The melodies seemed to live inside them, ever at the ready.

"This next one is called 'The Boys of Bluehill,'" I said. "It's a traditional English fiddle tune."

Suddenly I sensed the energy shift. As soon as I uttered those fateful words, a low grumbling began to ripple throughout the audience. Clearly they were displeased with my introduction.

I started to fidget. "Isn't it"—I asked nervously—"an English fiddle tune?"

My stomach dropped. Why would I be so fast and loose with the history of their traditional music? It's not like I was in Minnesota!

"No!" someone called out brusquely. "It's Irish. The tune was written right here in County Clare!"

I froze. Embarrassment and shame knotted themselves in my stomach.

"You think it *sounds* like an English tune?" someone else chimed in, their voice mocking.

A wave of titters bounced around the small room.

Now that I thought about it, the tune *did* sound Irish, through and through. In fact, it was ludicrous for me to assume anything else. I quickly fessed up. "I'm sorry, I was just guessing," I said. "But I can promise you I'll never make *that* mistake again!"

The audience chuckled at my admission. They had clearly forgiven me for my ignorance, and the rest of the set was a joyous affair. Nonetheless, several concerned Irish citizens gathered around me afterward, and I got quite an earful about the origins of "The Boys of Bluehill" that night.

WE FINALLY MET up with Low in Belfast for the first of three shows where I'd be opening.

To my dismay, accessibility was extremely lacking at these venues as well. The stages were all over four feet tall, with nary a ramp in sight. The greenrooms were, as I'd witnessed in the States, typically upstairs or in the basement. Bathrooms were almost always inaccessible. Thankfully, with my lighter manual wheelchair, these barriers were more manageable than they would have been if I had brought my heavy electric wheelchair with me. But it was during this portion of the trip that I started to realize the extent of the inaccessibility of music venues.

It was an issue of global proportions.

Though Martin Atkin's book *Tour:Smart* had mentally prepared me for many aspects of touring, I realized there was no equivalent guide for disabled musicians. It felt as though Paul, Leah, and I were constantly troubleshooting as access issues ambushed us. And it was becoming clear that this wasn't just reality in Duluth or Minnesota or even the United States. No, the *entire world* was full of inaccessible stages.

The next day we took the train to Dublin, and a few hours later the three of us set out from our hotel for my second show with Low, which was at a medieval cathedral called Christ Church. Our moods were merry and bright as we traveled down the bustling sidewalks that chilly evening. It was early December, but already the streetlamps and shop windows were adorned with strings of Christmas lights. We delighted in the countless storefronts and pubs that could have passed for set pieces from the Shire in *Lord of the Rings*.

We must have looked a bit ridiculous as we crossed over the River Liffey on the Ha'penny Bridge. Leah was pushing me in the folding wheelchair I had brought overseas, which had previously been owned by a friend's grandmother (it was ancient and much too big for me). It had no seatbelt, so I was strapped in with a literal man's belt wrapped around the back poles and buckled under my chest. Paul trudged alongside us, loaded down with my violin, merch, and looping pedals.

The concert was sold out, and a hush fell over the large audience as they waited for the music to begin. My opening set went well, in part because the acoustics in that cavernous stone cathedral were amazing. As usual, Low's set was akin to a religious experience. Alan's intense delivery of the lyrics and his sparse, thoughtful guitar parts were the perfect complements to Mim's steady drumming and soaring harmonies. It was inspiring to witness the high level of musical mastery they demonstrated each time I saw them perform.

We closed out the tour in Kilkenny.

That night's venue was a packed club with retro furnishings. Ahead of the show, Mim invited us to hang out with the band in their greenroom, which could only be accessed by a flight of stairs.

It wasn't often that we got to hang out with the cool kids, so Paul carried me up. Neither of us mentioned the staircase. I'd never spent much time with Mim in person, in part because she seemed a little intimidating to me. She had a paradoxically docile and commanding presence onstage, almost otherworldly. In the greenroom, however, she quickly made us feel welcome. To my surprise she was relaxed, frank, and funny. She curled her long brown hair as we chatted about the tour so far. It was reminiscent of hanging around my older sister as she got ready for prom.

To my amazement, and a twinge of jealousy, the venue had provided Low with a huge spread of healthy food—including a blender for making smoothies. They certainly weren't living on pub grub, like us! Of course, they were the headliners at a big venue, so smoothies were a reasonable request. But I couldn't help feeling a bit miffed. *Apparently,* I mused, *if you're a big enough artist, venues actually care about what you put in your rider. I wonder how big you have to get before they'll provide a ramp to the stage?*

Soon enough the house doors opened, and Paul, Leah, and I made our way back downstairs. Paul wheeled me backstage until my set began.

It was already the last night of the tour, which was bittersweet. Despite the lack of access, I had enjoyed all the shows, and I'd absolutely loved visiting other countries. But I was starting to feel restless in the manual wheelchair, and I was eager to return to my own chair back home. I'd definitely gained a new appreciation for the mobility and independence that my electric wheelchair provided me.

I played my six-song opening set to a receptive crowd. As planned, Alan joined me on guitar for "Bird Song," and on a whim, I decided to teach the audience Alan's vocal part. Their voices rang out beautifully, in unison with Alan's. To my complete surprise, though, when we got to the end of the song, the boisterous audience wouldn't stop singing. They kept repeating Alan's lines — some were even adding their own harmonies to the mix.

I was momentarily flummoxed, but soon shrugged it off and joined in the fun. I tried to end the song a second time, but to no avail. I could see smiles on the faces in the crowd as they sang. It was quite clear this feisty group of Irish music lovers intended to continue with Alan's half of the sing-along, even as I mounted a third attempt to end it. Who knows how long they would have kept going without intervention? Alan finally regained control of the room by shooting them a stern glare over the top of his guitar. His glower was met with hearty laughter and applause.

28

The (Nearly) Impossible Staircase

THE NEXT THREE years were all about touring. Paul and I were on the road about nine months out of the year, never home for more than three weeks at a time. We were absent for birthdays, weddings, Fourth of Julys, Halloweens, and Thanksgivings. For the most part it was worth it, though we did miss our families and friends. Since Paul and I always traveled together, we never really felt lonely—just disconnected from our lives back home.

During this span, we drove coast to coast multiple times. Our day-to-day life vaguely resembled that of over-the-road truck drivers. We lived on coffee, corn nuts, granola bars, La Croix, tacos, and beer. We spent hours together each afternoon in the van, urging traffic to keep flowing so that we could make sound check. We passed the time with conversation, channel surfing the radio, and—for two glorious weeks—listening to the *Lord of the Rings* audiobook. I performed about twenty concerts each month. Once the drive times were factored in, we didn't have much room for anything else but food and sleep on show days.

Fortunately, we were great at making the most of our rare days off, exploring our surroundings like schoolchildren on a field trip. We gleefully spotted a dolphin off the Atlantic Coast of Florida. We solemnly paid our respects at Gettysburg National Cemetery. We even enjoyed an oceanside dinner of raw oysters as we marveled at the flaming sunset over Ventura Beach, its hues as rich as a ripe Georgia peach.

The shows themselves were enjoyable, though frustratingly unpredictable in terms of attendance. Since I was booking with small venues, I had to do all my own promotion. As such, I could never tell how well a show was going to do until the evening arrived. Thankfully, my uneven ticket sales typically balanced out enough by the end of every tour, so we always broke even, which at the time felt like enough.

The one constant was the lack of accessibility. A select few venues took my request for access to the stage seriously and built ramps out of plywood before I got there. This warmed my heart to no end and made me start to believe the music industry was changing after all. But the majority of venues didn't do anything whatsoever to remedy a lack of access. Instead, they'd cheerfully suggest that the bartenders lift my chair up onto the stage at the beginning of my set. That was the simplest solution, to them, at least. For me, it compromised both my safety and my dignity.

When I started out, I felt obliged to make do with this unsavory workaround. But the longer I toured, the more I realized that nothing was going to change if I kept letting venues lift my wheelchair instead of building the ramp that was technically a legal requirement on their part.

In a perfect world, the government would help venues pay for accessibility modifications. But the ADA is currently an unfunded mandate, which means that business owners must cover the costs of improving accessibility in their buildings on their own. Unfortunately, the out-of-pocket expense for these much-needed renovations can be high. That cost is always the excuse venues give to justify their inaccessibility.

However, it's now been over thirty-five years since the ADA was signed. Venues that won't or can't invest the money to become accessible are keeping progress jammed up. The clock is ticking; people like me still can't get in the front door or use the bathroom at countless businesses across the nation. I think it's time for our government to finally try something different: Help to fund this important law.

EVERY WEDNESDAY AFTERNOON, I had a check-in call with my booking agent—usually from the van—to discuss what shows were on the horizon. During one such meeting, I received the alarming news that one of the venues he'd recently booked wasn't accessible.

Like, at all. As in, it was in the basement. Without an elevator.

"I understand if you don't want to do the show," he said, with regret in his voice. "But it's one of those places that's a big deal in the folk world. It's an honor to get asked to play there, frankly."

The venue had hosted Joan Baez, Bob Dylan, Nanci Griffith, and Regina Spektor.

I was torn. On one hand, lugging my electric wheelchair up and down a whole flight of stairs would be a lot more difficult, not to mention risky, than lifting it on and off a stage. What if my chair got damaged, or worse, what if Paul slipped while carrying me to the basement? *That* could be deadly.

On the other hand, playing a concert at this storied music venue might create some much-desired buzz. Although the Tiny Desk Concert had brought a big burst of initial press, it had since quieted down significantly. Now I was out on the road in earnest, struggling to sell tickets like any other indie folk artist. The dream of making it seemed as elusive as ever.

Maybe if I headlined this well-known venue, a music journalist would come and write a glowing review! This could lead to even bigger venues, or getting signed to a label. In the end, the allure of success drew me in and snagged me.

I said yes to the gig.

IT TURNED OUT that this decision was not without consequences. From the moment I agreed to play at this wildly inaccessible venue, I was racked with guilt. I began to envision a host of nightmare scenarios. What if a wheelchair user buys a ticket and isn't able to get inside once they show up? What if someone falls because they have difficulty balancing on the stairs?

In those days I still hadn't met many other disabled artists, but I did know one. Kalyn Heffernan is a fantastic rapper from the hip-hop outfit Wheelchair Sports Camp, who has the same disability as me. I had met her during my first month out on the road when she attended my afternoon sound check before my first show in Denver. We clicked instantly. I decided to call her for moral support.

"I feel so bad," I lamented. "I'm not sure I should have agreed to play there, but now it's too late to back out."

"I get it," she said. "Disabled musicians are always between a rock and a hard place. Hopefully your fans will understand."

"What do you mean?"

"Well, I had something similar happen to me at a festival once," Kalyn explained. "It was our first year there as a band and we got an official showcase. Only one problem: It was up a flight of stairs."

"They wouldn't move you?" I asked.

"Nope," she said. "I talked to them about it, and they said it was too late to alter the schedule. So instead, we played a short set in the parking lot before heading up to do the gig. But people were still upset that we agreed to do the show at all. Afterward I got a few angry emails from fans."

"Why were they mad at *you*?" I asked, genuinely perplexed and a tad defensive. "It's the festival's fault—*you* didn't pick the venue, it was assigned! Your fans should be mad at the festival."

"Nah." She gently dismissed my indignation. "Those fans had the right to be mad. If I say that I care about Disability Justice, then it seems pretty hypocritical for my band to play shows at music venues where disabled people can't even get in the literal door."

I knew she wasn't wrong, as painful as it was for me to admit.

WHEN MY SHOW at Club Inaccessible arrived, I was a ball of nerves. A few days earlier, my booking agent had told me that at least one wheelchair-using fan had decided not to purchase tickets because of the lack of an elevator. I wanted to call that guy to apologize. I wondered with dread how many other people had decided not to attend for the same reason.

Regardless, once we got to the space I had to switch into action mode. The first order of business was getting my wheelchair down the steps and onto the stage. Paul and I were talking with the venue staff, trying to troubleshoot a route. Just then, Reid showed up. Reid is the kind of music supporter who always donates to my Kickstarter campaigns and never misses a show in the area.

We'd made plans to have dinner together before the show, but before enjoying our bowls of soup, we roped him into dragging my two-hundred-sixty-pound wheelchair down that whole flight of stairs. I felt absolutely awful watching four people struggle to carry it. I wondered why society still deemed it acceptable for disabled musicians to be reliant on others to get on and off the stage. You would never see four dudes lugging Paul McCartney or Beyoncé or anyone else onstage. To make matters worse, after dinner Paul quietly whispered to me that a disabled woman had navigated the stairs on crutches.

"Did she make it in OK?" I asked, horrified.

"Yeah, it seemed like it," he said, "I mean those stairs are *steep*."

"Oh my gosh, this sucks so bad. Does she seem mad about it?"

"No," he mused. "She commented about the stairs, but she didn't seem angry or anything."

Selfishly, I was relieved to hear that she hadn't been visibly fuming, but I still felt hypocritical.

The show went fine after that, but it didn't lead to my pipe dream of good press and overflowing audiences. Besides, I couldn't stop thinking about the man who wasn't able to attend, or the lady with crutches who could have easily fallen down the stairs on her way into the venue.

How had this happened in the first place? My booking agent had clearly dropped the ball—access should have been one of the *first* topics that he discussed with potential venues. Upon further reflection, I realized that every show he'd booked without a ramp to the stage was proof that he hadn't taken my accessibility needs seriously or pushed the venues hard enough. I felt like I'd dodged a bullet this time, but I really had to reassess my protocol going forward. From now on I'd need to do a lot of extra investigating with my booking agent before confirming any shows.

I resented the additional workload, all because music venues were so unmotivated to prioritize accessibility. Indeed, it seemed the music industry was content to place the burden of access entirely onto disabled artists rather than evolving with the times or taking responsibility for their legal obligations under the ADA. It was unfair, but what other choice did I have?

Although it would still be almost a year until I formulated a set of guidelines for myself around venue accessibility, that night was the tipping point. If I wanted things to change, I would have to be part of the solution.

29

The Legend Herself

A FEW MONTHS after my run-in with the stair-studded venue, I was asked to speak and play at the State Department. I am a politics nerd at heart, so the opportunity was thrilling. It was likely the closest I'd ever get to my childhood dream of interpreting for the UN.

When the morning arrived, we rolled our rusty 2002 Ford Econoline up to a wrought iron gate. Our van must have looked a sorry sight compared to the rest of the vehicles on government business that day. Nonetheless, we received admittance from an armed security guard.

The State Department employee who had arranged for my visit met us outside and escorted us into the Harry S Truman Federal Building. We'd sent in our passports ahead of time for background checks, but we still had to run our bags and my violin through an X-ray machine. Someone inspected my wheelchair and swabbed my hands as Paul walked through a metal detector, as if we were traveling through an airport. Once we'd been cleared, a security officer verified our passports. Then he printed name tags and attached them to lanyards, which we were told had to remain visible at all times. The whole thing felt very official.

Next, he led us to the space where I was going to play—a small, brightly lit employee library. Paul set up my music equipment at one end of the room and we did a brief sound check. I lingered in the corner, waiting quietly by our host's side, as there was no greenroom. Eventually people started filing in, all dressed in business attire, looking serious and a bit preoccupied.

A few minutes before the event started, a woman in an electric wheelchair entered and parked herself right in the front row. She was dressed in a colorful floral shirt and blue linen slacks, with an elegant scarf wrapped around her head. She looked to be in her mid- to late sixties. I wondered who she was.

I didn't have to wait long to find out. "That's Judy Heumann," our host leaned over and whispered to me, with a hint of reverence in his voice. "Do you know who she is?"

"I've heard the name before," I lied. "But remind me who she is again?" I felt foolish for not admitting that I didn't know her. I hoped he couldn't detect my ignorance.

"Judy is a well-respected disability activist. Many people call her the mother of the Disability Rights Movement," he explained. "She worked in the State Department during the Obama administration, as Special Advisor for International Disability Rights."

How do I have no idea who this woman is? I wondered.

In the last moments before the program began, I googled "Judy Human" (which was corrected to *Heumann*) and quickly scanned her Wikipedia page for highlights. If I met her afterward, I didn't want to come off as completely clueless.

I learned that Judy had contracted polio as a child and that in the mid-1970s she'd helped to organize a protest called the 504 Sit-In. I'd never heard of that protest before, not in high school or college or anywhere else. Apparently she'd also helped to found several important disability rights organizations and had served under two presidents—yet she had completely escaped my awareness until that day. I made a mental note to read more about her after my show.

I quickly stashed my phone when it became clear that we were about to begin, and listened dutifully to my introduction. A polite round of applause signaled the time for my brief talk. I'd been asked to share a little about my personal history, but the main focus of the event that afternoon was inclusion in the workforce—in my case, including disabled performers and artists in our society. I still hadn't developed a clear set of accessibility guidelines for venues at this point, but I knew that a commitment to inclusion was the first step to wider change.

I'd been asked to perform a couple of songs after my talk. I had chosen "Watch the World Unfold" and "Someday We'll Linger in the Sun" as my first two, and I'd been debating the third since I'd arrived that morning. We were scarcely five months into Donald Trump's first term as president, and the nation was in a solemn mood. I really wanted to believe that "Bird Song," a sing-along, would foster a sense of hope and community among those in attendance.

But the group of about forty individuals, quietly sitting in their folding chairs, looked serious, stressed, and perhaps a little impatient.

Maybe a sing-along is exactly *what they need!* I thought to myself, stubbornly hopeful. I forged ahead and taught them "Bird Song."

That was a mistake.

Only about five of the forty people in attendance actually sang, Judy Heumann among them. The rest stared ahead uncomfortably, with lips pursed so that no music could escape. Some even had their arms folded tightly across their chest, in an act of musical defiance. One man checked his watch. The song's four minutes were achingly, embarrassingly slow, but it was too late to change course. I made it through the song by picking out those few, brave singers. But I should have trusted my initial instincts. A State Department gig was a different beast than a show in Ireland. Why did I make them do a sing-along?

When the event concluded, several attendees came up to say

hello. After the hubbub died down, our host introduced me to Judy. This made me nervous. I knew I was massively unprepared to speak with this disability rights legend whose existence I'd just become aware of thirty minutes prior.

Thankfully, Judy was direct and warm, and did not quiz me on her accomplishments. Instead, she complimented my music.

"Can we get a picture together?" she asked, like any other fan.

"Of course!" I said, "Let's do it in front of the room, by the flag."

The two of us posed side by side in our electric wheelchairs, next to an American flag. Before the picture, she reached over and put her hand on top of mine. Her sweet gesture took me by surprise. It was almost motherly—comforting and reassuring.

Our guide led a small group of us downstairs to the employee dining hall for lunch. We ate together at a long folding table, reminiscent of a junior high lunchroom. I sat next to Judy.

I'd been gifted the opportunity to pick the brain of one of the most influential disability rights leaders in the history of the United States. I didn't want to miss the chance to learn from her, to ask her questions about her life.

"What are some of the biggest changes you've noticed when it comes to disabled kids, as opposed to when you were growing up?" I asked, before taking a bite of pasta salad.

"Oh, so much has changed," Judy answered thoughtfully. "I grew up before elevators, ramps, and curb cuts. We had to fight for those in the seventies and eighties—they just weren't commonplace. Anyway, that meant getting around my neighborhood as a child was extremely difficult. And disabled students were segregated from their peers in school. My elementary education was down in the basement, in a separate classroom just for disabled kids. The coursework wasn't the same. It was a school in name only."

I had often pondered how different my own life would have turned out if I'd been born a mere thirty years earlier, like my friend Russ from Access Theater in Duluth. Accessibility certainly wasn't perfect when I was growing up—nor is it now—but I didn't feel trapped either, and I navigated my childhood world quite freely with my electric wheelchair. By the time I was in kindergarten, my school had an elevator, and it was understood that I'd be learning among my peers. Judy's childhood was something I never had to experience, mostly because of the ADA.

Later I would learn that the 504 Sit-In—orchestrated by Judy, the activist Kitty Cone, and several others—was one of the first nationally recognized protests by disabled people. Not only that, but it is *still* the longest sit-in at a federal building to date, with more than one hundred fifty mostly disabled participants taking over a building in San Francisco. The protest received crucial support from a diverse array of organizations, including the Black Panther Party, the Gay Men's Butterfly Brigade, Glide Memorial Church, and even the International Association of Machinists. It lasted over three weeks, and it resulted in accessibility requirements for all government buildings, including public schools. Judy would go on to be a key advocate in the ADA's passage and to work on disability rights internationally.

But at the time, I was too proud, or too ashamed, to ask her point-blank what her involvement had been in the Disability Rights Movement, so I focused on her childhood instead.

"That must have been really hard, to grow up in such an inaccessible world," I said.

"In a way," she reflected, "the hardest part was how people talked about disability back then. It was very negative. Even as a child, I got the message that your disability was something you should be ashamed of or try to hide—certainly not embrace."

"Do you think you internalized any of that?" I asked, well aware that this was a pretty personal question for someone I had just met.

"I don't think so—or, at least, I tried not to internalize it," she said. "But sometimes I am a little jealous of the younger generation."

This surprised me. Judy seemed so self-assured, so dignified.

"The messaging around disability is changing," she continued. "Kids these days don't seem to view their disability as a bad thing. It's just part of their identity from a very early age. They're even encouraged to embrace their disability, which is great. Sometimes I wish that had been the case when I was growing up." Then she added, "Of course, not *every* child is encouraged to explore their disability identity—especially if we're talking globally. But I still think things are changing, slowly but surely."

I agreed with her analysis, but I felt a deep sadness knowing that she had carried this burden of negativity around with her as a child.

"But enough about me," she said, obviously changing the subject. "How is your music career going? Are you enjoying traveling?"

"Yes!" I said. "My husband, Paul, helps me on the road; we've loved seeing so much of the country together."

I hesitated, not sure how much to tell her about our accessibility struggles. I didn't want to come off as a whiner. But surely Judy would understand the stress of traveling in a wheelchair? I had gleaned enough to know that she'd traveled all over the world.

"I really like playing shows," I said. "However, a lot of the venues aren't accessible, for me *or* audience members with disabilities."

Judy nodded empathetically. She likely had more than her fair share of accessibility horror stories, but she let me continue.

"Most of the venues are old," I said, "so they weren't built with access in mind. But that doesn't exonerate them forever. They're not renovating; they're not doing anything, really. And I feel gross, as a disability advocate, playing in these spaces." Then I went on, wanting to gauge Judy's reaction. "I've been thinking—I probably need to make a commitment not to perform at venues that aren't wheelchair accessible anymore."

I assumed that Judy would wholeheartedly agree with me.

But instead she asked, "Wouldn't this limit your ability to

book shows? And wouldn't that limit how you earn income as a musician?"

"Yes," I said, feeling a little thrown off. "But if I keep doing these shows, nothing's going to change. Or at least not fast enough."

"Look," she said pointedly. "I think it's honorable for you to want to play at accessible places. But you're still at the beginning of your career. Let the more established disabled musicians, people like Itzhak Perlman, set those high standards. They have the clout and the resources to make it happen. It shouldn't be on you."

"Really?" I asked, protesting weakly. "I feel bad. Irresponsible!"

"Don't feel bad," she insisted. "Eventually you'll be able to do it too. Don't put so much pressure on yourself now. You're young!"

Deep down, I wasn't sure if I agreed with her. Wasn't it on every person to contribute whatever they can in their sphere of influence, even if it's small? Or even if it's a sacrifice? If I didn't do my part as a disabled artist, how could I ask others to care?

I didn't have the answers to these questions, but I did know I couldn't accept Judy's view as my own without critical analysis. Nonetheless, I appreciated her compassionate response and listening ear, as well as the reminder that life is nuanced indeed.

"Really?" I questioned her once more for good measure.

"Really," she replied definitively. Case closed. She moved on yet again. "Have you ever played with Itzhak? He's a friend of mine."

"No," I said, starstruck. As the only other disabled violinist I had heard of, he was definitely on my radar. But I hadn't met him, or even seen him in concert, let alone *played* with him.

"I should introduce you," she said casually. "You'd have a lot to talk about."

I smiled to myself, thinking how strange it was that life had led me to this moment with Judy Heumann, this International Woman of Intrigue. I felt grateful indeed for the unexpected gifts that touring had brought so far.

30

Accessibility Is the New Punk Rock

THE CONVERSATIONS I'D had about accessibility with Kalyn and Judy wouldn't leave me alone. What *were* my responsibilities as a disabled musician? Although in a perfect world I'd be playing shows that were 100 percent accessible, I didn't feel that I had the capacity to make that happen in reality. I barely had time to think as it was, let alone overhaul my touring strategy.

For months I rolled the proverbial can down the road, until one afternoon Martin Atkins called me with an unusual request.

"Gaelynn, it's good to hear your voice!" he bellowed with his characteristic enthusiasm. "I have a tiny favor to ask of you."

My heart skipped a beat, as I never knew what to expect from this man. Martin was one of the busiest people I'd ever met. Aside from giving talks around the country about his book *Tour:Smart*—the same one I'd devoured before hitting the road—he was always dreaming up shows for his band Pigface and new, albeit unconventional, opportunities for his music business students. He'd once created an internship that included living on the tour bus for a full week while Pigface was on the road—what better way to gain real-life, behind-the-scenes experience?

"Sure," I said, nervous that it would involve a last-minute trip out to Chicago. I was rather enjoying the brief time we had at home.

"I'm writing the sequel to *Tour:Smart*," he explained. "It's called *Band:Smart*. So much has changed since that first book was released. For one thing, social media! Everything is online now. But beyond that, *society* is changing—like disability, for one."

This was certainly intriguing to me! Since we'd first met, Martin and I had discussed my frustrations with access on the road a few times. I'd always wondered if he was just humoring me as I vented.

"I want to make sure the book includes practical advice on how to make the music industry more accessible," he explained, clearly leading up to his pitch. "And I thought to myself, who better to write this section of the book than *you*? It doesn't have to be long! An essay, a top-ten list—whatever feels right. I just want to include practical ideas that any musician or tour manager could implement when they're planning the next tour. Disabled or not."

My heart softened. Martin *had* been listening to me!

"When it comes to punk and industrial music," he mused, "the ethos was very DIY. We were countercultural, operating outside the establishment. We booked our own shows in basements and warehouses, and we welcomed all types into the fold. It was a beautiful community in many ways, except there was one glaring problem that none of us seemed to notice: Most punk shows weren't even *remotely* accessible. So we were totally excluding people with disabilities, even though we *wanted* to be inclusive. How fucked is *that*?!" Martin loved a good f-bomb.

Even though I was a folkie rather than a punk rocker, I had seen this phenomenon play out in my own music career. On every tour, Paul and I were struggling to make things work at venues that weren't accessible. Meanwhile, all around me, nondisabled musicians were carrying on as if everything was fine. No one else was doing the work. No one else seemed to even notice. It touched me that Martin had begun to recognize this discrepancy, and, what's more, that he was willing to *do* something about it.

"I appreciate the DIY aspect of punk," I replied. "In a way, I think *accessibility* is a new kind of counterculture—it's not really mainstream yet in the music industry, but individual artists and agents and managers can be part of the solution, even if mainstream society doesn't care."

"I've got it!" he exclaimed. "'Accessibility Is the New Punk Rock'!"

"Perfect slogan," I laughed. "Let's get that baby on a T-shirt!"

CREATING A LIST for Martin's book helped me clarify my own goals around accessibility. The truth remained, which Judy had hinted at earlier, that I wasn't a big enough artist to demand 100 percent accessibility at all of my shows. This was especially true when it came to offering closed captioning and ASL interpretation at every single concert. I simply didn't sell enough tickets to justify the expense, because I'd never break even. But there was plenty I *could* commit to.

First off, I would no longer play shows at places that couldn't be safely accessed by people who use mobility devices. This meant the front door and the room where the stage was located either had to be free of steps or have an elevator.

Second, the venue had to have at least one accessible bathroom, available to both men and women. I had been carried to the bathroom too many times over the years. I didn't want to inflict this undignified and dangerous circumstance on any disabled guests at my shows.

Third, if the venue didn't have a ramp to the stage, I would ask them to build or rent one. If the venue wouldn't do that but was otherwise accessible, then I would simply play my set on the floor. I'd no longer allow people to lift my chair onto the stage.

My reasons for this third guideline were twofold. One, it was unsafe to be lifting my chair (and me!) onto the stage. Two, if I performed on the floor when there was very clearly a stage behind me, it would send a subtle but powerful message to the crowd. I wouldn't actually have to *say* anything for them to figure out what was missing—a ramp! The optics spoke volumes, and those venues didn't come out looking too good. As it turned out, once I began to adhere to this rule, many venue owners opted to *build* ramps, lest they be embarrassed by an obvious lack of access.

Fourth, if I was playing a concert or giving a talk that had a larger budget, I would work to have ASL interpretation or closed captioning—or both—available for my set. It may seem counterintuitive, but Deaf people are often huge music fans: The communal gathering, the vibrations of the music, and the lyrics all combine to make for an enjoyable show, if access is provided. Sometimes I facilitated these accommodations myself, and other times the venues took care of it.

It's important to note that under the ADA, communication accommodations like ASL interpretation and closed captioning are legally the responsibility of the venue, especially when requested in advance. This means that venues should have some of their budget set aside to cover these accommodations whenever requested. It shouldn't be coming out of the artist's pocket.

Fifth, I would keep improving the accessibility of my shows as my career progressed. I look forward to the day when I can have an access coordinator, an ASL interpreter, a captioner, and an audio describer (someone who narrates the action onstage for blind people) at every performance. After all, the ADA is only the legal baseline—the sky's the limit for accessibility!

Although this list of guidelines ruled out a bunch of venues nationwide as future concert locations, it also gave me peace of mind. Gone were the days of debating whether to take a gig at a basement venue. It was the start of my punk rock era. Now, my greatest hope was that others would join me.

31

Tabula Musica

IN THE SUMMER of 2018, my connection with the State Department yielded some unexpected and exciting results. I was invited to travel to Switzerland as part of the Arts Envoy initiative, a government-sponsored exchange program aimed at fostering cross-cultural understanding.

Although the concept was new to me, the State Department had been carrying out soft diplomacy missions like this since 1956. During the Cold War, the US started sending "Jazz Ambassadors" abroad to promote American culture, values, and ideals. These were big-time musicians, such as Dizzy Gillespie, Louis Armstrong, Benny Goodman, Ella Fitzgerald, and Duke Ellington. But instead of undermining communism, my main goal would be to promote the ideas of disability rights and inclusion, which are still underrepresented globally.

For this visit, I'd be a guest artist performing with Tabula Musica, a fully integrated orchestra in which half the musicians were disabled and the other half were nondisabled allies. In contrast to my previous overseas tours, the State Department would take care of all the travel details, from booking our flights to planning our daily itineraries. All Paul and I had to do was pack and show up.

A couple of weeks before flying to Switzerland, I had a Zoom meeting with the orchestra's conductor, Denis Huna, to discuss the song arrangements I had emailed him a few days earlier. Denis was about my age, with curly dark hair and a friendly smile. He assured me that the concert would be a breeze.

"Just be on time for rehearsal!" Denis said before signing off.

I grimaced. I'm pretty much always running late for something, because I never factor in enough time to get from point A to point B.

"I'll try!" I replied. Then I confessed that being prompt wasn't exactly my strong suit.

Denis looked suddenly serious. "Those stereotypes about Swiss clockwork? They're true!" he warned. "These people are punctual."

"OK, I'll be on time," I promised, only half-convincingly.

"Good!" he said brightly. "See you soon!"

Now that we'd met, I was no longer nervous about the concert, but a new fear had taken its place: sleeping through my alarm!

WHEN WE LANDED in Switzerland, a foreign service officer from the US embassy met us at the airport and rode the train with us to Bern, where we'd be performing. I was relieved to find that the trains were indeed accessible, as promised. Otherwise, transportation would have been a nightmare since I'd decided to bring my electric wheelchair with me this time. Thinking ahead, I packed a dual-voltage battery charger so that Paul didn't have to carry around a heavy converter box in our luggage.

The next day I had my first rehearsal with the orchestra, and to my chagrin it was first thing in the morning. I was still weary from traveling, so I slammed down two cups of coffee when I got out of bed and attempted to get ready as quickly as possible.

Even with our heroic efforts, Paul and I still missed our intended tram. I was sure that we were going to be late for rehearsal.

"Hold on," Paul said. "It's only three minutes until the next one. The Swiss have public transportation dialed in!" He was clearly impressed by their efficiency.

We made our way to the building, and just before entering the rehearsal room, I glanced down at my phone. It was 9:59 a.m. We were sixty seconds early! Head held high, I entered, expecting to see the ensemble members mingling in front of their open cases. Instead, they already had their instruments in hand, and Denis was standing at the conductor's podium. My face flushed. They'd been waiting for me. I could've kicked myself.

Rehearsal at ten had obviously meant arriving fifteen minutes early. Once again, I hadn't properly factored in the travel time. What I wouldn't give for *Star Trek*'s beam-me-up technology right about now!

I scurried over to a corner with Paul to unpack my instrument. Violin finally in hand, we were finally ready to begin.

"This is Tabula Musica," Denis announced, gesturing to the musicians with pride.

The ensemble was composed of twenty-five people. A few of the members were visibly disabled, but others had hidden disabilities or were simply allies. Most were playing the usual suspects in a chamber orchestra of this size: violins, violas, and cellos. There was also a guitar, an oboe, a flute, and—new to me—an adaptive instrument called the Skoog.

The Skoog was a squishy black cube with large, rounded buttons on the top and sides. Each button was a different color—orange on the top, and red, blue, yellow, and green on the sides—and each one played a different note. When the buttons of the Skoog were pushed down, the corresponding notes would sound for as long as pressure was maintained. The Skoog allowed people with limited fine motor skills, including small children, to make music. I had never seen an adaptive instrument in an ensemble before.

"Let's try to get through as many pieces as possible today," Denis said enthusiastically, as he set a music stand in front of me. "We've been working on your music for a few weeks, so we should be nearly ready to go."

To my delight, the chamber orchestra was great. It sounded like any other string ensemble of that size, pleasant but not overpowering. Yet I knew there were electronic instruments mixed in among the wooden ones. How did they blend in so well? What parts were they playing?

The rehearsal flew by, and soon the orchestra members were filing out the door, with polite nods and smiles in my direction.

Denis remained in the room, and in a few minutes, two women in their early thirties walked in and introduced themselves. Nadine was Denis's wife—she had curly golden-brown hair and light blue eyes. Her demeanor was gentle and friendly, though she wasn't as outgoing as Denis. Linda, Tabula Musica's administrative assistant, had long brown hair, smiling eyes, and a feisty, playful energy. Within minutes she was already teasing us and cracking jokes, as if we'd been friends for years.

Paul and I set out with this amiable trio to find some food and an afternoon coffee. The conversation flowed freely from topic to topic. Once in a while, they had to stop and search for a specific, obscure word, but otherwise, there was hardly any language barrier.

I was secretly jealous that they'd been exposed to so many different languages throughout their lives—Switzerland has four official languages, after all: German, French, Italian, and Romansh. Students are expected to learn one second official language in school *in addition to* English. In Bern, where we were visiting, people primarily spoke German.

We took the tram to the medieval village of Old City, whose architecture looked as if it had been lifted from a page of an illustrated storybook. Denis told us that there had been a fire in the fifteenth century and that Bern had been rebuilt from stone instead of wood. Gray-green sandstone buildings were roofed with orange clay tiles and sported picturesque chimneys. There were a few cathedrals and a castle in this idyllic hamlet, their copper spires turned green with age and bell towers covered with elaborate ornamentation.

This fairytale city had been built up around a crook of the gently flowing Aare River. Its waters were an impossibly bright turquoise hue, lending a magical energy to the landscape. It was different from Lake Superior, whose color mirrors the sky and changes day by day. On cloudy, windy afternoons, the lake is a steel blue, dotted with whitecaps. On sunny mornings, the glistening water is a cheery cornflower blue, and on still evenings it reflects the soft pink hues of the sunset. But I've never seen my lake turn aquamarine. I couldn't stop from gawking at this captivating river, backed by steep forested hills.

Eventually, our meandering stroll took us to a small café with a lush patio. It was located right next to the riverbank, surrounded by a small grove of trees. We sat at one of the round wrought-iron tables outside, and the waitress came to take our order. We started with a round of beers and a plate of fries for the table, both rare midday indulgences for me on the road. I was grateful we had the night off so that Paul and I could get to know our hosts.

Once we were settled, happily munching on deliciously greasy fries, I asked Denis why he decided to start Tabula Musica.

"Because I didn't want to become a professional violinist," he answered, laughing at his own joke. I must have looked confused, so he explained.

"My dad was a violinist in Macedonia. He was quite famous there, in the classical world, at least. When I was a teenager, he sent me to Juilliard, thinking I would follow in his footsteps. I studied with some very exceptional teachers, but I didn't want that to be my life."

"Why not?" I asked. I felt an unwelcome pang of jealousy at all the opportunities he'd been afforded in his childhood. Juilliard sounded like a distant reality to me, given my low-income Midwestern upbringing.

"My dad dealt with so much pressure during his career, and he was always so serious. He died of a heart attack at the age of sixty. I didn't want that kind of stress to consume my own life."

"I'm sorry, Denis," I said, worried that I had awakened painful memories. *Appearances can be so deceiving,* I thought.

"Thank you," he replied. "It's OK. When I graduated from Juilliard, I returned to Macedonia. I worked in a large facility that housed disabled people. It was an awful, inhumane place. Like a prison. I don't like to think about it."

I was upset to learn that Macedonia locked away its disabled people. But I also knew that, unfortunately, the US wasn't without its own atrocities in this regard. Meeting Judy Heumann earlier that year had sparked an interest in disability history, and much of what I'd learned so far horrified me.

Among the most disturbing of my discoveries were the so-called State Schools. These were state-run institutions with appalling conditions that housed thousands of disabled people — including many children — with intellectual disabilities.

One such institution was called Willowbrook, located on Staten Island. It opened in 1948, and by the mid-1960s it had become severely overcrowded and dangerously understaffed. The disabled children and adults living in this notorious facility experienced worse treatment than most livestock. They did not have enough food to eat and often went without clothing. Some were left alone for hours in oversized cribs, while others huddled on the floor of sparsely furnished rooms, smeared in their own excrement. Disease and distress ran rampant in this unsanitary and inhumane environment.

Many people died in this horrifying setting, but their real cause of death — neglect — was often obscured. For years, this barbaric treatment of disabled children and adults was hidden from public view. Willowbrook did not permit visitors, including the press, into the private areas where this inconceivable hell on earth existed.

In 1965, Robert F. Kennedy visited Willowbrook. Afterward, he described it as a "snake pit" to reporters and demanded change. Unfortunately, lasting reform did not materialize. But seven years later, an intrepid TV reporter named Geraldo Rivera made his way into the back hallways of the institution, urged to visit by a doctor there. The airing of Rivera's shocking exposé on the facility triggered widespread public outcry and a class-action lawsuit, but it *still* took fifteen more years of dedicated disability advocacy until Willowbrook State School was finally shuttered in 1987. That was only three years after I was born—certainly not the distant past.

As painful as it is to acknowledge, Willowbrook was not an anomaly. State Schools equally as terrible and inhumane operated in many states until reforms slowly started in the mid-1970s. No wonder disability activists have long been calling for the closing of state-run hospitals and institutions! Again, I thought, *Why didn't I learn about Willowbrook in school?*

From what I could tell, the institution where Denis had worked in Macedonia was basically a carbon copy of Willowbrook. "I had hoped to be able to make change from within," Denis said. "You know, provide the residents with music classes or something."

His face darkened at some haunting memory. "But the problems were too big, too ingrained. I eventually quit and moved to Switzerland."

"So what inspired you to start Tabula Musica once you got here?" I asked.

"While I'd been caring for those disabled adults, I noticed something: They responded to music! Not necessarily in a formal way," he said, "because most of the people living there were nonverbal. But when I'd walk them down the hallways, I'd experiment with timing my steps to different beats. They would follow my lead, even if I switched up the rhythm."

This experience reinforced his belief in the universality of music.

"Everyone has music inside of them," he said. "We just have to figure out how to access it. That's the foundation of Tabula Musica."

Over the course of the next few days, I would learn that Denis was quite masterful at bringing this lofty principle to fruition. For starters, he used the Skoog instrument he had shown me earlier to enable two adults with Down Syndrome to participate in the orchestra. He'd written parts for them that blended in with the other instruments. Whenever it was time for them to play a note, he would hold up a card with the correct color on it. They would squeeze the Skoog on that color for as long as he wanted them to hold the note, then he lowered the card when it was time for them to stop playing. These Skoog parts were simple enough for them to follow, yet an integral part of the ensemble.

Another musician in the ensemble was a middle-aged autistic man who played the acoustic guitar. He wanted to participate, but the volume of the orchestra was overstimulating and stressful. Denis, true to his mission, thought of a creative workaround. He set up a couple of microphones onstage to pick up the sound of the ensemble, and he had the man wear heavy-duty noise-canceling headphones that were plugged into the soundboard. Then Denis asked the sound engineer to feed just a little bit of the orchestra sound into the guitarist's headphones. That way the volume was adjustable, and the man could perform without getting overwhelmed.

Another gentleman had cerebral palsy and did not have good fine motor control, but Denis found an adaptive instrument that he could play. It's called the Soundbeam, and it works by placing the hand in front of its ultrasonic sensor. This sensor detects any hand movements, big or small, and translates them into musical pitches. The farther away the hand moves from the sensor, the higher the note sounds. The coolest part of the Soundbeam is that it can be programmed for different keys to match specific songs. Even the size of the pitch intervals can be adjusted. People who don't have fine motor control, including children, can preset the Soundbeam so that every note it plays fits in within the song's chord structure.

I wasn't focused on these adaptations during our rehearsals since I had to practice my own parts. It wasn't until the night of our big concert that I would be able to appreciate the full impact of Denis's careful planning.

The evening of the concert finally arrived. The performance started off with a few other pieces, but I barely heard them. I was just trying to keep my nerves in check backstage. Next came my suite of five songs with the inclusive ensemble. The set went well, though it sped by in a blur.

After I put my violin away, Paul and I snuck out into the concert hall to find some empty seats. I wanted to catch the grand finale—to experience Tabula Musica from the audience's perspective.

It was truly a sight to behold—at first glance, they appeared and sounded just like any other chamber orchestra. But if you looked a bit closer, the genius of inclusion became more evident.

There, in the front row, was the autistic guitarist with his noise-canceling headphones. To the left was the Soundbeam player with cerebral palsy, raising and lowering his arm to make harmonies that blended in with the orchestra. On the right were two adults with Down Syndrome, dressed in concert black with their Skoogs in hand, watching Denis intently. Throughout the piece, Denis discreetly held up the colored cards for them with one hand, while conducting with the other hand. It was so subtle, so integrated, that no one in the audience probably even noticed.

Denis had found dignified and thoughtful ways to include people who have traditionally been excluded from mainstream music ensembles. Watching them, I felt a deep longing rise up in my belly—the wish that everyone could have instructors like Denis and Mrs. Sommerfeld.

I was lost in the beauty I was witnessing when, to my surprise and delight, I heard the Soundbeam loud and clear. I had forgotten that Denis had planned a Soundbeam solo toward the end of the last song. The man with cerebral palsy was now a veritable firestorm. His wiry arm was flying up and down over the Soundbeam, creating a pulsing string of musical scales. His enormous smile and contagious, star-power energy were palpable all the way to the back of the room. A spontaneous round of applause broke out as the audience shared his joy and reflected it back to him.

The finale came to its close. The members of Tabula Musica took a few bows from the stage, dressed in their formal black attire, and the audience clapped loudly in appreciation. It struck me how, in this moment, the Skoog players with Down Syndrome were being celebrated in equal measure as their nondisabled, flute-playing peers. This elegant inclusion was rare, but Denis had shown me through example that it needn't be an uncommon phenomenon. Another way was possible. The clapping continued, until one by one, the audience members began to rise in a standing ovation. That's when I started to cry.

Tabula Musica ignited my passion for Disability Culture that night, even though I didn't have a name for it quite yet. The concert wasn't just an "inspirational" show for the audience—it was much more radical than that. Each member of the ensemble had been invited to fully embody and embrace their unique identity. And when these musicians came together to perform, they exuded an authentically joyful, welcoming, and creative energy that everyone in the audience could experience. It was clear that Tabula Musica was bigger, better, and more expansive *because* of disability inclusion, not despite it.

32

Meeting Your Idols

EVEN AFTER I won the Tiny Desk Contest, I never dared to imagine that someday I might cross paths with the musical loves of my formative years. In 2018, however, I was asked to open for The Decemberists at the Palace Theater in Saint Paul. To say that I was ecstatic is an understatement. College-age me would never have believed what life had in store!

The Palace was a recently renovated historic theater that seated twenty-five hundred people—definitely not my typical venue! The idea of opening for The Decemberists was more than a little nerve-racking. I figured it would be less intimidating to do the set with backup, so I invited a few of my closest Minneapolis-based music buddies to play with me. To my relief, they happily agreed. It would be fun to share the experience with them. I carefully curated our six-song setlist for maximum impact. The flow had to be just right if our short performance was going to make an impression.

We wanted to look sharp for our big gig, so we got all dressed up—me in my fanciest dress and them in their best suits. The day of the show finally came, and we arrived at the Palace in midafternoon. After sound check, we hung around backstage with The Decemberists. I was surprised to discover they traveled with a record player and a pile of board games to make their downtime more relaxing and enjoyable. The band was extremely friendly and made us feel welcome.

Our set went as well as I could have hoped, the crowd cheering for their homegrown openers. We rejoiced together in the greenroom before watching The Decemberists play from backstage. When the end of the show was approaching, the stage manager led me back onto stage so that I could improvise with the band for the encore. I thought I'd never stop beaming after that night.

A year later, my dream scenario materialized again when Wilco asked me to open their Minnesota show. My guitarist and keyboard player were both huge Wilco fans, so I invited them to join me. Once again I picked a banger setlist, and we wore color-coordinated dress clothes. This time Wilco invited me to play violin on not just one, but *two* songs during the encore. I could hardly believe my good fortune!

Before the show, Jeff Tweedy had asked me to practice the encore with the band. Wilco was crammed into a dressing room backstage as Jeff strummed his acoustic guitar and sang. I wanted to pinch myself during the entire jam session.

For the first encore, "An Empty Corner," it was just Wilco and me playing, but during the second song, "California Stars," Wilco invited my two bandmates onstage to play tambourines. Several times I glanced back at them. They were standing on either side of the drum kit, wearing the widest smiles and dancing along to the music as they shook those tambos. Soon Jeff nodded in my direction, and it was time for my solo. My fingers and bow knew exactly what to do as I started improvising harmonies with abandon. When my solo ended, I turned it back over to the band, and the audience roared. I looked at the crowd and grinned, letting myself soak it in properly—a moment of bliss.

A FEW MONTHS later, I was performing a solo show at the University of Michigan. Just before the concert began, I noticed an intellectually disabled girl sitting in the front row, presumably with her mother. She was wearing a floral print dress, and she had a violin case resting by her feet.

I lost track of her until the middle of my audience sing-along, "Bird Song," when a minor commotion broke out. The young girl was crying and seemed very agitated—her mom was trying to calm her down. Next thing I knew, the girl had sprung out of her seat and was pacing in the aisles. That's when I saw an usher approach. I hoped they wouldn't ask the girl and her mother to leave halfway through. I think one way to be truly welcoming to disabled folks during live performances is to recognize that not everyone is able to sit quietly through an entire concert.

I thought back to a night early on in my touring career, when a staff member from a local group home brought two disabled music fans who had cerebral palsy to my show at a venue in Iowa City.

This pair so enjoyed the concert that they were literally unable to contain themselves—they loudly vocalized their glee throughout the show at the back of the room. To the uninitiated, it might have seemed like they were not paying attention or that they were being disrespectful, but I knew better. These two were having a ball, and this was how their bodies expressed delight.

I brought myself back to the moment at hand.

Before starting my last song, I did a quick scan of the rows closest to the stage. Relieved, I saw that the mother and daughter were once again seated in the front row, listening attentively.

After the show ended, the two of them made their way over to the edge of the stage.

"Can we come up to meet you?" the mom asked hesitantly.

"Sure!" I said, as I waved them up.

"And can my daughter show you her violin?" she inquired.

"Of course!" I said. I love any chance to talk to a kid about music.

The mother led her daughter up the stairs and brought her face-to-face with me. The girl, who had looked perfectly at ease by the end of the concert, suddenly seemed stiff and anxious.

When I said hello, the girl immediately started to cry—big, wet tears rolled down her cheeks. I wasn't sure how to respond.

Her mom jumped in. "Don't worry, she's not upset. She's just excited. She listens to your music every night as she falls asleep. In fact, you're the reason she wanted to start playing the violin in the first place."

Upon hearing her mother explain the situation, the girl's face started to relax a tiny bit.

Then it dawned on me. She hadn't been *sad* when she'd jumped out of her seat. Far from it—she'd been overcome with emotion!

"Were you excited to sing 'Bird Song' with me earlier?" I asked.

The girl nodded through her tears, smiling faintly when our eyes locked.

"Well, it's so nice to meet you!" I said cheerfully.

She nodded again in reply, her smile widening.

"And I'd love to hear you play your violin," I prompted. "But only if you feel like it, of course."

She beamed radiantly, then opened up her violin case and started to play.

33

Sunday Sessions

PAUL AND I were getting ready to head out for a two-week tour to Denver and back, against our better judgment and the protestations of my mother. Of course, almost *everyone* was nervous about traveling then: It was early March, 2020. Paul and I tried to convince ourselves that we'd be able to stay safe as long as we came prepared, so we loaded up the van with music gear, merch, luggage, food, face masks, and hand sanitizer.

A heavy cloud hung over Paul and me as we made our way out West. The news about COVID, which was quickly spreading across the country, seemed to grow more dire by the hour. I was having serious doubts about following through with the tour. On our third drive day, I called a college friend—now a doctor—for advice. The first show was scheduled for the next evening.

"Yes, people can stay home if they feel like it," she explained. "But not everyone *will*, because they want to see you play. So don't leave it up to them to make the decision. Keep them safe!"

Although disappointed, I agreed with her assessment. I got busy calling the venues to let them know I was canceling my shows. All those months of tour planning were evaporating before my eyes.

That night, I drank several glasses of white wine with some crackers, cheese, and a pouch of tuna. Through a bleary wine haze, Paul and I watched the news in our hotel room. President Trump had shut down air travel. By the next morning, he had announced a national emergency, and the business lockdowns began. *Well*, I thought, *I guess the tour would've canceled itself!*

With that, Paul and I began our long, eerie drive back to Duluth.

YOU MIGHT SAY that adaptability is one of my strong suits. Dealing with broken bonesx, surgeries, and inaccessible venues over the years has instilled a tendency to adjust accordingly when things don't go as planned. Thus, I was pretty quick to pivot during the COVID lockdown.

Luckily, my career as a musician and public speaker was quite translatable to the virtual format, so Paul and I managed to keep our heads above water, financially speaking. And because I worked from home, Paul and I were able to isolate and avoid getting COVID. This was critical, since my reduced lung capacity put me at a higher risk for serious complications from the virus, especially before vaccines came along.

That spring, I felt exceedingly grateful to be living in beautiful Duluth, nestled in our cozy studio apartment by the shores of Lake Superior. Paul and I took neighborhood strolls together almost every day, and I was amazed by how much flora and fauna there was to see within a mere mile of our home. I witnessed delicate flowers bloom and fade and berries ripen and decay throughout the season. I spotted deer, raccoons, foxes, bald eagles, and even a great gray owl. After three years of near-constant touring, it felt especially grounding to be rooted in one place for longer than a few weeks.

Despite these blessings from nature, Paul and I both carried a lot of extra stress with us.

By June 2020, there was statistical evidence that people with developmental disabilities were at higher risk of dying from COVID than pretty much any other group in the US. This was partly because many of them lived in group homes. If their staff members weren't taking precautions to avoid COVID in their personal lives or wearing proper masks at work, then they could easily spread the disease to the residents of these group homes. On top of that, many folks in group homes have health issues that make them even more susceptible to severe illness and death from COVID.

This news alarmed and angered me. It felt like a confirmation of what I feared most, that some people weren't doing all they could to protect those most vulnerable to the disease. I couldn't understand why this wasn't front-page news, why carelessly jeopardizing the lives of disabled people wasn't seen as a human rights issue. Infuriating as it was, this revelation also galvanized me. Even if I couldn't convince everyone to take COVID seriously, I vowed to make positive changes wherever I could. During the summer of 2020, I led a grassroots campaign for a mask mandate in my hometown. It started with an open letter to the mayor of Duluth, asking why our city was dragging its feet on a mask mandate when other cities around the state had already enacted them. My letter was printed in our regional newspaper and circulated widely online.

This local advocacy gave me a sense of agency during an extremely frustrating time, and thankfully, a mask mandate was eventually passed. I was reminded that it doesn't take legions of people to bring about change. Often, social justice movements are led by a small but dedicated group of citizens—many of whom are minorities themselves.

DURING THE FIRST year of the pandemic, most of the people I cared about were on the same page as me in terms of being cautious—even though our country was politically divided on the national and even state level. After vaccines became more widely available, I started to notice that my friends and family once again began to live as though COVID was no longer a threat—despite the fact that cases surged randomly and that long COVID was being reported.

It became uncomfortable to discuss my continued vigilance against COVID, and I was starting to get the impression that people I cared about didn't take my concerns very seriously. After all, I had been labeled a worrier for most of my life, ever since I dragged out those heavy volumes of Encyclopedia Britannica to research diabetes and brain tumors as a child. I started to second-guess myself: *Maybe we were simply being irrational. Why were we so worried, if no one else seemed to be?*

In the end, I determined that medical trauma was the root of a great deal of my fear around COVID—and that it wasn't uncalled for, given the circumstances. The news stories from the early days of the pandemic were doubly traumatizing: First, I read about hospitals rationing ventilators, giving them to only the "healthy" candidates. Later, articles stated that the "only" people at risk of dying from COVID had preexisting medical conditions—as if their deaths were somehow permissible. Had my friends and family ever experienced the same sense of helplessness that I knew all too well—whenever a medical expert I'd trusted was wrong or, worse, dismissed me because of my disability—then they no doubt would have felt wary too.

The pandemic continued to claim a disproportionate number of disabled souls as the months dragged on, but those deaths received very little press coverage. Instead, the news focused on what some politicians called "Reopening America." My disability had suddenly put me at odds with mainstream culture in a major way. I began to feel increasingly invisible, expendable even. This was a huge shock to my psyche, given how I was raised in such an affirming community. I had simply never imagined I would become so isolated in my own hometown. An aching sense of loneliness took hold of me.

It was as if Paul and I had moved to a different planet—Planet Disability. I felt wildly out of orbit with the rest of society. Maybe life had always actually been this way, but I'd just never noticed. Maybe the sting of structural inequality had been buffered by my wide net of caring friends and loving family. But now this sense of community was fraying at the edges.

The disconnect grew only larger with each passing month. Masks became a thing of the past, and testing soon followed—once these main lines of defense were removed, I felt more vulnerable than ever. Meanwhile, my friends went back to concerts, restaurants, and bars. Text chains and social media feeds were replete with pictures of fun times that I never experienced. Family gatherings and holidays were a nightmare to navigate.

I was beside myself that most people could move on from COVID so easily, forcing vulnerable populations to navigate a world that had largely forgotten about them. My medical trauma reared its ugly head yet again—grief and fury threatened to pull me under almost daily.

A few thoughts did help me to maintain some of the equanimity and feelings of grace and benevolence that seemed to flow so easily before the pandemic. First, I tried to have compassion for those with whom I disagreed, to refrain from judging them for what I perceived as bad choices.

Easier said than done, I'd think, in my more cynical moments. But whenever I went inward, I would recall the words of Jesus: "Do not judge, and you will not be judged. For in the way you judge, you will be judged; and by your standard of measure, it will be measured to you." An internal audit quickly revealed my own darkness and bad behavior over the years, so why did I suddenly think I had the right to hold my fellow humans in contempt for their own follies?

As I approached my own judgmental attitudes with a bit more honesty and awareness, a second realization slowly dawned on me: *You can care deeply about a cause, but ultimately you can't expect everyone else to care about it as much as you do, or to work as hard as you at solving it.* This truth was difficult to accept at first, but once I made peace with it, a burden lifted that I hadn't realized I was carrying.

My life experiences have led me to believe that Disability Justice is a moral imperative, and that our country's COVID response disproportionately harmed people with disabilities and chronic illness. Nonetheless, it's unrealistic of me to assume that every single person—or even most people—will view COVID through the same lens of urgency that I do. I just don't know that human beings have the capacity to care about everything all at once and still lead a life of joy. That reality doesn't justify inaction or willful ignorance, but it does open up a small space for humility.

Now I feel a greater kinship to other changemakers whose causes often get overlooked or outright dismissed—such as climate change, animal rights, and racial justice activists. No doubt they, too, feel this tension as they fight for their respective causes in the face of overwhelming apathy. It's never easy to go against the grain, even if you know deep inside that you are right.

This period also taught me the importance of being an empathetic ally, one who is willing to listen, and then to act whenever possible. But it also pushed me to stop demonizing others for their lack of personal experience. The best—ultimately, only—way for me to change hearts and minds is to set an honest example through my own thoughts, deeds, and words.

The only thing I can control is my own behavior. But I believe that if integrity, respect, and compassion guide my interactions, then there's a chance people will be open to learning from me. It is education and respect, not anger, that will one day win the fight for justice.

ONE OF THE main things that kept me going during the pandemic was my online concert series. I hosted my first live YouTube show on March 20—exactly one week after the lockdowns.

The video was grainy and poorly lit, and the sound was terrible. I was streaming live from my Chromebook, and I didn't yet own a USB microphone—or even a proper webcam. But what my online concert lacked in technical expertise, it compensated for in charm. I told dad jokes between songs, Paul made a brief cameo, and I even appealed to Stephen Colbert to reach out about an interview, wielding my full-sized Sting replica from *Lord of the Rings*—its gleaming blade inscribed with Elvish text—as my extremely nerdy calling card. He did not respond, though it was a pretty funny segment.

The first show managed to bring a couple hundred scared people together to experience something joyful, if only for an hour. The live chat was hopping from start to finish, and I was delighted to see that folks from all over the US and even England, Scotland, and Germany had tuned in for the show. Though scattered far and wide, folks seized the chance to connect.

Buoyed by the success of that first live stream, I immediately launched a weekly concert series, gradually upgrading my computer equipment as I went. As the pandemic stretched on, I had to think of ways to keep the show interesting—there were only so many setlists I could arrange from my repertoire of roughly forty songs. With a great deal of sweat and tears—luckily, no blood—I grew increasingly tech savvy, and I figured out how to invite guests to my show.

My YouTube series—aptly named *Sunday Sessions*—hosted dozens of musicians whom I had met on the road. Each artist played three tunes, and I interviewed them between songs. The online audience could type their questions into the live chat too, making it an interactive discussion. Topics ranged from the artists' creative process to more personal matters such as grief, addiction, and the value of community. Our conversations were heartfelt and honest, but not overly serious—there was a lot of laughter throughout. I always ended the concerts by playing a few of my own songs.

Sunday Sessions ran every single weekend for eighteen months, and I recall those afternoons with fondness. The concerts gave me a semblance of routine as well as a much-needed feeling of purpose during a very disorienting era. I loved how the magic of the internet connected me directly—and in real time—to other artists and music fans, two things I dearly missed. The series had a small but faithful audience from all over the world, and I soon discovered that many of the attendees had their own connections to disability. As the pandemic rolled on, I hoped my shows would give people a place to get inspired, find new music, and feel a bit less alone each Sunday afternoon.

34

Ramping Up RAMPD

"HEY, BEFORE YOU log off, can I get your number? I'd like to pick your brain about a project I'm working on," said Lachi, one of the fellow Zoom panelists from the day's event. "I'll call you in a few."

"Sure!" I said, very curious to hear what creative plans she had up her sleeve.

It was early spring of 2021, and I'd just finished participating in a virtual panel discussion about disability in the music industry, hosted by the Recording Academy. Almost a dozen of us were on the panel that day—disabled musicians spanning disparate genres, spread out across the country. For the past hour we'd fielded questions and shared our perspectives on how access and inclusion could be improved. The discussion was aired on the Recording Academy's Facebook page.

Lachi had organized and moderated this particular event, but it was, in fact, the third time that the two of us had been on a panel together. During the pandemic, pretty much every nonprofit was doing virtual discussions, and when it came to disability and music, we seemed to be the natural go-to's.

Lachi is a Black songwriter and recording artist from New York City who is legally blind. She has a confident speaking voice, quick sense of humor, and a big laugh. On Zoom, she looked much more put together than me, with formal clothes, stylish hair, and polished makeup. No matter how dressed up I got, I could never seem to ditch the folksy Northwoods vibe. The fact that my kitchen had been in the background the entire time didn't help, but it was that or the bed. Such is life when you're Zooming from your studio apartment.

I had never met Lachi before doing these virtual events. And even though our life experiences and musical styles were markedly different, everything she said during our panels about disability inclusion resonated with me.

Fifteen minutes later, my phone rang. It was Lachi, as promised.

"Hey girl, it's me," she said breezily. "It seems like we should get to know each other, since people keep hiring us to be on panels together." She chuckled.

It was indeed a small world when it came to disabled musicians.

"I liked the points you made today," she went on. "Especially about the need for venues to build accessible stages. It's good for me to remember that. I have different access needs, with my vision loss. That's why folks need to hear from lots of different disabled people, not just one!"

"I couldn't agree more," I said. "And I am so glad you mentioned that some recording software is hard to navigate with a screen reader. I didn't realize that. They need to do better!"

Try as I might, there's no way I will ever fully understand the nuances of all the different disabilities out there, and what that means for access.

"What's the project you wanted to run by me?" I asked, now intensely curious.

"I know this is out of the blue," she said, "but I am launching an organization to support disabled music professionals, and I am wondering if you want to be the cofounder."

I was floored. I had long dreamed of such an organization, but the idea of actually launching one felt overwhelming. I had never felt equipped to try—not yet, anyway.

"And get this: It would be named RAMPD—Recording Artists and Music Professionals with Disabilities," Lachi said, delighted by the acronym. "I know, right?! God gave me that name."

"I love it. It's perfect!" I exclaimed. "What would the organization do?"

"It's still in early stages, so nothing's set in stone," she answered. "But I am thinking it could be modeled after the Recording Academy. There are quite a few nonprofits that connect disabled people to music on the amateur level—recreationally, that is. But there's virtually nothing for disabled artists once we decide to make music our career. We're left to fend for ourselves."

"Yes, we are!" I responded. "And I feel like I'm always winging it. I don't think most people realize how much extra work it is to try and make sure shows are accessible. It gets exhausting."

And lonely, I thought. *What I wouldn't give for other musicians to join the cause.*

To my surprise, a lump rose in my throat.

Most of the musicians I knew personally didn't seem to factor in accessibility when booking venues. They played the same inaccessible stages year after year, instead of seeking out new, more welcoming spaces to perform. It often felt like I was fighting for access all by myself.

I swallowed hard to keep from crying.

"No kidding," she agreed. "It's hard work getting venues on board! Plus, here's the thing. Most venue owners tell me, 'You're the only disabled artist I know besides Stevie Wonder.' Come on, *please*. Don't give me that!"

"If we all get together, eventually they'll realize that there are a bunch of us out here," I said. "So count me in!"

"Great!" she said. "I've been networking with folks behind the scenes—a few from the panel today, plus others. At some point I'll get us all together on a Zoom. Stay tuned for next steps!"

I was impressed by Lachi's confidence in tackling this daunting project, boldly deciding to make her dream a reality. I was excited to join her. The music industry was overdue for a revolution.

ABOUT A MONTH later, Lachi followed through on the promise of a Zoom meeting. She had handpicked a dozen disabled musicians, all with an impressive list of accomplishments in their respective genres, and dubbed us the Founding Members of RAMPD. I was surprised to find that I didn't know anyone yet, aside from those I'd met briefly on the Recording Academy panel.

There was no question that Lachi was in charge of this fledgling operation, but there was lots of idea sharing and lively debate within the group to determine the organization's direction. Some folks wanted a focus on advocacy, especially around accessibility. Some were more interested in getting disability covered in mainstream media. Others wanted more job opportunities.

My personal passion, as boring as it sounds on paper, was to create an online database of disabled artists. That way, music venues and other arts organizations could easily locate us and hire us for gigs. Plus, if we built up a large enough membership, it would be impossible for venues, booking agencies, and festivals to pretend that disabled artists were rare—and thus not a priority when it came to inclusion and access.

After a few brainstorming sessions, the group held an election to choose members of the executive committee: president, vice president, treasurer, and secretary.

I was camping with Paul that night, so I used my hotspot to join the Zoom meeting. My laptop rested on a picnic table, tall pines visible on the screen behind me. Most of the group was located in either New York or California, so my environs did not go unnoticed for long.

"Where are you, Gaelynn?" Lachi asked.

"In the woods," I said, with a touch of pride. "Paul and I are camping this week. Do you camp?" I asked her, not wanting to assume anything about her hobbies.

"God, no!" she said, to uproarious laughter. Then our meeting officially convened.

Naturally, Lachi was elected president. Next, I was elected vice president. A fellow Minnesotan, a pianist and disability advocate named Stephen Letnes, was elected treasurer, and a California-based entertainment strategist named Andrea Jennings was elected secretary. Before logging off that night, Lachi made an impromptu speech, congratulating us for showing up and doing the work—for launching the Disability Culture Revolution. We all clapped and cheered. And just like that, RAMPD was born.

THAT SUMMER, I decided to sublet an office just so that I could get out of the apartment. I wasn't yet comfortable working at coffee shops due to the lingering presence of COVID, but I was really tired of being at home all the time. My new office was a mere block away from where I used to teach fiddle lessons. This space, however, had an even more marvelous view of the Lake Superior shoreline. I adored taking little breaks to look up from my computer. I would gaze, awestruck, at the vast blue waters straight ahead, the picturesque lighthouse to my right.

I spent many energizing afternoons and evenings there, hammering out the contours of RAMPD. We had formed an executive committee, but we still hadn't clarified our mission statement or chosen our objectives for the year ahead. All we knew was that we were planning an official launch party so that we could introduce RAMPD to the wider world and start our first-ever membership drive.

The executive committee met weekly on Zoom, and often Lachi would call me right after the meetings ended to continue talking and scheming. It was an exciting time, filled with heady discussions about embracing Disability Culture and envisioning the kind of music industry we wanted to help create. By this point I fully owned my disability identity, but I was rarely surrounded by others who truly understood what that meant or knew the unique joys and challenges it presented as a touring musician. It felt astonishingly wonderful to have this outlet.

During one of the committee meetings, the four of us were trying to come up with a clear and concise mission statement. This was my strong suit—I have always loved writing and painstakingly rearranging sentences (nay, single words!) in my essays and lyrics alike. I had been listening to their spirited conversation on mute as I happily typed away. Shifting a word here, replacing a word there.

When there was a break in the action, I eagerly presented this sentence to the group.

"Tell me what you think of this," I said. "'RAMPD's mission is to amplify Disability Culture, promote inclusion, and advocate for accessibility in the music industry.' Short, sweet, and to the point!"

"*What?!* You just came up with that?" Stephen exclaimed. "It's great!"

"I love it," Lachi said.

"I'm wondering if people will understand what we mean by *Disability Culture*," Andrea mused. "Society's perception of disability still seems to be mostly negative."

"Excellent point," I replied. "Is there a good definition of Disability Culture we could reference?"

We googled "Disability Culture," and nothing we saw really fit the bill exactly.

We grew quiet.

Eventually the conversation regained momentum. As I listened, my mind wandered back to a poster I'd seen in a bathroom stall, of all places.

The infographic depicted culture as an iceberg. Its premise was that what we normally think of as culture—like food, music, and art—is just the tip of the iceberg. Other, more subtle aspects of culture—such as views on relationships, friendship, time, beauty, family, competition, and cooperation—form the larger part of the iceberg, hidden below the surface.

The poster made no mention of disability, however—and as far as I could tell, *Disability Culture* wasn't yet a mainstream phrase. But it was clear to me that disabled people *did* share a loose, albeit diverse, form of culture. That's why so many of us identify with terms like *crip time* and *interdependence* and *#DisabledAndCute*—and, for me, why the music and paintings of disabled artists are so meaningful, somehow voicing the secret longings of my own soul.

If only we could define Disability Culture broadly enough to not alienate people who have different experiences of disability, I pondered. And then I started to type. A few minutes later, I had what felt like a reasonable attempt at defining what I'd so long implicitly cherished.

"Guys, can I read this to you?" I asked, and they nodded. "OK, here goes."

Disability Culture is a celebration of people who identify as disabled, while acknowledging the vast diversity of the disability experience and each person's inherent and equal worth. It is unapologetic, creative, innovative, adaptable, imaginative, and rooted in problem solving. It is based on the premise that disability needs to be seen, respected, included, and celebrated. It includes our worldviews, our perspectives, our contributions, our art, our words, and our music. Disability Culture, at least in part, is a vibrant and thriving counter-response to the exclusion, marginalization, and oppression historically and currently experienced by many disabled individuals.

"Great wordsmithing, G!" Lachi said, grinning.

"Someone needs to be feeding you grapes right now," Stephen joked. "It's divine!"

"Yeah, that's an amazing definition!" Andrea exclaimed.

"You've got me thinking, should we try defining *disability* too?" Lachi asked. "So people understand *exactly* what we're talking about?"

"Another great point," I responded. "Let's see what the current definition of *disability* is."

We search online, but each definition had words like *impairment* and *limiting*.

"Maybe we should try writing our own here, as a group," I proposed. "We can make it broad enough so that people can feel like identifying, and we can avoid the language we hate."

"Sure!" they replied.

So we got to work, creating a definition that used inclusive, neutral language. We added and subtracted and argued our points and laughed a lot. Twenty minutes later, we were finished.

For the rest of the night, I couldn't stop grinning.

It's hard to overstate how important this meeting was for me. Here I was, a disabled artist and activist who had toured the country and spoken to thousands of people about the importance of inclusion and accessibility in the arts—yet all the while, I had never felt that society's view of disability matched my inner experience. I don't feel *impaired* or *limited* or *less capable* than anyone else. Still, society had passed these ideas down to me and expected me to define myself as such. And the world hadn't even acknowledged a culture to which I could belong. It felt so good to take the words back and build them into something that felt inherently true to my life experience.

Like slipping into Cinderella's magic gown and realizing I was lovely all along.

35

The Bard and the Lute Factory

BY THE END of my second year of touring, fans had started to ask when I would write a memoir.

"Maybe someday," I'd reply wistfully. "But when will I ever be home long enough?"

When everything ground to a halt with the pandemic, I finally found that perfect window of time for a writing sabbatical—I even created a whole new email address, complete with a sternly worded auto-reply, to filter out booking requests. I'd saved up some cash and planned to hunker down to write a book at our studio apartment by Lake Superior.

Between writing sessions one afternoon in 2021, I came across an email that I couldn't ignore:

> We are theater producers and we would like to speak with you about composing music for a Broadway show. We are hoping to set up a call to discuss the project, so please reply ASAP to let us know if this is something you are interested in pursuing.

Most people would be elated to receive such an email, but in my mind, writing the memoir was a do-or-die proposition. I knew that as soon as I got back to touring, it would be nearly impossible to find enough uninterrupted time to put words on paper. And I desperately wanted to do that.

Besides, I had a few misgivings about composing an entire score, even if it was for Broadway. Was it *actually* Broadway? Or was it just a random theater in an alley off a street that happened to be called Broadway? And how serious was their offer, anyway? Would it pay mainly in exposure, the dreaded currency of all musicians?

The other thing was, if this really *was* for Broadway, I was terrified by how much work it would be. The idea of juggling a book deadline while composing a score felt intimidating, basically impossible. I knew how all-consuming theater was because the world in which my parents had raised me revolved around it.

Curiosity finally got the better of me. Could it really be Broadway?!

By email, I agreed to a phone call the following afternoon. I was *determined* to make a clear-headed decision about this. The play had to feel like the right choice, with the right people, for the right price.

Shortly before the call, the producers emailed to let me know I would be talking with the director himself. I felt unprepared for this one-on-one meeting.

At the appointed hour, I was sitting outside on our little wooden patio attached to our studio apartment. To my right, tall pines swayed in the warm summer breeze. Ahead of me stretched a freshly mowed lawn and the calm blue waters of Lake Superior.

The hustle and noise of New York City felt worlds away as I answered my phone. *Be tough,* I said to myself as I hit Accept.

"Hello, my name is Sam Gold," said the voice on the other end of the line. "It's so nice to meet you, Gaelynn. I'm a big fan."

He sounded genuine, friendly, and almost unsure of himself. His name was not familiar to me, but his voice drew me in instantly.

"Hello, Sam! It's nice to meet you too," I said. "Thanks for making time to talk with me so soon."

"No problem! Well, as you know," he started, his voice relaxing slightly, "I'm directing a show on Broadway next year, and I want you to do the score. I've been listening to your music ever since you won the Tiny Desk Contest, and your sound would fit the mood I'm trying to create perfectly. Wait, the producers told you which show, right?"

"Not yet," I replied. "I've definitely been wondering!"

"Oh, wow! It's *Macbeth*. Are you familiar with that play?"

"Vaguely, but it's been a while," I said. This wasn't entirely a lie—I was 60 percent sure our class read it in high school English.

"Well, the main thing is that this production won't be a period piece. I want to do a fresh interpretation with lots of dark, moody music—not, like, Scottish period music," Sam explained. "And if you're familiar with my directing style, you'll know that I prefer really minimal staging, set design, costumes, and sound design."

"Um, I am not really familiar with your work," I said sheepishly. "I'm sorry."

I couldn't believe how badly I was blowing it! Why did I never think to research these people ahead of time—had I learned nothing since my first encounter with Alan Sparhawk?

There was an awkward pause after my confession, but Sam recovered quickly. "I guess I assumed that my reputation preceded me. Sorry. You can look me up after our meeting."

(I did. He is a Tony Award–winning director.)

"My background is in avant-garde theater, so I tend to go for a minimalist aesthetic. That includes sound design. To give you an idea: One time, the only sound effect I used for an entire play was the sound of a single light switch," he said, laughing. "But for *Macbeth*, I want the music to be central to the play. I'm hearing lots and lots of music woven throughout. I want it to be textured and dark and intense. I remember listening to your orange album on the subway one day, and there's this instrumental number toward the end…"

"'Metsäkukkia?'" I ventured. "From *Learning How to Stay*?"

"Yes, that's it! When I heard it, I knew that was the sound I wanted to create for this play. I think you'd be perfect for it."

"That's a traditional Finnish fiddle tune, but I wanted it to sound like the apocalypse," I said with a grin. I was pleased that he had not only followed my music since the Tiny Desk Contest, but that "Metsäkukkia" had spoken to him. I loved that arrangement.

I could feel myself getting hooked by his creative vision. It did sound like a fun project. Suddenly I remembered my mission for the call: to investigate and be a deliberate decision-maker!

"This all sounds really cool," I said, "and I'm definitely interested in the type of score you're describing, but I need a little more information before I can make such a big decision."

"Of course," Sam replied. "What other questions do you have?"

I felt the ripples of anxiety nipping at my toes. I had no idea how to negotiate a theater project, especially one in New York.

"First off, what kind of budget do you have for music?"

"Sorry I can't be more helpful," Sam replied, "but that is a question for the producers. The director is usually kept out of finance discussions."

Strike one. "OK, then my second question is, how long would the project take? And would I have to travel to New York?"

"We'd need you in New York City at least a couple of weeks before tech starts and then hopefully you'd be able to stay for rehearsals all the way until opening night—so six weeks total?"

"Wait, I wouldn't be playing it live every night? Does that mean it would be pre-recorded?" I asked. The idea of doing the same show every night for three months straight had admittedly made my head swim.

"Yes," Sam continued. "You'd attend some rehearsals, go and record your ideas at a studio here in New York, and then help to place them in the show."

OK, so it *wasn't* live. But then a new wave of dread washed over me. Recording sessions were long and tedious, as I knew from making my own albums.

"Well, is there any way I could get a head start in Duluth so I don't have to record the whole soundtrack during rehearsals?"

"I don't see why not! That's another question for the producers."

I knew the last question I wanted to ask, but I was dreading it.

"Please don't interpret this the wrong way," I started in awkwardly, "but this is a huge undertaking that would take me out of Duluth, away from my current projects, for well over a month. And I'm writing a memoir. If I were to say yes, do you think this project would be worth the effort and time commitment, career-wise?"

I cringed. I'd never asked this question before, but I was out of my depth.

Sam paused and cleared his throat softly. I was frozen in fear.

"I can sense your hesitancy, Gaelynn," he said, "but yes, I do think it's a good career opportunity. I mean, it's Broadway!"

"Like, *actual* Broadway?" I asked.

A not-so-small part of me was still wondering if this was legit.

"*Yes,* actual Broadway!" he said emphatically. "Like in a big, beautiful theater that holds nine hundred people. Every night, nine hundred people will be introduced to your music, eight times a week for three months. I want this play to help you expand your audience!"

In the midst of all my objections, I hadn't stopped to ponder this. I felt a burst of excitement as I envisioned a real, live audience stirring in the dark, waiting in anticipation for the curtain to rise.

"I don't know what else to say that I haven't told you already. It can't get much bigger than this in the theater world," he said, clearly grasping at straws. "Daniel Craig is playing Macbeth."

The name Daniel Craig meant nothing to me—I live under a rock when it comes to pop culture. I assumed he was probably a movie star. I tried to play it off. "Oh! What's he been in again?"

"James Bond."

At that point I did a literal face-slap. I don't know why it took so long to trust what I was hearing. "I get it now," I said. "I'm really sorry to question you so much, but it's just a huge commitment. Can I talk to my husband first and then I'll get back to you?"

"Of course," Sam said.

My check-in with Paul was brief. "Why wouldn't you do it? Obviously you should do it, Gaelynn!" he said. I was certainly relieved that Paul was on board, but I still had one last phone call to make before I could come to a final decision: my parents.

I was extremely nervous to tell them about traveling to New York City while the pandemic was still raging nationwide. I was essentially still living in lockdown. I assumed my mom would not want me to head smack-dab into the middle of one of the world's largest cities.

But my mom's reaction surprised me. "Of course you're going to say yes, right?"

SAM SENT ME an audio recording of the first read-through and the script. I did not procrastinate on my Shakespearean homework. First I read *Macbeth for Dummies,* then I read the original script while listening to the actors' voices.

By this point I'd looked up Daniel Craig, and indeed I could recognize his booming British voice on the recording. I felt guilty, because this rare Daniel Craig listening experience was clearly being wasted on me. My idea of a celebrity crush was more Gandalf than James Bond.

As Sam suggested, I marked down all the points in the script where I could imagine music supporting the scene, like a movie soundtrack. The next week, we met on Zoom to compare notes, scene by scene. Ultimately, we identified fifty possible places for music cues. It was now my job to create them all.

It was November 2021, and rehearsals would begin March 1.

I still wasn't totally sure I'd be able to conjure up musical themes that were interesting enough to build into a full score. But thankfully one morning in the bathtub (where I do my best work), I started hearing four distinct melodies that all interlocked. It was like a more complex version of "Bird Song," only dark and brooding. I knew I had just found the themes for the witches and Macbeth.

That afternoon I created a very basic demo of the four parts weaving in and out of one another and sent it to Sam. To my utter relief, he loved them. From then on, I kept my voice memo app handy to capture inspiration wherever it struck, and soon I had a theme for Malcolm's army, Lady Macduff, and Banquo. But I still needed music for Lady Macbeth.

Several days later I was meandering down the sidewalk in my wheelchair and found myself absentmindedly singing the song I had written a few days earlier, called "Perfect." It was a melancholy tune about not realizing the true significance of one's marriage until it's too late.

We were so busy painting
We didn't see the corner
Some days we both felt trapped there
But still, the nights were warmer

Just then it hit me: *This* was the Lady Macbeth theme—not an instrumental melody, but a *full song*. I rushed back home and recorded the roughest of demos to email over to Sam. He wrote back a few hours later. "My wife and my daughter and I just listened to your song, and we're all lying in bed, crying. I love it."

THE MAIN THEMES were there—now I had just three months to record fifty music cues. I had decided to work with the Duluth-based audio engineer Jake Larson, the same quiet person who had helped me record my first solo album in that deconsecrated cathedral seven years earlier.

By day, Jake works with his father in a brick warehouse in Duluth, where they build medieval instruments and wind old-fashioned gut strings. Jake let me use their workshop after hours to avoid studio fees. He'd set up microphones and audio gear to transform the space into a makeshift recording studio. We worked several nights a week for three full months. It felt appropriate—like fate, really—to create music for The Bard's words in a veritable lute factory!

Not that the music was in any way traditional, in a Renaissance sense. For each cue, I recorded multiple tracks of the violin and stacked them on top of one another. To make the music sound less classical and more atmospheric, I often had Jake distort the sound of my violin with software plug-ins—the weirder the better. Lower or raise it an octave or two? Reverse the tracks? Make the violin like a heart monitor, or make those pulsing notes sound more like Morse code? Yes, to all of it!

We built each cue layer by layer, track by track, with plenty of experimentation along the way. Each cue usually took about an hour to record—we'd do three or four of them per session. By the end of the night, we were mentally exhausted.

Usually Sam approved about two-thirds of our cues. Then they got passed on to a few other Minnesota musicians I had recruited for this gig: Dave Mehling on keys, Jeremy Ylvisaker on guitar, and Al Church on drums. I asked them to get as atmospheric and weird as they wanted, especially toward the end of the play, when Macbeth descends into darkness. Later I'd piece their parts together—picking and choosing which bits to include, a kid in a musical candy shop.

For the cues that Sam rejected, it was back to the drawing board. I was just relieved he wasn't turning away more of them. I'd mapped out a calendar of cues, and we had very little leeway. We were barely going to finish by the deadline. But I was on a mission. There was no way I was going to turn up in New York City with only 60 percent of the music recorded!

In the midst of this recording frenzy, I received an unusual email from a nondescript address, asking if I would be interested in recording some vocal harmonies on Michael Stipe's new single, "Give Me a Hand."

By now, it should come as no surprise that I had to google Michael Stipe, but even my below-rock domicile hadn't kept me oblivious to the band R.E.M. I wrote back: "Thank you so much for reaching out! I would love to do that. Please just let me know the next steps."

A mere hour later, I received a reply: "This is Michael. I love your voice, and I am so excited you are going to sing the harmonies!"

This all felt a bit too surreal. Either way, I decided, *what could it hurt to record some vocal tracks?*

The next afternoon, the lyrics and a demo arrived in my inbox. I listened to the song—a catchy, lo-fi pop song with great lyrics and excellent opportunities for harmony.

Elated by this unexpected good fortune, I called Jake to tell him.

Our *Macbeth* deadline was looming nigh, but we weren't about to turn Michael Stipe down. We recorded his song during our next session. To my great relief, he seemed pleased with it. I wondered if I'd ever get the chance to meet him.

After that brief detour, it was a race to the finish—the soundtrack was due in less than a week!

The last couple of cues were the longest ones. The fight scene between Macbeth and Macduff totaled almost seven minutes, the winding layers and booming and screeching finally crawling to an end as—spoiler!—Macbeth dies. That single cue took three days to record.

During our final evening session, I recorded the vocals for "Perfect," the very last cue of the play.

Behind the scenes
We just wouldn't let it go
Wouldn't let it go
To pieces
Who knew we'd dig our own graves here?
No other would tend them with such great care

I wasn't prepared for how poignant the lyrics would be to sing, and during one of the takes I started crying. I felt embarrassed at becoming so emotional in front of Jake, but I guess it's a hazard of the job. I wiped away my tears, composed myself, and sang it again.

That last session with Jake was on February 28, 2022. There wasn't much time to celebrate, however, because Paul and I were scheduled to leave for New York the next day. It was a hectic turnaround, loading up our van with everything we'd need or want for the next six weeks. But I didn't mind—in fact, I was glowing inside. Jake and I had managed to finish the score on time!

I had been so focused on the recording process that I hadn't even really allowed myself to internalize what was coming next: Paul and I were Broadway bound!

36

Broadway Baby

PAUL AND I left for New York on March 1. We had allowed ourselves a leisurely travel schedule—I wasn't due to attend my first rehearsal until five days later. I cozied up with my trusty Chromebook in the van and prepared for a long, relaxing, and uneventful ride.

But apparently that's not the way Broadway rolls, because on our very first day of driving, I received a long list of edits from the stage manager over email: *Cue 6: need it to end 10 seconds earlier* and *Cue 13: needs to be approx. 45 seconds longer*. Jake had promised to remain available through opening night in case I needed him to make adjustments to the cues. Thus began a daily exchange of music edits, right from the van. Needless to say, it was a working commute!

We arrived in Brooklyn during rush hour. The producer was waiting for us at the rehearsal space. Play practice had just ended, but a few cast members were hanging around outside smoking, including an actor in a manual wheelchair. It was Michael Patrick Thornton, who played Lennox. He immediately rolled up to introduce himself, and I got the sense we were both excited to see another disabled person in the mix.

Sam Gold, a middle-aged man with curly brown hair beneath a baseball hat, was among the smokers. Spotting me, he broke away from his conversation.

"Hello, Gaelynn!" he said excitedly. He shook my hand warmly. "I'm so glad you made it here! We're done with rehearsal, but come inside—Daniel wants to meet you before he leaves."

What?! I was definitely *not* prepared for this. I was still in a driving daze and I felt like a slovenly mess—I hadn't even put on makeup that morning.

The producer held the door open for me as I made my way inside.

Suddenly, there he was. Daniel Craig was sitting on a bench against the mirrored wall, wearing casual clothes and a stocking cap. As I entered, he jumped off the bench, came up to me, and gave me a bear hug. I definitely hadn't been expecting that. Or how crystal blue his eyes were.

Daniel seemed genuinely pleased to meet me and came across as a very friendly person. Our brief introduction thus accomplished, the producer promptly escorted us to the hotel so that we could get settled in before starting work the next day.

During rehearsals, I was stationed at a long folding table located in the back corner of the room. The large empty space had been lined with folding chairs and filled with props. The walls were coated with pictures that Sam had taped up—mostly costume inspiration and set design ideas. I was seated with the sound designer, Mikaal Sulaiman, a tall, wide-shouldered man who only ever wore black clothes—including a black scarf and his signature black baseball cap. Mikaal was already an award-winning sound designer and composer at this point, and *Macbeth* would soon add a Tony nomination to his extensive list of accomplishments.

His assistant sat between us and operated the music cues from her laptop, which was plugged into a speaker on top of the table. Mikaal instructed me to take notes on any edits I wanted to make to the music, but warned that the staging and cue timings wouldn't be finalized until we got inside the theater. Mostly, we were at those early rehearsals to give the director an idea of the available music, and to help the actors adjust to hearing the score as they recited their lines.

This meant that I got a front row seat to some pretty fabulous theater. It was interesting to witness the creative process behind the scenes. Ruth Negga, the Ethiopian-Irish actress playing Lady Macbeth, was captivating. Compared to Daniel Craig, she was tiny, with the build of a gymnast or a ballerina. Her impish, intense, and eventually frenetic energy played well off the red-blooded-turned-bloodthirsty persona that Daniel was creating as Macbeth.

One night, toward the end of rehearsal, Daniel brought out a whiskey bottle, and his assistant—who was always there in the shadows—produced a stack of tiny disposable glasses and filled them each with a shot of the amber liquid. Daniel invited anyone who wanted one to join him in a toast.

Unsure at first if his invitation included the crew, I waited until I saw the sound assistant grab a glass. Daniel said a short toast, and we all raised our miniature glasses to cheers. I downed the fiery liquid as quickly as possible, as I find straight whiskey to be a tad overpowering. Everyone lingered a little bit longer than usual that night, talking and laughing in small clusters.

Once Daniel was gone, Michael wheeled over to me.

"Did you like the whiskey?" he inquired, eyes gleaming under his dark trilby hat. "Daniel asked me to help him pick out a bottle."

"Yes! It was good," I said, hoping he wouldn't ask for flavor notes. I'm no connoisseur, after all.

"I recommended that brand," he continued, "but I was talking about the hundred-dollar version. That bottle cost a thousand!"

"What?!" I croaked incredulously. "I wish I'd known that before I guzzled it!"

He laughed as he rolled away. Truthfully, even if I had known, it wouldn't have made a difference. All whiskey is wasted on me.

IN TERMS OF editing the music cues, I did most of my work in the evenings. The expectation on Broadway was that the director's requests would be addressed by the next rehearsal, but some of these changes were massive. Together Jake and I spent most nights and weekends on Zoom, restructuring the cues to meet the production's needs.

The hours were long, and the pressure was high. One night we found ourselves on the ledge when Jake snapped at me uncharacteristically, "How many more of these are we going to have to do? Every cue?" to which I desperately howled, "I don't know! Maybe?"

I went to bed that night worried he was going to quit on me, and I almost couldn't blame him. This was so much more work than either of us had imagined! Thankfully, Jake was as committed to finishing the project as I was.

After two weeks of daytime rehearsals, we transitioned over to the Longacre Theatre, where the play would take place. Paul and I packed up our suitcases and moved across town to Hotel Edison in Manhattan, right in the heart of the theater district.

We had two rehearsals each day, split up only by a dinner break. By this point, the weather was warming up a little, and Paul and I loved making the most of our breaks by dining at one of the makeshift outdoor patios that nearly every New York restaurant had built in response to COVID.

These little huts were as unique as they were plentiful. Some were merely unpainted plywood shacks thrown up in a rush, and others were clearly designed with care. Our favorite patios had garlands of fake flowers strung around the entrances, pretty curtains adorning the walls, and—most important—heat lamps that could be activated during chilly or rainy weather. Hurley's Irish Pub was next to the theater and boasted all three features, so it swiftly became our haunt of choice.

Mikaal and I sat next to each other at the back of the auditorium during rehearsals. The prop shop built us little wooden tables that were balanced on top of the row in front of us. We used them to take notes, by the faint glow of clip-on reading lights.

The days were long, but luckily I found a delightful way to escape the monotony of rehearsals: union-regulated smoke breaks! I didn't actually smoke, but I had discovered that many cast members would gather in a blocked-off alley just off the theater for a cigarette. This was my long-awaited chance to bond with the actors—namely, Michael, Ruth, and the trio of witches. We'd tell each other amusing stories and trade jokes to decompress.

I was expected to attend the previews as well. Ticket holders had snagged their seats for these performances at a reduced price to basically witness a work in progress. During each preview, Mikaal and I sat in the back of the theater and took notes of the things we still wanted to tweak. Then we waited for the chance to speak with Sam and make our case for the proposed changes.

Sam's time was very limited, because every department was asking for his attention—lighting, set design, projections, costumes, props, fight scenes, blood—and of course music and sound. Frustratingly, this meant Mikaal and I barely had any time with him.

After months of intense labor, my patience was admittedly at an all-time low—and it showed, whenever Mikaal and I didn't agree on how the cues should sound in the theater. The line between sound designer and composer was often blurry, and our differences in opinion led to a few tense conversations. But since we're both professionals, we managed to keep things mostly good-spirited during that last week before opening. Eventually, Sam found a half hour to settle our unresolved disagreements—after all, as director, his opinion was the Law of the Land. Some of the final changes were gutting to me, but along with everyone else in the cast and crew, I gritted my teeth and pushed myself to make it to opening night intact.

BACK WHEN WE started tech at the theater, I had texted Michael Stipe to let him know I was in the area. I thought it would be cool to meet him in person, but I didn't hear back from him.

Oh, well, I thought wistfully. *The stars didn't align.* Soon my unreturned text was lost in the mental crush of music cue edits.

In the middle of that final week, when I was hanging on by a thread, I received a voicemail from Michael.

"Sorry I didn't reply to your text," he said. "I've been out of town."

He continued: "Maybe we can find some time for you to re-record those vocals, so I can be in the same room while you do it. Give me a call if you can, and we'll try to make it work."

My brain nearly short-circuited at the thought of adding another thing to my plate, but I couldn't bear to turn him down. I texted back: *I'd love to find a time to record! Is Monday an option?*

Michael was available then, so I booked us an evening recording session at Power Station, which (I'd learn later) has a storied reputation for cutting many famous albums. Truthfully, I chose it for more practical reasons: It was one of the only wheelchair-accessible recording studios in Manhattan.

By Monday, my excitement to record with Michael Stipe had won out over my *Macbeth* stress.

Paul and I met him in the entryway of the nondescript studio building. Michael was surprisingly cheerful in person—none of that angsty seriousness or self-importance one might expect, given his remarkable rock-and-roll history.

The sound engineers were ready to start when we arrived. Paul helped me position the microphones and headphones, then he joined the others in the console room. The soundproof door that separated us was made of glass, so I could see Michael swaying back and forth to the music, sometimes gesturing with his arms like a conductor as I sang.

Halfway through the session, Michael came into the vocal booth to debrief.

"I think I'm hearing you sing 'give me a hand,'" Michael said. "But if you listen closely, I'm really pronouncing it 'gimme a hand.'"

I hadn't noticed, but there it was, clear as day.

For the rest of the recording session, Michael coached me between takes, asking for subtle tweaks on breath control, timings, and even my energy levels while I sang. I was so grateful for this incredible master class in performance and recording; his enthusiasm and joy for music were contagious.

When he had everything he needed, we called it a night and went to celebrate with a round of beers at a local spot that Paul and I had started frequenting for its late hours.

The front wall of the bar was a glass garage door, which was fully raised because of the warm weather. We parked ourselves at a high table that ran along the now-open wall, our backs to the bar as we breathed in the night air.

We talked, laughed, and shared stories about our experiences growing up, music, politics, pets, photography, food, cooking, our favorite books—whatever came to mind. We finally parted ways after midnight, but by then I knew we were leaving as friends. I was so glad I'd made time for the session during my most stressful week in New York—it turned out to be exactly what I needed.

BY OPENING NIGHT of *Macbeth,* I was running on caffeine, adrenaline, and anticipation.

That morning, I went to my final dress fitting. The costume designer had kindly agreed to make me a special dress for the occasion. It was a gorgeously iridescent purple with embroidered flowers all over it, designed to fit my short stature perfectly. It even had a piece of fabric used in Lady Macbeth's golden gown—arguably the coolest costume piece in the whole play—peeking out from the bottom hem!

Two hours later, Paul and I, as well as our parents—who had flown in earlier that morning—were all dressed up outside of the

Longacre. My dad strutted like a proud papa peacock in his tux, which I'd only ever seen him wear in plays or during his children's weddings.

There was a mix of cast, crew, family members, and celebrities milling around the PR tent in front of the theater. I beamed as I introduced our parents to Michael Stipe and his guests—I'd managed to procure him a few coveted tickets at the last minute. The producers were passing out mini bottles of champagne to everyone. To my horror, as we all clinked our little bottles together, I accidentally splashed champagne on my new dress. I was momentarily distraught until Michael joked, "It's not a real evening gown until you spill champagne on it!"

Photos and interviews were conducted inside the PR tent, which boasted the red carpet (in truth, it was hot pink) and a huge step-and-repeat backdrop with the word MACBETH printed all over it. I went through the tent one time by myself, then Michael convinced me to go with him for a second round of pictures. "The press loves a two-for-one!" he said. And apparently, he was right—that was the photo that got published the most.

We finally entered the theater and took our seats. I gazed at the throngs of people waiting expectantly in this gorgeous space, just as Sam had foretold a year earlier. The energy was charged as the lights dimmed. My eerie music rang out, setting the mood for the action onstage.

By this point Paul and I had seen the show so many times we practically had it memorized, but watching it with my parents sitting next to me was a completely new experience. Their eyes sparkled whenever the music entered a scene and they glanced over, delighted, during the particularly dramatic cues.

As I sat there in the dark, all the stress of the months before washed away—in its place, a sweet mixture of relief and pride rose up in my chest. *This must be what it feels like to get a master's degree in music*, I thought, smiling. My work here was done, and I was happy with it!

Macbeth was dead; the play was nearing its end. I nervously held my breath. To me, the last cue was the most important. It was the song I'd written, the Lady Macbeth theme, "Perfect." Sam had cried when I'd first sent him the demo, but try as we might, we just couldn't find the right recording of me singing it to include in the show. No matter the instrumentation—guitar, piano, or a cappella—it was too jarring to have a disembodied voice over the speakers.

Sam ultimately decided to have a cast member perform it from the stage. At first I was heartbroken when I found out that I wouldn't be the one singing the final cue. I loved that song—it was the most raw, vulnerable thing I'd ever written. But I eventually had a change of heart. The young actor who would be singing it was a genuine, caring person. She knew how much the song meant to me and wanted to make me proud. She asked about the song's meaning, and we even practiced it together. Now I was more than just at peace with Sam's decision—I was excited about it!

This was the first time she'd be singing it for a full audience.

The moment was finally here. She began, her voice sweet and sincere, as the cast quietly gathered onstage for a moment of repose after the long and bloody battle. As she continued to sing, you could almost hear the audience relax, dipping into a moment of reflection about mortality and the pressure to succeed at all costs. She finally came to the last lines of the song:

Wish I had known
It wasn't meant to be
Wasn't meant to be
Perfect.

The play was over, but for a few moments, no one moved or made a noise. The theater was suspended in a sacred silence, save for the sound of sniffles scattered throughout the crowd.

Then the clapping started, slow at first but quickly building momentum. Soon after the entire room of theatergoers rose to their feet in a standing ovation. I beamed at Paul, who was sitting next to me. "We did it!" I said triumphantly, squeezing his hand tight before leaning in for a quick kiss.

The applause kept going. My mom turned toward me, still clapping in her seat. To my surprise, she had tears in her eyes. "That song was the perfect way to end it," she said. "Just beautiful."

37

Trust in Your Ripple

AFTER OPENING NIGHT of *Macbeth,* Paul and I packed up the van and started our long drive home from New York City. It was bittersweet to leave, but as we covered more distance, the open space and green woods felt like balms to my soul. My heart belonged to Minnesota, after all.

On the last night of driving, we stopped somewhere in Wisconsin. I had scoured Google Maps, finally locating a wheelchair-accessible Irish pub with a patio. Most of the restaurant patios remained closed—spring had barely even begun in the Midwest—but we were still trying to be extra cautious about COVID.

It was a chilly evening, but fortunately the waiter was willing to humor us. He led us out to the empty patio with metal chairs and tables. Paul and I each ordered a Guinness and a cup of French onion soup, plus a plate of fish and chips to share. It didn't take long for the food to arrive, and it was unexpectedly delicious.

We were relaxing and chatting over our second beers, no longer feeling frozen or caring how weird it looked to be sitting alone on the patio in jackets while everyone else was warm inside.

Suddenly, my phone rang. To my surprise, it was Judy Heumann.

Judy had kept in touch through occasional phone calls and emails, checking in once a year or so to see how things were going with my music and advocacy. She always asked if there was anything she could do to support me. She loved connecting people—if she had a good match for me, she'd type up the introductory email right in the middle of our phone call!

In 2020, Judy gained mainstream recognition after being featured as a central character in the Oscar-nominated documentary *Crip Camp,* which told the story of a group of teenagers who met at a summer camp for disabled kids in the late '60s and early '70s. Judy herself had been both a camper and a counselor there in her teens. Several of these disabled campers (including Judy, of course) went on to stage the 504 Sit-In that took place in San Franscisco in 1977.

I cried big, wet tears from start to finish the first time I watched *Crip Camp.* It was thrilling to see footage of Judy as a young woman fighting against the system with such passion and poise. Although I knew she had helped to push the Disability Rights Movement forward, I hadn't fully appreciated just how hard Judy (and everyone involved in this advocacy) had to work to secure the civil rights that now seemed so fundamental to my daily life—or the risks they took so that I could have a better future. And I'd never seen anything even close to my life experience represented on screen before with such honesty or depth. It was a truly beautiful film.

Judy and I had texted and spoken on the phone a few times since the movie had come out, but the pandemic had kept me from playing in DC, where we could have reconnected in person.

Still, I cherished her surprise calls.

I picked up the phone. "Hello, Judy!" I said. "How are you doing?"

"Hello! I'm getting into a cab," she said, jumping to the point, in typical Judy fashion. "I just saw the show. *Macbeth.* I loved it, Gaelynn."

I grinned. I could hear the noise of the New York City streets, now over a thousand miles away. The cab pulled up and I could hear her drive her wheelchair up the metal ramp.

"Hold on a second," she said.

I smiled to myself as she greeted the cab driver, as Judy's penchant for multitasking during calls was something Lachi and I had joked about before. Since Paul and I were the only two people outside, I put the call on speakerphone so that he could listen in on the conversation.

I was glad she'd traveled all the way from DC to see the show, and even more touched that she'd taken time to call me afterward.

"I'm serious, Gaelynn," she said, suddenly back with me. "The music was beautiful. I'm just so proud of you. I want you to know that." She paused, her voice cracking. "I'm getting emotional."

Tears sprung to my eyes.

After all the time and energy she had dedicated to the disability community over the years, it felt pretty surreal to hear Judy Heumann say that *she* was proud of *me*—for making music, of all things. Scoring a Broadway show felt insignificant when compared to her lifetime of monumental contributions to disability rights.

She was one of the people who made my life possible. Without Judy, I wouldn't have gotten a public education with my peers—most likely, I wouldn't have been introduced to the violin at all.

I remembered hearing an interview that Judy had given about a year earlier.

"Growing up," she said, "I studied piano and voice. I was a good singer. I auditioned for Juilliard."

I didn't know Judy had been a singer. She'd never mentioned it during our conversations.

"My parents, they loved my voice and they supported it. Still, they felt I wouldn't be able to make a career in the theater. But Ali Stroker—she was the first wheelchair user to be on Broadway and win a Tony Award—she's in her thirties now. She's broken a big barrier in theater. But in the '60s and '70s, it wasn't going to be me, unfortunately," she mused. "It would've been fun."

I detected a hint of resignation in her voice during that interview—regret, even.

I came to understand that all the activism that Judy had done—was still doing—was out of love for my generation. *Activism* hadn't been her dream job—her dream job had been musical theater! But simply because of when she'd been born, that dream wasn't available to her.

Despite how frustrating and inaccessible the music industry is today, the fact remains: I can still pursue music professionally. Whereas Judy's childhood dreams were deferred indefinitely.

Judy took up the mantle of activism so that disabled people like me could pursue *their* dreams without the same barriers she had faced. She wanted disabled kids everywhere to be free from oppression, stigma, prejudice, and abuse. To be seen as equals and to have the same chances in life as their nondisabled peers. To go to school, take dance classes, be in a play, or compose music for Broadway, even—to pursue whatever it is that makes their hearts sing.

Maybe that's why she was calling to tell me she was proud of me—I was living the dream she never could. I hoped it gave her comfort to know her work had not been in vain. In the span of a single generation, so many new doors and opportunities had opened up for disabled people.

"Anyway, how are you doing?" Judy asked once she'd composed herself. "Are you back in Minnesota? Is Paul there with you"

"We're almost home!" I said. "We'll get there tomorrow. And Paul's right here! You're on speakerphone, actually. I hope that's OK."

"That's fine. Hi, Paul!" she said brightly. She always included him in conversations.

As we talked—or tried to talk—Judy was also in the middle of instructing the cab driver on how to tie down her wheelchair.

"There," I heard her say, directing him. "Not there, a little lower."

I could hear the metal buckles of the tie-downs clanking in the background. I cringed for her. I'd dealt with many drivers over the years who didn't know how to properly operate their safety equipment. But her assertive tone with the cab driver made it clear that Judy could handle herself.

"I'd better go," Judy said with a sigh, the teeniest bit of exasperation in her voice. "I have to tell the driver where to hook the tie-downs. Anyway, great work. Safe travels home, you two."

That call from the cab was the last time I ever spoke with her.

Sadly, Judy Heumann passed away on March 4, 2023, at the age of seventy-five. I had heard through the disability grapevine that she was in the hospital, but I couldn't quite believe that she might actually die. Judy always triumphed eventually—it was just the natural order of things.

The news of her death touched everyone I knew in the disability community, just as Judy's life and actions had touched each of our lives in meaningful ways. A huge light—a genuine lighthouse to many of us—had been extinguished. I felt adrift.

All I wanted to do was talk to other disabled people. I called every disabled friend I could think of the week she died—Lachi, Kalyn Heffernan, and many others. We cried, we shared stories, we laughed, and we talked about where our beloved community needed to go now that she was gone.

To be clear, Judy wasn't the first disabled elder to pass, nor will she be the last. She wasn't the most important either—we are all equally valuable. But she touched my life personally, and her death impacted me and many others tremendously.

Judy's funeral was held at her synagogue in DC. Hundreds of people attended in person and several thousand more joined virtually, including me. It was one of the most beautiful services I've ever witnessed. Family and friends, mostly disabled, shared stories I had never heard before. Some of them were empowering, others hilarious. The theme was connection—Judy had so clearly connected, supported, and uplifted thousands of people behind the scenes. I was grateful that I had gotten the opportunity to know her even just a little bit during her time on this planet.

Since Judy's passing, I've often thought about how much younger disabled people owe to the previous generations of disability rights activists—people like Justin Dart Jr., Johnnie Lacy, Patrisha Wright, Ed Roberts, Kitty Cone, Mary Lou Breslin, Frank Bowe, Brad Lomax, Corbett O'Toole, Margot Imdieke Cross, Harriet McBryde Johnson, and so many unsung heroes. The lives of disabled Americans would be virtually unrecognizable today if these brave activists hadn't organized and been willing to put in twhe work to fight for change.

Many wonderful activists since then have continued their legacy, including Anita Cameron, Alice Wong, Rebecca Cokley, Vesper Moore, Andrew Pulrang, Gregg Beratan, Ingrid Tischer, Mike Ervin, Lawrence Carter-Long, Keith Jones, Mia Mingus, Sandy Ho, Vilissa Thompson, Haben Girma, Imani Barbarin, and Lydia X. Z. Brown—as well as the visionaries we've recently lost, including Stacey Park Milbern, Lois Curtis, Tinu Abayomi-Paul, and Patty Berne. These bright lights—along with countless others—have carried the Disability Rights Movement even further, making sure it becomes more diverse and inclusive through the lens of Disability Justice.

Disabled musicians and artists are also making change.

Art creates reverberations off the walls of the heart; it bypasses the brain and hits the receiver directly in the soul. Art can lead to more compassion, understanding, and awareness, and I am grateful to be part of its magic. I hope that my work in the music industry will make it easier for those who follow me, and I hope that my music leaves a trace of added beauty in the world.

For one day soon, a whole new generation of disabled artists and activists will travel the paths my contemporaries and I are constructing today. Every generation builds upon and expands the work of the last, until finally the great goal of equality has been realized.

EVERY LIFE IS filled with ups and downs, joys and sorrows, tragedies, and victories. Mine has been no exception. Countless times, my disability has shown me that it is truly possible to build a life that is enriching, creative, joyful, and authentic—no matter what my body or mind is going through. There isn't a moment I would trade away my disability. It makes me who I am, as an artist and a person, and it has taught me so many important life lessons over the years.

For one, I know in my bones that every human being deserves care and support. I am convinced that equality is the underlying, universal principle on which all disability activism must ultimately be built. When I measure my actions against the principle of equality, it becomes clear that the only way to live this truth fully is to practice loving everyone—even people I may dislike, disagree with, or struggle to understand.

Each time we interact with someone, it sets off a chain reaction. The words we choose and the way we treat people create ripples in the lives of others. This means we have the powerful ability to produce either love and peace, or fear and anger. Our daily interactions—while seemingly insignificant on the surface—all add up over time. In subtle and not-so-subtle ways, they shape the future of our lives and the lives of others. Indeed, they are shaping the future of our planet. That's why being loving and kind to others is of the utmost importance.

Disabled activists have shown me that you don't have to be rich or famous to make change, nor do you have to be mighty in numbers. Many of the biggest turning points in history have been fueled by small groups of everyday people, such as the handful of leaders who grew the 504 Sit-In into a powerful protest—which is still a shining example of activism today. So don't worry if your numbers are small or if your efforts aren't getting widespread attention at first. Focus instead on maintaining your integrity. The rest will follow.

Living in this disabled body has also taught me that disability *is* diversity. It is a unique and complex experience that shapes the lives of people from every single walk of life, across the globe. It has been a part of the human experience since the dawn of time; the more recent celebration of disability as an integral part of our cultural landscape is long overdue. Disabled artists are helping to shape and guide how our society views and includes disability in many important ways: through their music, theater, film, visual arts, dance, and writing. But *all* disabled people—not just artists—can set a powerful example by having pride in their identity and embracing authentic connection every day.

In a society that seems hooked on blaring bad news, it can feel like kindness barely moves the needle. But no matter what the future brings, we must not fall prey to despair. Kindness always matters. Whenever we share goodness, love, beauty, or light with others, we tip the scale away from darkness. Whenever we care for our neighbor, these ripples of service spread far and wide.

We may not get to see the full impact of our earthly efforts, but I believe our ripples do coalesce somewhere further upstream. Eventually our collective energy will create waves of real, lasting change. So let us not grow tired of doing good, even if progress is slow. Trust in your ripple.

ACKNOWLEDGMENTS

IN DECEMBER 2024, I sent this manuscript to a group of twelve beta readers, and I was surprised to discover that the number one piece of feedback was "Too many names!" If writing a memoir has taught me anything, it is that I have so many people to thank for being part of my life—so many, in fact, that I want to start this section by acknowledging that some really dear people got far less page space in the end than they deserve. I guess that's what happens when you stitch together snippets of a life (and your memoir isn't a trilogy).

In particular, my cousins Rachael Stigsell and Carolyn Rich—who were my bonus sisters growing up—barely got mentioned. This pains me because I love them so dang much and lots of my favorite memories involve them. My best friends from high school (The Van Girls) also went unnamed, but Hailey Golds, Rachel Schachter, and Allison Schoenecker are still such big parts of my life and I'm very grateful for their love and laughter. College roommates, PCAs, teachers, mentors, coworkers, bandmates past and present, fiddle students, fellow touring musicians, disabled artist-activists, in-laws, relatives, and friends—I am grateful for each of you. Thanks for loving me and supporting me, and for all the beautiful memories. You have truly blessed my life.

But as far as this book is concerned, I must first and foremost thank Leigh Stein, my wise and patient book coach, who helped to coax this puppy along ever since March 2021, when it was a mere twinkle in my eye. I am so grateful for her help with the book proposal and the first three drafts—she offered tons of spot-on guidance during our Zoom meetings and also diffused my angst with laughter whenever the process felt overwhelming (which was pretty often).

I would also like to thank Emma Parry, my kind and encouraging agent at Janklow and Nesbit. I am so grateful she contacted me in October 2021 after I (foolheartedly) announced I was writing a memoir on my website, "due out in 2022" (hahaha). Oh, how little I knew about publishing a book! Luckily, Emma knows a lot. Thanks for believing in my work, for taking me on, and for helping this memoir reach a much wider audience than I could have on my own.

I am grateful to my editor at Algonquin Books, Maddie Jones, for guiding this book to its final iteration. Her thoughtful feedback made this manuscript so much better. Thank you for patiently answering my endless questions, and for sharing your energy and enthusiasm as we prepared for the release date. I also appreciate the editing assistance that Jovanna Brinck provided, and the eagle-eyed copyediting by Leslie Keros. Thank you to my managing editor Brunson Hoole, as well, for carefully shepherding this book through the release process.

As I mentioned, I sent the very first rough draft to twelve beta readers, and their impact on the memoir you have just finished cannot be overstated. They helped to shape the final contours of the book, and it is infinitely better for it. So, a huge thank you to my friends Kalyn Heffernan, Rachael Stigsell, Leah Nelson, Jenna Kowaleski, Karolyn Gehrig, Rachel Schachter, Sara Langbert, Corry Duffy, Beth Bartlett, Nathasha Alvarez, Hailey Golds, and Naomi Anderson. I truly appreciate your taking the time to read the book and share your thoughts.

Several drafts later (there were six in total), I started to worry because I'd included more disability history than I'd originally planned. So, at the last moment, I sent the manuscript to a few scholars and well-versed disability activists to fact-check it for me. They generously took the time to read the entire memoir, and on very a tight deadline. Thank you to Ginger Lane, Meesh Sara Fradkin, Ashley Shew, Warren Rosenblum, and Mara Mills for helping me clarify the stories I included from the Disability Rights Movement—your expertise was invaluable.

Writing a book isn't a solo project—far from it! But in addition to everyone who helped with the editing process, there were many others who supported my creative endeavors behind the scenes while I was working on this memoir. None more so than the amazing Carrie Craig, my longtime assistant, whom I also consider a dear friend. Thank you for keeping my email inbox from exploding and my social media up and running, and for providing a listening ear and a hefty dose of wisdom and compassion whenever I felt stretched too thin by multiple projects.

Thank you to Jake Larson, audio engineer extraordinaire, for all your work getting my latest album, *Music From Macbeth*, ready to release in the midst of it all. And thank you to Richard Carter for booking shows (and playing guitar!) for the subsequent *Music From Macbeth* UK album release tour. Neither project would have gotten off the ground without you two.

A great deal of thanks is also due to the Arrowhead Regional Arts Council, Minnesota State Arts Board, Whippoorwill Arts, and the Disability Futures Fellowship for providing me with financial support for my creative projects, including this memoir. Your work is essential to helping artists thrive; I'm grateful that you recognize the importance of diverse voices in the arts.

And of course, thank you to the wonderful people who have supported my work through Substack and attended my shows online and in person. I have loved connecting with you over the years, and I truly appreciate all you do to uplift the arts. I hope to cross paths with you soon!

I would be remiss not to thank my wonderful friend Leah Nelson for being part of my life since our first meeting at UMD back in 2006. Thanks for all the pizza nights, couples' dinners, and girly chats and for your good-natured vibes whenever you're #TravelingWithTheTresslers. Thank you for letting me vent about this book and for encouraging me when editing it felt impossible. I am grateful for your gentle spirit, loyalty, optimism, and sense of humor — not to mention your videography skills (I'm forever indebted to you for those, obvs). I love you, dude!

To my siblings, Ben Anderson, Corry Duffy, and Greg White. I sure lucked out having you three as "sibs"! You are such special people, and I love you very much. I enjoyed revisiting memories of you while writing this book — it was not lost on me how much joy you added to my childhood. I'm proud of who each of you has become, and grateful for our friendships today.

To my amazing parents, Tim and Peggy White. Thank you for raising me to believe that I am loved, worthy, capable, and free to explore all the creativity life has to offer. I can't imagine being raised by anyone else — your devotion, spark, kindness, and can-do spirits are exactly what this disabled kid needed to thrive. Thank you for your loving care, fierce advocacy, intelligent guidance, and endless encouragement from childhood to today. I'm so lucky to have you in my life as an adult; you are two of my very closest friends. I love you, Mommi-o and Daddi-o!

And finally, to my remarkable and loving husband, Paul Tressler. I'm so grateful that we met during that open mic night in Duluth, and that you have stood by me through life's twists and turns ever since. Your genuine kindness, intelligence, wisdom, compassion, dedication, growth mindset, love of learning, reverence for nature, and quirky sense of humor all inspire me. I am lucky to be your wife, every day of any year. Thank you, especially, for holding down the fort while I wrote and edited this memoir. I know I wasn't always a delight during this process, so thank you for giving me grace and forgiving me whenever I went off the deep end. You are my lifeboat, my refuge, my best friend, and my favorite traveling companion. I am looking forward to many more adventures together. I love you so much, and I thank the Creator for you.